CHINA MYSTERIES

CHINA MYSTERIES

Crime Novels from China's Others

Jeffrey C. Kinkley

University of Hawai'i Press
Honolulu

© 2024 University of Hawai'i Press
All rights reserved
Printed in the United States of America

First printed, 2024

Library of Congress Cataloging-in-Publication Data

Names: Kinkley, Jeffrey C., author.

Title: China mysteries : crime novels from China's others / Jeffrey C.
 Kinkley.

Description: Honolulu : University of Hawai'i, [2023] | Includes
 bibliographical references and index.

Identifiers: LCCN 2023011329 | ISBN 9780824895204 (hardback) | ISBN
 9780824896751 (kindle edition) | ISBN 9780824896744 (epub) | ISBN
 9780824896737 (pdf)

Subjects: LCSH: Detective and mystery stories—21st century—Themes,
 motives. | Detective and mystery stories—20th century—Themes, motives.
 | China—In literature.

Classification: LCC PN3448.D4 K563 2023 | DDC
 809.3/8720935851—dc23/eng/20230323

LC record available at https://lccn.loc.gov/2023011329

Cover art: Olivier Tabary/Shutterstock.com

University of Hawai'i Press books are printed on acid-free paper and meet
the guidelines for permanence and durability of the Council on Library Resources.

*For those whose efforts to build bridges across cultures
were dashed during the COVID-19 pandemic*

Contents

Preface	ix
Acknowledgments	xi
Abbreviations	xiii
1. Introduction: Mystery Novels from the Second Sino-Western Honeymoon	1
2. Birth and Anatomy of a Genre	15
3. China: Places and Problems	50
4. Actors: Personas and Partners	86
5. Retrospection: History and Nostalgia	117
Appendix: The China Mysteries in Three Lists	149
Notes	161
Bibliography	183
Index	201

Preface

Crime fiction in Chinese, replete with intriguing local crime scenes and story lines, suddenly returned to the People's Republic of China (PRC) in the 1980s, ending a 30-year ban. It was as if the works appeared out of thin air. Curious, I "investigated." By the time my findings went to press in 2000, whodunits starring PRC police detectives were being published in the West, too. These were original works in English and French, not translations from the Chinese. Soon all kinds of authors were writing them and they were being read worldwide— only not in China. I grew curious all over again. This book is the result.

My critical reaction to these "China mysteries not made in China" began with delight, at Qiu Xiaolong's debut Inspector Chen novel (2000). A poet and scholar from the PRC, Qiu had come to the US and begun writing whodunits in English, with his native Shanghai as the setting. In time I perused a hundred more China mysteries with contemporary themes by Qiu and 40 other authors, some likewise raised in Chinese milieux, the majority not. Professional training made me scrutinize these cross-cultural works not just for infelicities but also for errors, bias, and misunderstanding, particularly of the sort attributable to cultural and political difference. They were there for the finding, but so were intriguing plotlines and China-related aperçus. Most of these mysteries are good reads and also perceptive, in my opinion. Some are fast-paced. Many are witty. A few, by Zhang Xinxin, Alban Yung, and Nury Vittachi, are satirical, even farcical, deserving other kinds of analysis, yet the authors have not eschewed the "detective fiction" label for these works. My aim now is to comprehend and analyze this multinational spectacle. I see here a new genre or subgenre of popular fiction that among other things illuminates hopes and fears from a second honeymoon of China and the West following their several-year trial separation after the June 4, 1989, massacre in Beijing. Historical, analytical, and comparative questions abound, for mystery writing has long drawn strength from reader interest in unfamiliar places. How did these overseas China mysteries arise, almost as suddenly as crime fiction had in the PRC some 20 years earlier? What is distinctive about these novels? Are there reciprocating works in Chinese from PRC authors,

x   Preface

about murders in North America, Europe, Japan, and Thailand? Not many, I think. The PRC crime fiction market today is dominated by foreign crime novels translated into Chinese and local authors' mysteries solving crimes in China. The PRC's own crime fiction has evolved since I last wrote about it and the pages below occasionally cite it for comparative purposes, but it comes from a separate publishing world, even if some works have now crossed over into ours in translation.

Only a few mysteries described in this book are in Chinese, yet I feel instructed by Shu-mei Shih's Sinophone studies, about writing culturally indebted to the China Mainland and created outside of it—"decentered." Here I have eliminated *language* as a necessary generic or cultural defining factor. This is an age of multilingual actors, ubiquitous translation, mixed and transforming identities, cross-cultural exchange, and potentially unbounded internet discourse. Genres are always in flux, too. Yet customary distinctions among crime, detective, mystery, and mystery thriller categories pale by comparison to what the novels below have in common. Then again, I see these works as belonging to a particular moment in time.

This is an academic book with plot spoilers. We mystery lovers, however, and theorists, too, know that a good plot deserves rereading even when we know the ending.

I spell the names of fictional characters and places as the authors do, but cite real places and organizations in conformity with standard usage, for example, Discipline Inspection Commission, not Disciplinary Inspection Committee. Authors who publish under different names are referred to by their original name; their pen names appear in the Bibliography and Appendix. For Japanese authors, I accede to English-language publishers' practice, putting the author's surname last.

A year that appears in parentheses after a book title indicates the first year of the book's publication, sometimes in a foreign translation that preceded publication of the book in its original language.

Acknowledgments

Many thanks go to my beloved wife and first reader and editor, Susan Corliss Kinkley, who is more familiar with global mystery fiction than I will ever be. Coincidentally, it is she who introduced Chinese fiction to me when we were both fourteen, in a book report on the Chi-chen Wang translation of *Dream of the Red Chamber*. My brother Gregg J. Kinkley and my son Matthew Kang Kinkley are a continual source of encouragement. Qiu Xiaolong and Zhang Xinxin have furthered my knowledge of China and its literature ever since I met them at a Shanghai conference in 1986. Diane Wei Liang and Harriet Gilbert hosted me on a 2007 trans-Atlantic BBC radio program, in which my personal 15 minutes of fame came when I spoke on *China*'s mystery fiction. Dinah Lee Küng provided information through correspondence. Lisa See and Daniel Nieh gave stimulating talks at the Powell's Book Stores in Beaverton and Portland, Oregon, respectively, and answered a couple of my questions. Portland State University, its library, and its Institute for Asian Studies, directed by Prof. Suwako Watanabe, provided research help. I was buoyed by friends at the Northwest China Council, including John Wong, Amy Richter, and Victor Lam; the Portland-Suzhou Sister City Association; and colleagues at the University of British Columbia, particularly Christopher Rea; the University of Leeds and its Centre for New Chinese Writing, thanks to Frances Weightman and Sarah Dodd; the Shanghai International Studies University, Hongkou Campus, with special thanks to Dean Sun Huijun and Zhang Bei; Brigitte Duzan; Don Baham; Scott Savitt; William Tay; Columbia University; and St. John's University, my former employer. Bertrand Mialaret, at http://mychinesebooks.com/, and Paul French, at http://www.chinarhyming .com, are among the few critics who write about China-related crime novels. Two other indispensable resources are *Paper Republic,* https://paper-republic.org/ and Kirk Denton's MCLC Resource Center, https://u.osu.edu/mclc/.

I am very grateful for improvements made to the manuscript by my expert editors Stephanie Chun, Wendy Bolton, and Gianna Marsella; my outside readers; and other staff at the University of Hawai'i Press.

ABBREVIATIONS

CCP   Chinese Communist Party
DSD   Domestic Security Department, under the MPS
MPS   Ministry of Public Security
MSS   Ministry of State Security
PLA   People's Liberation Army
PRC   People's Republic of China
PSB   Public Security Bureau(s), the regular municipal police forces, under the MPS

1

Introduction

Mystery Novels from the Second Sino-Western Honeymoon

Why read—or write—a mystery or crime novel set in contemporary China? For the plot, and to learn about China, readers on our side of the newly descending curtain between China and the West would likely say. Because there is a market for such books, the writers might respond, and probably should. The People's Republic of China (PRC) has its own market for crime novels by local authors and today a few are read globally, in the original Chinese and in translation. This book's focus lies elsewhere: on mysteries that unfold *in* the PRC but are written and read everywhere *but* there. How and when did these works appear? What are they like? What goes into them? To the authors and readers: Why mysteries, why China, and why you?

This book lays claim to be the first acknowledgment and analysis of a particular genre (or subgenre) of popular fiction: an out-of-China or ex-China body of fiction so discrete it might be deemed "overdetermined." I call it "the China mystery" (in contrast with "the Chinese mystery"), with the understanding that the term designates crime, detective, and mystery thriller novels that are set in the China of our times but were not written or published under its dominion.[1] These works have emerged from Western lineages of the modern novel and popular genre fiction, with Chinese contributions, and they depend on a commercial Western publishing regime that is shaped by cultural, national, political, economic, institutional, and target-audience factors. Yet these works straddle conventional academic categories defined by nation or language; native, foreign, diasporic, or expat provenance; and popular vs. highbrow appeal. Most works discussed here were composed in English—over 80 and counting. Fifteen others were written in French; four in Chinese; three in German; one in Swedish. Most are available in English versions, except those written in French. The Francophone world, however, has its own strong market for and venerable history of *policier* novels or *polars*: police procedurals, crime sagas, and thrillers. I looked for leads to PRC-sited mysteries in Japanese and several mystery-loving languages I cannot read, only to come away empty-handed, although that might reflect inadequacies of my searches.[2] Deliberately excluded from analysis here

1

2   Chapter 1

are spy thrillers, true crime novels, historical detective fiction,[3] Chinatown, Taiwan, and colonial Hong Kong mysteries,[4] and works with science fiction (SF), alternate history, horror, supernatural, paranormal, and fantasy themes.[5]

China mysteries complicate the notion of "world literature," which is typically a tale of actual and potential centrifugalism—of works, genres, and national literatures spinning outward across national and cultural boundaries.[6] The China mystery originates from centripetalism. Multinational and multicultural authors, including ex-PRC nationals, converge on a common source of attraction, the China Mainland, where they negotiate political and cultural obstacles. A centrifugal progress toward global readership ensues, occasionally joined by new, native-author spinoffs from the Mainland nucleus. These are but analogies, although they need not pertain only to mystery novels. Both the nucleus and the periphery retain the ability to alter their polarity and thus their relationship. China, the core, mightily retains the power to determine who are its Others, which it finds both inside and outside its borders. The Others living outside China constantly reevaluate their relationship with the nucleus, evading capture by its gravity and politicomagnetic force and even hoping to avoid being fixed in place until observed, like Schrödinger's cat. Sometimes they imagine themselves and China itself as other than Other. I must leave it to different scholars to look for comparable territorial, linguistic, and political configurations elsewhere. Mysteries set in South Asia, for instance, are read in that region's many vernacular languages, in English translations of them, and in works originally composed in English—within South Asia and outside—by natives, Desis, and foreigners. And there is politics, from home and abroad.

Qiu Xiaolong is the favorite author of contemporary China mystery aficionados outside China. A Chinese American who writes poetry in Chinese and mysteries and poetry in English as his second language, Qiu has sold two million mystery novels, translated into 20 languages. Many of his most avid fans read him in French or Italian translation.[7] I once imagined he and Diane Wei Liang, the best-known PRC-born authors in the genre, would dominate my inquiry, but they joined a publishing phenomenon in progress. Under the tent now by my count are more than 100 mysteries by 38 authors or two-person teams, 41 authors in all. Not quite a third are women. This book's Appendix lists the authors and their relevant works in three categories.

The majority of books at issue here star a Sherlockian Great Detective who solves crimes in a series of mystery novels. Chinese police officers and ex-cops who get leads from former colleagues are typical heroes. Also pursuing crime are judges, procurators (state's attorneys), and agents of the Chinese Communist Party's Discipline Inspection Commission and the clandestine State Security

Mystery Novels from the Second Sino-Western Honeymoon   3

service, organizations outside of and able to pull rank on the regular state judicial apparatus. The lead detective might have a trusty subordinate—even a foreign collaborator—as "Watson." Perhaps as *her* Watson, for some of the detectives are women, not quite a third of the main protagonists. It takes extraordinary insight to create a credible hero who works for a PRC security organ. Hence another plot formula in our subgenre takes an alternate path by having an intrepid civilian hero, perhaps a foreigner, puzzle over a crime *in loco inquisitoris*. I call this the China mystery sub-subgenre with a "beset citizen" hero. Anyone asking questions about crime in China without a badge, however professional, is bound to feel beleaguered; private investigation of crime is not permitted. (In fact there are civilian sleuths in PRC popular fiction, too, but they are cronies of the police.) One series investigator who enjoys the protection of a foreign passport is a smartly outfitted lesbian Chinese Canadian forensics accountant, Ian Hamilton's Ava Lee. She has criminal associates in China and is skilled in martial arts. I doubt one can find a hero like that in any crime novel written in the PRC. I still get carried away following her carefully plotted exploits. A disgraced and very beset Chinese ex-cop can solve crimes, too, while avoiding the local authorities. In the imagination!

"Inside China information" helps bring readers and writers together. Readers want it; authors like to share it. China has its own secrets,[8] and social consciousness is a signature tendency of crime novels by acclaimed European, American, and Japanese authors. Some literary historians trace the noir social crime novel to Raymond Chandler, who was educated in the UK and said he "had to learn American just like a foreign language."[9] Yet, journalists and displaced Chinese writers well know that there are many book formats to choose from, including the memoir and the nonfiction "China book."[10]

Qiu Xiaolong says he took up the detective story because it provided a ready-made structure well suited for what he, a scholar-poet, wanted to say about his native land.[11] Some professors have assigned his books in their social science courses. Diane Wei Liang, another native, likewise found "crime fiction" "an ideal format to examine the social and economic changes that are at the center of modern life in China." She had already written a memoir, but in that genre, "There isn't a screen behind which one can hide, to cover up emotions or justify actions—everything is raw."[12] From Michel Imbert, in France: "Not being Chinese, it seemed to me fairer to write using Western literary structures: the *polar* and *noir* novel. These genres allow description of society and ways of life deeply rooted in urban settings."[13] Christopher West, a China mystery pioneer, writes: "I like the mystery genre as a vehicle for discovery of other cultures—Tony Hillerman is a great hero of mine" (referring to Hillerman's Navajo Tribal Police

4   Chapter 1

mysteries, published 1970–2006; Hillerman was not himself Navajo, though he ran his manuscripts past Navajo friends to check for accuracy).[14] Eliot Pattison's mysteries set in Tibet are frequently compared to Hillerman's. A fictional Navajo ethnographer of her people comes to explore Tibet in Pattison's *Prayer of the Dragon*. "Underlying the murders, thefts, and other crimes in my books," Pattison says, "is very much an attempt to explain the East to the West."[15]

When Peter May's seven "China Thrillers" were reprinted in 2018, a reviewer called them "a series that is part mystery and part cultural history," echoing the author's own retrospective opinion of 2016: "I view the books now almost as modern historical documents."[16] China in David Rotenberg's detective novels has been called "a character in and of itself."[17] He followed with an 800-page historical novel called *Shanghai* that was "supposed to do for that city what James Michener's books did for Hawaii and James Clavell's novels did for Japan."[18] After penning her acclaimed contemporary China mysteries, Lisa See also slightly changed direction and wrote the atmospheric historical novels set in China that made her truly famous. Duncan Jepson went the other way, from China-themed historical fiction to mystery fiction: "I wanted to try to write to a broader audience and I felt a crime story might give me that opportunity."[19] Brian Klingborg's Inspector Lu Fei mysteries are the ne plus ultra, providing running commentary (artfully done) on Chinese urban and rural culture, political institutions, crime statistics, average farm acreage, and unique Mandarin and Burmese vocabulary, delivered in a second omniscient voice like a Greek chorus. Sometimes it pities the hero. Except for Peter May, all these authors had connections with China before they became professional fiction writers, and May, too, traveled in China and met Chinese police officers before he published his China procedurals. Do authors who see themselves as mystery writers first and educators only second consider their works' information dividends essential to their craft?

Probably so, and likewise authors of other kinds of suspense narratives, technothrillers, historical novels, and science fiction.[20] A noted example is Tom Clancy's 1984 thriller, *The Hunt for Red October,* originally published by the academic Naval Institute Press in Annapolis, Maryland. Many readers perused the book to learn about life on Soviet and American submarines. World-ranging detective and spy novels serve up the pleasures of a travel diary for armchair urban flaneurs[21] who surf the internet or once browsed the *Information Please Almanac*. One of our China mysteries names global, not Chinese, historical personalities known for their photographic or eidetic memories (technical terms are a bonus) and another lists famous people who are vegetarian.[22] We get lessons in pharmacology, genetics, pathology, Chinese pistols, cigarette brands and which rank of Chinese official smokes them, and the names for different

Mystery Novels from the Second Sino-Western Honeymoon 5

fireworks bursts. A full online search of detective novels turns up a hundred titles that embed recipes in their plots. Several of our China mysteries come close; Nicole Mones publishes her Chinese recipes in an online supplement.[23] Information exchange can go either way. After Sherlock Holmes tales entered China in 1896, Chinese translators of Western crime fiction added their own factoids and explanations of exotic and everyday Western culture, forensics, and science to inform their readers.[24] Mysteries assume less responsibility for factual accuracy than nonfiction genres like the travelogue, yet readers accord mysteries some trust in their recreations of place and culture, more than science fiction or historical fiction. One difference from the days of Poe, Conan Doyle, and the early Chinese whodunit writers is that mysteries and best sellers today tend to be full-length novels, not short stories. The genre or subgenre here is distinct in four other ways.

Four Characteristics of These China Mysteries

1. The setting is China, and it is "recent." In the PRC, "contemporary China" denotes post-1949 times, but the mystery novels here—and I was not at pains to narrow the field by picking and choosing—were published and, with two exceptions, have plots situated within a shorter time frame: China's period of "reform and opening up" after 1978, following the death of Mao Zedong in 1976, and usually a couple decades or more after that. The pioneering works appeared in 1984 and 1985, with plots set in 1983 or shortly after: *A Death in China* by Carl Hiaasen and Bill Montalbano and *The China Lovers* by David Bonavia and John Byron (Roger Uren). Today those novels look like outliers. All the other China mysteries were published in the 1990s or later, most with plots unfolding in China's era of hyperkinetic economic development after 1992, when economic restructuring and international exchanges resumed after three years of political crackdowns following the June 4, 1989, Beijing massacre. Christopher West's first Inspector Wang mystery appeared in 1994 (in the UK; only 1998, in the US); it has a 1990s plot. Apart from West's second work in his series (1996, UK; 1999, US), all the other contemporary China mysteries have come into print only since 1997, and just a few have plots set in the earlier post-Mao days. Michel Imbert's Judge Li mysteries unfold in 1978–1982, Lee Barckmann's China mystery in 1987, and Deborah and Joel Shlian's in 1989. Those works, all published in 2004 or later, bore a retrospective aura from the start. Since 2008, Qiu Xiaolong has put out four books of linked short stories and vignettes about Inspector Chen Cao's "old childhood neighborhood"[25] as background for that character.[26] Imbert has written what I think may be the only China mystery confined to Mao's

6   Chapter 1

China (set in 1953–1972), *Les disparus du laogaï* (2010). Chapter 5 below discusses it as a historical mystery! Other works with historical themes analyzed in that chapter include a few in which detectives explore the past to solve new crimes and Qiu Xiaolong's twelfth whodunit (2020), a new Judge Dee novel set in the Tang dynasty. It is a companion and interpretive key to—indeed originally part of—what I refer to as his thirteenth mystery (2021), set in 2019. Qiu's latest Inspector Chen novels suggest that China has passed another historical watershed, into a new age of Xi Jinping.

The paucity of contemporary China crime and mystery novels written outside of China, ca. 1949–1996, lasted longer than the 30-year *ban* on such works within the PRC itself, ca. 1949–1979. Robert Hans van Gulik (1910–1967) wrote Judge Dee whodunits in the 1950s and '60s in English and they have delighted readers ever since, but their plots unfold centuries ago.

It seems unlikely that global curiosity about China was greater in the 1990s than during the Cultural Revolution and Vietnam War years of the 1960s; than during the euphoria of the first honeymoon of the PRC and the West, when China began to "open up" in the 1970s; or during the 1980s, when Chinese intellectual ferment climaxed during an internationally telecast 1989 democracy movement in Tiananmen Square. Detective novels set in locales having a special mystique for Western readers blossomed in the 1990s, although Hillerman was popular earlier. Judgments by publishers must have ushered in the China mystery genre. Beyond that, apart from deficits of access and understanding that took years to rectify, it is almost as if the mystery authors had to pass through a period of mourning after the 1989 massacre before writing upbeat tales set in the PRC. That nation's course seemed to be gelling in what would be called the "Beijing Consensus" or "China Model," a full-scale appropriation of an "Asian" development plan based on export-driven market economics and authoritarian politics previously known in Taiwan, Hong Kong, Singapore, and South Korea. China joined the World Trade Organization in 2001, supply chains were integrated, and cultural exchanges proliferated, of students, teachers, technology, arts, and ideas. Some writers in the West spoke of China becoming more capitalist and having a more democratic future.

China was more open than ever in the later 1990s to communication, travel, and temporary residence, for foreigners and its own people. The following decade saw the rise of "new, harder-to-control forms of expression, such as blogs, independent documentary films, underground art movements, and social media."[27] The 1997 handover of Hong Kong to the PRC was another boon to mystery writing.[28] Perhaps for all these reasons, the China mystery blossomed during a "second honeymoon" of the PRC and the West. The 2010s then saw

Mystery Novels from the Second Sino-Western Honeymoon   7

leaner, meaner, more noir thrillers depicting an urban China as complicated and corrupted by new wealth and global interconnections as any society. To a Queens, New York City ex-con, Shanghai is the perfect place to go off the grid: "a landscape in flux, growing fast enough for there to be opportunities, but not so fast that a person couldn't remain out of sight" (Kirk Kjeldsen, *Tomorrow City* [2013], Ch. 21).

2. These works come from outside the PRC. Publishing them there would be problematic. Translation of Qiu Xiaolong's first three Inspector Chen novels from the original English into Chinese for publication in Shanghai confirmed this. Qiu was a former Shanghai homey, but censorship was so heavy (two-thirds of a chapter was deleted in one instance, damaging plot logic) that he put further translations on hold, and that was in a more liberal time.[29] His works evince love of Chinese people, places, and culture, but are devoid of official or even nonofficial nationalistic overtones. Online posts in China faulted him for not understanding the more advanced China of *today*, catering to foreigners, etc.[30] One can imagine what a PRC readership would think of the mysteries by other authors. We all love to spot anachronisms and bloopers in films. Many China mystery authors explain what a PRC native would consider common knowledge and novels featuring China as a place for self-discovery might seem odd to a Chinese audience. Few influential critics or professors in the PRC value crime fiction. Publishers and their CCP (Chinese Communist Party) overseers control the domestic market.

3. The novelists have an abiding personal or professional interest in China, combined with an outsider's consciousness and inability to feel like a PRC citizen. They did not pick China simply because it seemed like a good place to write about mystery, conflict, and intrigue. Qiu Xiaolong, Zhang Xinxin, and Diane Wei Liang were born and raised in the PRC. They live abroad, more or less in self-exile since 1988 or 1989. All were allowed trips home within a decade of leaving China. Probably they could reside and even publish in the PRC again, subject to conditions—some knowable, like heavy self-censorship, others not necessarily knowable in advance. The younger author An Yu was born and raised in the PRC and she resides there again part-time, but she wrote and published her novel in the US. Alban Yung, Lisa See, Duncan Jepson, and Daniel Nieh have some Chinese ancestry; Leo Ou-fan Lee and Chan Ho-Kei exemplify full Chinese ancestry and a Chinese cultural coming-of-age outside of but close to Mainland China. Most of the other authors have substantial experience and often years of residence in the PRC, as foreign correspondent, businessperson, student,

8   Chapter 1

teacher, or consultant, with subsequent return trips. A half dozen of them studied China in college or graduate school. Carl Hiaasen is the exception. He had little or no China experience of his own, but worked with a collaborator who did, Bill Montalbano. One might combine the Chinese emigrants and foreign sojourners in China under the label of **reciprocal** or **convergent expat authors** if the terms were clearer and the word "expat" did not so often suggest people living in culturally isolated communities. Caricatures of expats in China and Chinese immigrant enclaves abroad enliven certain novels discussed below. The authors know such communities well and view them with skeptical eyes.

Yet no author here belongs to Mainland Chinese society these days, not even the four born in the PRC.[31] The other authors never belonged. Most are however from multicultural societies: the US, UK, France, Canada, Singapore, and Hong Kong. Jan-Philipp Sendker is a German-born journalist formerly posted to the US and Asia. Henning Mankell, a Swede, admired the Chinese revolution, but came to China only to visit. His second home was Mozambique.

Lisa See and Peter May, during their relatively brief but multiple visits to China, saw PRC public security officials up close. But the authors featured in this book, unlike so many mystery writers in the PRC, are not publicly known to have worked as security or intelligence officers in any nation's service (I have not either)—Roger Uren and James Church are exceptions—and few if any of the authors ever worked for a PRC-owned enterprise. Alban Yung enjoyed access to the French embassy in Beijing, Ian Hamilton has been a Canadian civil servant, and a couple of other writers' early sojourns in Asia look a little mysterious. Eliot Pattison, Shamini Flint, and Duncan Jepson are international lawyers. Even so, the mysteries and crime sagas here are not the place to look for specialized knowledge about PRC police or legal procedure, Chinese Communist Party thinking, or the practices of criminal organizations. In my opinion, comparable novels written in the PRC, including the many penned by current or former security professionals, are not much more informative about such topics.[32] For their part, the China mysteries produced over here seldom provide deep and persuasive critiques of global capitalism (likewise, mysteries written in the PRC). We love the authors on both sides because they are good at fabrication—at storytelling that makes improbable and exciting events somehow convincing. Ordinarily incredible scenarios become real as the writers make crosscutting subplots come together and sew up every loose end. Local color and "information" help out, as the glue or binder.[33]

Outside my inquiry are thrillers with espionage and sabotage themes in which a peripatetic hero visits China, such as the one-off adventure, bio-, naval-, and cyber-technothrillers set in China or Hong Kong featuring operatives like

Mystery Novels from the Second Sino-Western Honeymoon 9

Jack Ryan, Ian Ludlow, Eve Polastri and her nemesis Villanelle—they, too, have been to China—Nick Foley, John Wells, Harry Bosch, Lincoln Rhyme, Dirk Pitt, Neil Carey, Capt./Adm. Dan Lenson, Susanna Sloane, Jake Grafton, Joe Lennox, Ian McLean, etc., as purveyed by Tom Clancy, Lee Goldberg, Luke Jennings, Alex Ryan, Alex Berenson, Michael Connelly, Jeffery Deaver, Clive Cussler, Don Winslow, David Poyer, S. G. Kiner, Stephen Coonts, Charles Cumming, and David W. Rudlin, respectively. Jason Bourne fends off PRC bad actors in his second novel, by Robert Ludlum, and in his eleventh, by Eric Van Lustbader, creator previously of the China-involved secret agent Jake Maroc. Investors from the PRC appear in a 2019 Greg Iles Mississippi nailbiter, *Cemetery Road*. Jake Needham is an "old Asia hand," but his thrillers unfold in Southeast Asia. Barry Eisler and his spy series assassin, John Rain, are outside our category, as is best-selling British thriller writer Stephen Leather. His pre-handover Hong Kong thriller *Hungry Ghost* (1991) has Hong Kong spy and crime themes. William [Leonard] Marshall's Yellowthread Street series, which began in 1975, has European- and mixed-ethnicity cops investigating Hong Kong crimes.[34] Leather's and Marshall's works could be called "postcolonial mysteries," even if they are not literally "post." Later editions of Dean Koontz's thriller, *The Eyes of Darkness*, uncannily feature a scientifically engineered bioweapon called "Wuhan-400." In the original 1981 edition, it was named "Gorki-400," after a lab near a fictional Soviet town of Gorki. When the USSR dissolved, a 1989 reprint of the novel simply substituted the name of the Chinese city, which was known to have had a microbiology lab since 1956.

These other thrillers can be exciting and some incorporate creditable book research on things Chinese. However, besides the different generic themes, the Sinitic plot locales seem to me to reflect single-instance geopolitical interest. Someplace else could be substituted for China. Eric Stone's fourth Ray Sharp novel, on the other hand, is admitted to our fold; it really is about China and it yields dividends from the author's twelve years' journalistic experience in Hong Kong and Indonesia. Even though many of our China mysteries offer the attractions of travel diaries, they are not those of a stopover or tourist writer, although readers may see the matter differently or even wish they were.

4. These mysteries were written for a global mass market of middle-class readers outside the PRC. That must be the main reason why novels by authors who came to the West from China and those who viewed China from the West and its onetime colonies ended up with so many common themes. (Another reason would be the extreme difficulty of understanding the upper echelons of Chinese decision making and even the lower echelons of policing that intrigue most

10   Chapter 1

authors and readers of the genre.) The authors hope to attract, entertain, and inform the same body of readers, and they are advised by many of the same publishers, editors, and agents. Plus, the book industry does not abjure copycatting. Popular fiction readers are not expected to know much about China, and many who read these novels may be drawn to crime narratives set in any evocatively presented locale. The dominance of English, French, and translations from the English in China mysteries seems to me a dependent variable, following global marketing precedents. Editors have played a big role in shaping the language, content, and plots of many of the novels, particularly those by authors writing in English as a second language. Authors who can write in English enjoy many advantages. Why, though, do so few authors in Taiwan, Hong Kong, and other global Sinophone communities write PRC-sited mysteries in Chinese, to go with all the martial arts and historical or quasi-historical fantasy novels and media productions? Difficulty selling a Chinese-language contemporary mystery set in China must be involved.

Leo Ou-fan Lee wrote in 2001 that the prospering Taiwan book market did not even support original Chinese-language spy novels, though he, a major cultural figure and interlocutor, did get his own spy-detective novel printed in Taiwan. (It was released in Shanghai the next year, which is another exceptional case, though the book was not reprinted or widely promoted.[35]) The PRC and Taiwan internal markets for new detective and mystery novels are dominated by best-selling translations into Chinese of mysteries by Japanese authors who set their works in Japan. (Taiwan has in recent years printed mysteries set in Taiwan.[36]) Japanese mysteries can fascinate Chinese audiences and ours, too, but the eye is not on *Chinese* society—rather, on a global modern industrialized society common to Japan, Taiwan, urban Mainland China, and the West. Mysteries published in the PRC with Chinese settings strike me as even more culturally "abstract" or generalized. Keigo Higashino (Higashino Keigo in Japanese word order) is the favorite crime author in China.[37] His detective and other novels, with their unusual plot twists, battles of wits among relatively well-rounded characters, transcendental ethics that prevail in morally ambiguous situations, and close psychological observations, also have youth, schoolmate, and ghost themes popular with PRC readers. Japanese critics, perhaps too simply, call Higashino a writer of *honkaku* ("orthodox" or "original form") whodunits in the mode of Poe, Conan Doyle, and Edogawa Ranpo, unlike Japan's social realist mysteries that explore the dark side of society. Higashino's emphasis on the puzzle makes his crime fiction a good fit for China's readers. Also influential in the PRC are East Asian and Western media productions, including Japanese *manga* such as Gōshō Aoyama's *Case Closed* series starring

Mystery Novels from the Second Sino-Western Honeymoon   11

Detective Conan. Japanese mysteries depicting corruption and police cover-ups, like Hideo Yokoyama's international best seller *Six Four*, are politically taboo in the PRC.

That Japanese mysteries translated into Chinese lord it over native PRC authors' own mysteries on PRC best-seller lists, though the native authors' cops, killers, and prose are after all Chinese, provides a clue as to why I am now so attracted to China mysteries *not* published in the PRC. Liu Cixin, China's most famous SF author, prefers that bilingual readers take up his globally acclaimed *The Three Body Problem* in the English-language edition masterfully translated (and restructured) by Ken Liu rather than in the original Chinese. But to see the full "communist-capitalist" whipsaw, consider the setting of PRC crime novelist Zhou Haohui's *Death Notice*. When he wrote it in Chinese, the author meant for the locale to suggest a city in his native Jiangsu, perhaps Yangzhou, his hometown, or Nanjing. In the final print edition, however, the setting is anonymous, designated as "'A' City," to avoid objections from Jiangsu officials who would not want their bailiwick associated with crime. This sort of problem confronts other PRC writers. Zhou's workaround, using a placeholder letter from the Roman alphabet, is a common one. Small wonder that settings can seem generalized. When the book was translated into English, an American editor wanted more local color. The location was changed to Chengdu, a thousand miles up the Yangzi River, to entice Anglophone readers thought to be partial to Sichuan, famous for its spicy food and giant pandas. Or was it a bigger intervention when Liu Cixin's foreign editor had him change the gender of a major character in the final volume of his Three Body trilogy "for the sake of better 'gender balance'"?[38]

The Leo Ou-fan Lee, Chan Ho-Kei, and Zhang Xinxin novels cited in this book show that a good mystery can be written in Chinese without support or "guidance" from the PRC culture bureaucracy, to put the case ironically. Intriguing, necessarily apolitical crime novels published inside the PRC can win global readers if well translated and adapted. That includes He Jiahong's mysteries of 1995–1996. The author, a law professor at the Chinese People's University in Beijing with a 1993 graduate law degree from the Northwestern University law school in Chicago, created a lawyer-detective hero, which is unusual although not unprecedented in PRC fiction. He Jiahong's mysteries are cited in this book for comparative purposes, but they do not appear to have been written for the global capitalist market or to have much influenced it. The author says he was inspired by Scott Turow's legal thrillers.[39]

Better known in China and also deserving global readership are Chinese-language crossovers from the crime genre to highbrow fiction available in

12   Chapter 1

English from resident PRC authors Wang Shuo (*Playing for Thrills*), Liu Zhenyun (*I Did Not Kill My Husband; The Cook, the Crook, and the Real Estate Tycoon; Strange Bedfellows*), Song Ying (*Apricot's Revenge*), A Yi (*A Perfect Crime; Two Lives; Wake Me Up at Nine in the Morning;* "The Curse"), and Sun Yisheng ("The Shades Who Periscope Through Flowers to the Sky"). In French, one can read a puzzler published in the PRC by Zhang Xinxin before her self-exile, *Le courier des bandits* (The Bandit Courier; 1986),[40] and Ma Xiaoquan's *Confession d'un tueur à gages* (Confession of a Hitman). Even Nobel laureate Mo Yan's *The Republic of Wine* appears on some crime aficionados' lists. More generic 2010s mysteries from the PRC seem to favor psychopaths, dismembered corpses, profiling of serial killers, and forensic medical investigations. Some works can be read in excellent translations: *The Untouched Crime* (Zijin Chen), *A Devil's Mind* (Gangxueyin), *Murder in Dragon City* (Qin Ming), and the aforementioned *Death Notice* (Zhou Haohui). Mi Lei's intriguing mysteries, such as his *Profiler,* are available in roughly edited English editions. Mai Jia's *Decoded* has been well received abroad. It is a novel about a spy, not really a spy thriller.

Run-on narratives by Cai Jun and Murong Xuecun that gained traction with younger PRC readers online can also be read in Western languages. Cai's *The Child's Past Life* (2013) is a best seller of the crime-horror-ghost genre popular in the PRC. Cai feels that "suspense fiction" in Chinese was unknown before 2000; the 1991 Japanese novel *Ring* and its media adaptations were game changers for him.[41] Murong, like the more senior He Jiahong, has legal training. A cynical lawyer-confessor in Murong's 2008 cult hit, *Dancing through Red Dust,* iterates tales of judges and lawyers collaborating in barely disguised bribery, case fixing, profit sharing, pimping, blackmail, suborning, and setups leading to jail time for anyone who refuses to play the game—rather like a late Qing "exposure" or "muckraking" novel.[42] The content comes from stories lawyers told him, Murong says. Copious deletions from the Chinese were added back to the English edition. (Criticism of corruption was allowed; not of the legal system.) Cai and Murong may not be ready for Japanese or Western mainstream publication, but their windows on Chinese social attitudes, family relations, and taste in domestic and imported pop culture, including video games, are more up-to-date than in most mysteries written abroad. The authors express amazement at how much China has changed since the days of their youth in the 1990s. The interest of *The Child's Past Life* lies not so much in reincarnation fantasy or mystery plotting as in existential displacement like that in time travel and alternate history genres.

Quality?

How might one rate these mysteries? A genre novel faces difficulties winning highest literary honors. Measured against works by the crime fiction profession's award winners (in the West and Japan; the PRC lacks such awards), I give most of the China mysteries here fairly high marks for pacing, sense of intrigue, wit, and evocation of background; a little less for originality and memorability of the heroes, plots, and styles; and a further discount regarding their conveyance of Chinese interpersonal relations and dialogue. No works here are low-end pulps. Some have won or been nominated for awards by the West's mystery fiction associations; a few have won critical praise as general literature. Sinophiles like me, giving extra credit for cleverly expressed or *telling* (not most frequent) observations regarding Chinese culture and society, will want to award five stars to some China mysteries. The information dividends can be judged along two different axes: reliability, usually good, and insight or depth. The latter must serve different audiences: insiders who enjoy seeing familiar Chinese city street names and subway stops; complete outsiders who need constantly to be filled in on background; and readers in between, who may have visited China. Local color, to the novelists' credit, is more distinctive than Confucius Institute, Shen Yun, and diverse information services' dance and calligraphy performances that capitalize on exterior beauty without background meanings. A few of the China mysteries were printed by self-publishing or small presses. Being among the more personal creations—despite their sashays into some quite fantastic exploits—these mysteries have charm and fascination for those of us who were in the PRC when the authors were. These books, too, kept me turning the pages.

All sorts of readers are on the lookout for East Asian themes. Fans of online fantasy fiction in English, like fellow devotees who read in Chinese, seek out martial arts and "cultivation" novels and games populated by mythic "Asian" characters from exotic and fictitious eras, planets, universes, and the underworld—*that* underworld. Some such works are written in the US, UK, Canada, and Australia, by people seemingly without ethnic or identity affiliation with Asia,[43] while other such novels, by authors with Asian names, are continually being translated into English from Chinese and other Asian languages for reading online and even in print. Conversely, entire PRC online fiction subgenres are named for the European-style princesses, wizards, or vampires they feature. Harry Potter and *Game of Thrones* were big hits there. China has murder theater with audience participation, too. Yet readers in China, more than in the West and Japan, feel they are "above" customary fiction of crime and detection, apart

14   Chapter 1

from Agatha Christie's. It is a niche interest that today must compete with burgeoning online fantasy productions.

For the novels discussed in this book, set in the "real world" of China on planet Earth, some aficionados far from the fictional crime scenes appear delighted just to encounter common newspaper knowledge and snippets from Sunzi's (Sun Tzu's) *The Art of War*, judging by posts in Goodreads. Then again, the smallest detail could be a clue.

2

Birth and Anatomy of a Genre

This chapter explores how the China mystery arose and, after years of difficulty and delay, found a place in the West's commercial publishing industry. Recent scholarship on genre, popular fiction, and cross-cultural interpretation may serve as preamble to clarify the works' place within the larger world of popular fiction.

The generic attractions of a China mystery come clear on its opening pages, often on the book cover: plot themes (crime, investigation, jeopardy), setting (China), and time ("now"). Readability is another lure. So is a hint of established popularity, with more works to come. Once the subgenre found its niche in the 1990s, nine out of ten books were defined or redefined as belonging to a series. From the front covers: "An Inspector Wang Mystery," "A Red Princess Mystery," "A Zhong Fong Mystery," "An Inspector Shan Tao Yun Mystery," "A China Thriller" (by Peter May), "An Inspector Chen Novel," "*Une enquête du juge Li*" (A Judge Li Investigation), "A Mei Wang Mystery," "A Feng Shui Detective Novel," "The Handover Mysteries Volume Two," "Inspector Singh Investigates: A Calamitous Chinese Killing," "An Inspector Lu Fei Mystery," "Author of the Critically Acclaimed Inspector O Series" (under the author's pseudonym), or simply "A Ray Sharp Novel," "An Ellie McEnroe Novel," or "An Ava Lee Novel."[1] Those are the names of series heroes, not the authors. Paratexts (titles, blurbs, cover art) might promise a death, murder, killing, abduction, slaughter, mystery, or case; speak of a skull, skeleton, snakehead, thief, or fire maker; cite China, Beijing, Pékin, Shanghai, perhaps a jade or mandarin; depict a dragon, Chinese calligraphy, or Shanghai's landmark Oriental Pearl Tower; or ostentatiously deploy the color red.

The China mystery can be grasped as a whole because it is so discrete, in effect a microgenre, promising particular kinds of novelty within the comforts of thematic and formal reliability and relatability.[2] Of genre fiction generally, Sally R. Munt observes: "readers compulsively consume one novel after another, and crime fiction is a paragon of its type."[3] This book will argue that besides its recurring plot schemas, sense of contemporaneity, and interesting factoids about

15

16   Chapter 2

anything and everything from practically anywhere in the world, the China mystery favors particular crimes, locales in China, kinds of heroes, patterns of human relations, cross-cultural complications, and means of dealing with or bypassing China's modern history. The China mystery has its own beginning, in 1984 or really 1997, after a decade of near silence; a sometimes all-too-obvious educational side mission; and a demarcated range of reader circulation: the world outside the PRC, the scene of the action. That can be another attraction. One can read and write these whodunits and thrillers, with all their contemporary ramifications, without serious consequence. Whether the China mystery with all its predilections is equally overdetermined in its social, cultural, and political values and prejudices, overt and subterranean, raises further questions that this monograph can only begin to probe. These works do not extol PRC political viewpoints or opposition to them, but neither do generic crime novels written in the PRC. The Western market has not produced alternative China mystery genres—ones that might, say, unfold in the Mao era, ponder seemingly unbridgeable cultural gaps between China and the West, or focus solely on local crimes solvable through reconstruction of bizarre individual motives and odd coincidences without need of a global social vision, the forte of generic crime fiction written in China. To that extent, the overseas-produced China mystery presents a view of Sino-Western relations, not just of China.

In the academy, and well away from Chinese departments, concepts of genre, genres, and popular fiction are disputed in debates that have their own history, particularly when the subject is detective and crime fiction. Already in 1991, David Trotter wrote that "Detective fiction has become the most frequently and most heavily theorized of all popular genres" (66). Since then, fiction with crime themes has continued proliferating, diversifying, and mixing ("hybridizing") with other popular and postmodern fiction and nonfiction genres and audiovisual media trends, stimulating an academic field of crime fiction scholarship. It traces the multinational and multigeneric genealogy and "rhizomatic" differentiation of this writing, often seeking to "shift" ideas of crime fiction as a prescriptive genre in favor of "a field in flux where mutation, contamination and innovation take precedence over the purity of canonical forms."[4] This approach offers close readings of classic and postmodern works whose complexity invites metaphoric, ironic, transgressive, and metaliterary textual analyses. Such analysis can also be trained on commercial midmarket and downmarket novels; exempting them might reinforce misconceptions that popular fiction must be devoid of literary value, that literary pleasure and edification cannot coexist with formulas, archetypes, and salability, or that popular fiction has no influence on public opinion, international images, and highbrow culture.[5]

Birth and Anatomy of a Genre   17

We know from the Chinese experience that "crime fiction" is a broad subject-matter category whose very capaciousness can have implications under a system of literary control.[6] Equivalent terms exist in Chinese, without having achieved dominance, though neither have academic specializations in crime- or law-enforcement-themed fiction under any other rubric.[7] The subject is sensitive. I have written previously that crime and law themes, within law enforcement gestalts differentially conceived as paternalistic or adversarial, generated distinctive, even if cross-fertilizing, native-style and Western-style forms in Chinese fiction by the early twentieth century. And they did so again beginning in the 1980s, once the Maoist banning ended.[8] In the twenty-first century, diverse sorts of print, online, and broadcast books, films, TV series, *anime,* and games have lent China's crime-and-law-enforcement-themed media much variety. Many productions are original to China. Others are translations of foreign products.

Generic or metageneric differentiations still cut across postmodern ideas of crime fiction. One discrimination is of register or level, starting with reading or grade level,[9] which with other differences of text, dissemination, and public perception that Pierre Bourdieu refers to as matters of position and habitus, not to mention differences in ephemerality, reinforce hierarchical concepts of popular, mass-market, and middlebrow fiction and media.[10] (In the PRC, genuine and putative folk or *minjian* literature has stood as another alternative to "high" or canonical literature, and modern local operas with PRC cop heroes exist, but these have waned in the internet age.) The aforementioned Western scholarly shift in focus toward relatively original and high-end or literary crime fiction "challenges the distinction between literary and popular fiction," regarding it "as a relic of a previous, elitist view of literature."[11] On the opposite side in spirit, purview, and advocacy, even amid genre objectification, is Ken Gelder's enthusiasm for popular fiction (which he agrees "is, essentially, genre fiction") as a "literary field" "best conceived as the opposite of Literature."[12] Popular fiction, he reminds us, has its own cherished multigeneric, multinational, indeed time-honored genealogy going back to Walter Scott. And like literary fiction, the popular has its own perpetually fractionating micro- and nanogenres. Bernice M. Murphy photocaptured them during their 2015–2016 moment; Megan Walsh did the same for Chinese-language works in their 2021 moment.[13] Meanwhile Beth Driscoll has written of the middlebrow as a "magnetic" literary range with gendered characteristics that embody "women's shared reading."[14] (Matters of gender are considered in this book's Chapter 4.) Robert Rushing sees popular fiction providing the same kinds of repeating irresolution-as-enjoyment as highbrow works. And Peter Swirski has applied to crime fiction

18   Chapter 2

the twenty-first-century meme of "nobrow," indicating works aiming at both highbrow and lowbrow taste, not something in the middle.[15] Internet fiction authors who post several thousand characters daily remind us that subliterary fiction exists, too. An anomaly in theoretical study is the lack of attention to plots, except as embodiments of archetypes.[16] A plot with closure, and even so poised to be replicated in a future volume with the same hero, is a major attraction in crime fiction. One finds it also in China's never-ending episode-driven online fantasy sagas. Quite different are PRC author A Yi's more abstruse stories, like those narrated with dissociated consciousness in *Two Lives*. A Yi writes modernist fiction with themes of crime, pathology, and therefore police involvement (his former profession), not "crime fiction." He reads Camus, Faulkner, and Proust.[17]

This monograph holds that fiction's "wavelength" values are partly physical (aspects of readability and ephemerality can be measured), but also perceptual. And they vary not across demarcated boundaries, but continuously, across a spectrum: from subliterary (call it ultraviolet, invisible to critics), popular and middlebrow (violet, blue, green), to literary (red), and canonical (infrared). In Chinese, literary and canonical or classic works were once called *chun wenxue* or "pure literature." *Elements* of fiction (characterization, themes, styles, and types of them) can vary separately, each across its own spectrum. Moreover, when these elements interact, with each other and with changing taste, perception of the colors can change while wavelengths stay the same. Thus, gory imagery can shift upward from being an indication of pulp status when it becomes associated with ideologically important and overlooked negative social phenomena, as in postwar hard-knuckle crime fiction (Dobrescu, 45).

The contemporary China mysteries discussed in this book are mostly in the middle range, sometimes with upmarket redshift qualities. It is for convenience that I refer to the latter as crossover traits, crossing over variously into satire, comedy, irony, pastiche, or the contemporary social novel. The authors here vie for readers and Edgars, not canonization, and some are celebrated for their writings in journalism, nonfiction, the social novel, or poetry; their international law practice; or visibility academically and in the arts.[18] An educational function regarding a particular time and place can also belong to the historical novel, a genre largely bypassed in popular fiction studies despite its own considerable lineage, which ought to include Robert van Gulik's Judge Dee mysteries. Composed by a professional Sinologist (among his other callings), those works were born to be classics—to be remembered. We recall above all the hero, the works' pioneer status and authority in their field, and their interface with history.[19] The best China mysteries discussed in this monograph might hope for similar staying power, as fictive emblems of a unique time and place.

Other generic or metageneric fault lines, theorized more than 50 years ago by Tzvetan Todorov, separate thrillers (featuring present danger), whodunits (solving a mysterious crime committed in the past), and suspense novels (combining ongoing danger with mystery). Recent academic studies of crime fiction have not emphasized this differentiation, nor does this monograph, although marketing and sales surveys often do. Nearly every novel discussed herein investigates at least one past crime or mystery, adds thrills and danger, and is sufficiently driven by appeals to topicality that cold case inquests in the plot are usually triggered by new cases in the novel's present time. I take from Todorov the idea of "the story of the suspect-as-detective,"[20] which is usually but not always a subset of the "beset citizen" sub-formula.

Still other lines of categorization remind us that contemporary crime novels are corralled within the broad realm of realistic fiction. This monograph tends toward that position; it views both true crime narratives and mysteries with spectral or horror themes as distinct from crime fiction as generally conceived. Overlaps and comparisons are still of interest, for most China mysteries are at least partly rooted in an author's lived experience in China, and supernatural presences entered East Asia's own crime narratives centuries ago and remain popular with all kinds of readers still today. Zombies have meanwhile entered Anglophone novels set in China.[21] I persist in differentiating among real (nonfiction), realistic, and fantasy plots. Eliot Pattison's Tibet novels discussed in this book embrace local religious themes and tropes, but causation in his complex plots belongs to our usual world of materialist epistemology.

Voices and Where They Come From

Crime and mystery fiction depicting a setting distant from the works' place of creation and its intended readers is not new and many classics have been analyzed in that light,[22] but the globalization of settings for crime fiction plots has burgeoned particularly since the 1990s.[23] Writing pointedly marketed as multicultural is only slightly older. Eva Erdmann wrote in 2009 that "the crime novel of the last decades is distinguished by the fact that the main focus is not on the crime itself, but on the setting" (12). She added that "the distinguishing feature of Scottish or Greek crime fiction is not that it is written by a Scot or a Greek, but that it attempts to convey a Scottish or Greek atmosphere" (22). Her first point argues (more than I would) for geographical setting as the *main* genre characteristic of the contemporary crime novel; her second point, intentionally or not,

20   Chapter 2

makes a place for transnationally composed works like those at issue in this book. Some critics evidently agree with Erdmann's first pronouncement.[24] Academic analyses of location in crime fiction are bountiful. Geographers weighed in early on, and there is talk of a "spatial turn in literary studies" generally.[25] Crime fiction set in non-Western locales has however mostly been discussed in Western scholarship within scholarly discourses of postcolonial fiction, globalization, and world literature,[26] predominantly in symposium and reference volumes populated by entries about works by particular authors set in certain cities or within a particular national literature, supplemented recently by mobility and borderlands themes.[27] In the American field, novelist Jim Nelson feels that "modern mystery fiction has supplanted 19th-century American regional literature, sometimes known as 'writing of local color,' as its dominant form."[28] Erdmann, citing works by a Catalonian and an Israeli, posits: "the crime novel takes on the function of a new kind of *Heimatroman*," or "homeland novel."[29] Might mystery novels set in China and written by nostalgic ex-sojourners and self-exiles then be read as homeland fiction manqué? It is in native crime fiction published in the PRC that attractions of local color go missing, due to the recurring taboo on linking crime to particular jurisdictions. That applies even to the megalopolis of Shanghai. When Qiu Xiaolong's debut whodunit was translated for publication in Chinese, the location had to be rendered anonymous, as "H City." Street names were also disguised. This disadvantages in-country PRC authors. Sympathetic collaborating translators sometimes "add back" at least the city names when preparing English-language renditions of Chinese crime novels.[30] Highbrow authors like A Yi and Liu Zhenyun seem to enjoy more leeway in identifying the settings of their works' action.

Crime and detective novels can be set in the distant past, which, too, "is a foreign country." Mikhail Bakhtin is known for considering a particular time and space together, as a chronotope.[31] Thomas Leitch describes for "detective fiction" a progressive chain of creation linked to particular times and geographical settings: (1) the Great Detective School (associated with Victorian and Edwardian London, Paris of the Belle Époque, and their empires), (2) Golden Age puzzle mysteries or whodunits (English country estates between the world wars), (3) hardboiled detective stories (particular American cities in the 1930s), (4) police procedurals (other American cities, as pioneered by the radio program *Dragnet* in 1949), and (5) historical mysteries (Europe and the Mediterranean in ancient, medieval, and World War II times; this subgenre crested only in recent decades, Leitch argues).[32] Here one might add Robert van Gulik's relatively cozy Judge Dee novels and numerous multimedia hardboiled gangsters-in-paradise tales of prerevolutionary Shanghai. Leitch attributes reader acceptance of a "normalcy"

Birth and Anatomy of a Genre   21

of crime to the rise of the procedural (166; also Erdmann, 19–20). Lack of concern with statistical probability may well buttress the believability of crime fiction, necessary in the case of the PRC, where murder is rare. Similarly, English country estates.

The China mysteries discussed in this book generally draw on all the categories above except the historical one, though the authors must have read van Gulik's novels and been encouraged by his success. Most novels discussed in this book feature a hero who is as perceptive as a Great Detective. That goes not only for the police but also the foreign explorers in China, including those who came to escape predicaments back home. Second, most works have multiple murders or a constant stream of attempted murders, kidnappings, and rackets that normalize crime, just as in a procedural; half of our China mysteries *are* police procedurals. Whether the heroes are professionals or amateurs, there is interest both in solving the crimes and the process of getting there. The heroes, on the other hand, even the police officers, have, third, the hardboiled, sometimes impulsive inner resolve of a detective who walks the mean streets alone when necessary. That may seem unrealistic, but it is accompanied by broad social descriptions as in Euro-Japanese urban social procedurals. Some China mysteries even so manage to serve up reassurance about enduring cultural values that suggests, fourth, a latter-day Golden Age mystery with Chinese characteristics—a post-Mao "farewell-to-revolution" Chinese cozy. Instead of a country estate, the crime scene might be the Bund Park, a prewar Shanghai mansion, or a precinct of abandoned factories turned trendy Beijing artists' colony—the Dashanzi Art District.

More attention to the global character of crime fiction is a second intended shift advocated in recent scholarship. Under the auspices of the first shift, toward consideration of crime fiction as Literature, crime fiction has entered the field of "world literature" as David Damrosch defines it: works widely read across national, cultural, and linguistic borders.[33] International literary *influence* on both PRC-produced mysteries and our China mysteries produced abroad is also apparent, though hard to trace, like influence generally. Stewart King reminds us that readers, too, have a transnational strategy for reading crime fiction, from their preunderstanding that mysteries are unreliable narratives with misdirection in the plot.[34]

Yet, outside the Chinese cultural world, which for its part is not very interested in crime fiction studies, mention of crime fiction connected to China is infrequent, apart from Fu Manchu and Charlie Chan studies.[35] This calls for remediation on several grounds. (1) China has from the start of the twentieth century contributed Chinese-language crime novels to the conventionally generic

22   Chapter 2

global corpus and does so today. Some works are now read internationally, in Chinese and in translation. (2) China inspires crime and mystery fiction written around the world: the novels discussed in this book. These works, too, are read globally (except in the PRC), in their original languages and in foreign translations. (3) China for some centuries has had its own Great Judge literary forms depicting crime investigations and legal process.[36] They influenced premodern Japanese writing[37] and Robert van Gulik's mid-twentieth-century Judge Dee mysteries.[38] The latter alone have spawned Chinese media adaptations (enabled by early 1980s PRC Chinese translations of van Gulik's novels) and multiple whodunit book series in different European languages starring case-cracking Chinese officials and even a fictional eleventh-century Japanese samurai detective.[39] (4) China mysteries like those discussed in this book (more than domestic PRC mysteries without spy themes) feature transnational and cross-cultural plots, detectives, and investigative partnerships, even global legal and criminal organizations, though the criminals are seldom very convincing. (5) Transcultural and/or diasporic Chinese protagonists (positive ones) appear in crime novels written and set in locations across the globe.[40] A few PRC-born authors have composed—abroad—Chinese-language crime novels with foreign settings.[41] These would be the reciprocating "America mysteries" anticipated in this book's preface. They remain rare.

Still, questions of authenticity of authorial viewpoint and voice arise about works produced overseas.[42] Systematic misapprehensions of and prejudices against Asian cultures have been most famously analyzed by Edward Said.[43] Slavoj Žižek in 2003 wrote of parallax that results when authors view a locale from different places, with the "global detective story" as his example. He moreover posited as the "chief" distinction in the "global detective story" "the opposition between foreigners writing about a distant place and 'natives' writing about their own environs."[44] My study begins with a bifurcation just as stark and extraliterary, although different: publication inside vs. outside the country depicted. The political wall between the PRC and its Others inheres not just in the conditions of writing and publishing, but also in the bifurcation of intended readers with their separate knowledge bases, which might mimic the native vs. foreign authorial dichotomy—*if* authorial backgrounds and identities were so simple. Žižek takes as his examples "detective series set in Botswana, on Native American reservations, in the industrial Ruhr, in Venice and Florence, in Ireland, in Brezhnev or Yeltsin's Russia, even in contemporary Tibet."[45] Žižek goes on to name Alexandra Marinina, a native Russian detective fiction writer, and Eliot Pattison, a nonnative traveler in Tibet often mentioned in this book. We can guess at the other authors, but their positioning is complicated: Alexander

Birth and Anatomy of a Genre   23

McCall Smith, who is Scottish/Zimbabwean and Caucasian; Tony Hillerman, a Caucasian resident of New Mexico whose Lt. Joe Leaphorn sleuths in Four Corners country as a Navajo variation on a Caucasian sheriff Hillerman met in the Texas panhandle; maybe Jürgen Kehrer and/or Jan Zweyer, native Germans long resident along the Ruhr and nearby; Donna Leon and Magdalen Nabb, not native to Italy but by 2003 already resident for more than two decades in Venice and Florence, respectively; and perhaps Ken Bruen, an Ireland native who nevertheless is known for his extensive residence and teaching abroad. (The celebrated Dublin mystery author Tana French debuted in 2007; for the record, she is of American and multinational upbringing.)

Authors everywhere aspire now to a global audience and may write accordingly. Chinese-origin authors like Ha Jin who write nongeneric fiction in English as a second language explain Chinese cultural norms and probably limit the number of Chinese names in their works for the sake of non-Chinese readers. Cultural adaptations and simplifications for readers not native to the literary place of action appear notably in the craft of translation. Exhibit A is Robert van Gulik's first mystery, the *Celebrated Cases of Judge Dee,* the one he did not compose from scratch and thus called a translation.[46] Exhibit B might be most translations of Chinese crime fiction cited for comparative purposes in Chapter 1, artfully and compellingly rendered by Howard Goldblatt, Sylvia Li-chun Lin, and colleagues. PRC officials habitually accused native highbrow writers and filmmakers of catering to foreign taste during the latter's springtime in the 1980s. Their acclaimed avant-garde films were in fact best known overseas, though partly because distribution of them was restricted at home. The paramount factor in insider vs. outsider differentiation may yet reflect the audience targeted and the character of the publishing regime.

However, Žižek's point is not so much about divergence between native and nonnative creators as between Third World (his term) and First World authorial positions within a capitalist world system. This bears consideration. Industrialization is a major plot-mover in the China mystery, with the financial capital typically coming from the US. Moreover, PRC-origin China-mystery authors share the First World outlooks of their majority non-Chinese readers and writing colleagues.[47] One might however ask how many nonelite citizens in a Third World country read popular mystery fiction or ponder world systems relationships through it.

Many China mysteries (the majority discussed below) nevertheless present the spectacle of authors who were raised outside of Chinese families composing imaginary dialogue spoken by PRC citizens. The difficulty of an outsider author "passing" as an observer of the PRC as competently as an insider has been a

24   Chapter 2

major incentive for authors to add foreigners to their cast of characters in China mysteries. Seldom do non-Chinese authors dare to narrate a novel in the first person as a Chinese, as noted below in Chapter 4.

And yet our China mystery authors reenact certain scenarios familiar in the four-century history of translating Chinese literature into Western languages as illuminated by James St. André in his pathbreaking theory of translation as cross-identity performance.[48] That history began with pseudotranslations (works represented to the public as translations from the Chinese but really written *ab ovo* by the Western presenter). Among our contemporary China mysteries, some (not all) by Michel Imbert are similarly represented, as translations by him of mysteries by one Mi Jianxiu, who is fictitious. Cheryl West Petty publishes her China mysteries under the Chinese-sounding pseudonym Sha Li, though this, too, seems more like a playful alternate identity for herself than an imposture. Her novels' hero is very autobiographical; two back covers bear the author's photograph, one in the company of Qiu Xiaolong. Lisa See asserts the Chinese part of her Chinese American identity most insistently, presumably to answer reader doubts about it. Whereas the difficulty of a Western author meeting and conversing with a Chinese person furthered pseudotranslations in the eighteenth century, in the late twentieth century it was the ballooning volume of overseas person-to-person contacts that created a demand among common readers and their publishers that China be represented to them by real Chinese authors with Chinese names. We shall return to these matters later in this chapter.

St. André's insights can shed particular light on Qiu Xiaolong, Diane Wei Liang, and An Yu. Like Ha Jin and Xiaolu Guo, who write outside the crime genre,[49] they "perform as Chinese" for a mostly non-Chinese audience. This is not to say that they are acting to stereotype in their English-language novels. Qiu and Liang fit St. André's specially defined category of "masquerade" writers, or those who may feel uncomfortable with the identity they were born with (for Qiu and Liang, that would be their birth identity's political aspects, not its cultural aspects), but as writers assume their birth "identity" anyway, without giving up political doubts and reservations about it. As St. André says of figures like Gu Hongming and Lin Yutang, who brought aspects of Chinese culture to English readers through translations (216–217), self-Orientalism is too simple a way of seeing the writing of such cultural interlocutors. Meanwhile, Qiu Xiaolong must also "pass" as something he has never been—a PRC police officer.

The field of translation studies has also revived the idea of national allegories,[50] a concept that originally gained currency from a 1986 article by Fredric Jameson. He claimed that in Third World literature, "*the story of the private individual destiny is always an allegory of the embattled situation of the public third-world culture and society*" (his emphasis); that is, this fiction represents a national and nationalistic position in a capitalist world system.[51] Jameson's name was iconic among avant-garde Chinese intellectuals even before his 1985 semester teaching in Beijing, but his subsequent national allegory idea has been critiqued as reductionist, stereotyping (of diverse regional literatures as all Third World), and devaluing (Jameson used as his first example a story by Lu Xun widely considered canonical and even modernist). The national allegories' idea has however been revived as a tendency in global crime fiction studies, due to crime fiction's thematic immersion in particularities of place, especially since the dramatic rise of crime fiction in translation (stimulated by global fondness for Nordic Noir) and innovative scholars' awareness of translations that superimpose on their final product national myths and allegories fitting both the origin- and target-language countries being served.[52] To others, crime fiction's critical edge generally constructs a national allegory. A 2012 conference announcement put it this way: "Only crime fiction has the grit needed to bring to light both the dark underbelly of society and the malfeasance and inequities that hide in plain sight. It is in this sense that crime fiction can be understood as national allegory (to borrow Fredric Jameson's useful concept) because the truths it has to tell are ultimately all truths about the state of the nation."[53]

Analysis of the blind spots and distortions in transnational image making is a China historian's stock in trade, so the further question would be: What is China (the PRC) an allegory *of* in these works? The answer need not be abstruse: China is allegorized as a potential partner for the West in a future global commonwealth of liberal democracy, social egalitarianism, rule of law without favor, and universal enrichment under unfettered if sometimes problematic global capitalism, without class or nationalistic struggles—and without dissolving or homogenizing local cultures, instead bridging them and letting them improve each other. That would be the humanistic, possibly utopian vision of the second Sino-Western honeymoon. This vision would contain projections onto China of the authors' own hopes for and criticisms of Euro-American culture and society as they "translate" and interpret Chinese society along with its Others.

"Crime writing as a genre is a space that lends itself to exposing, denouncing, addressing and . . . constructing Otherness" (Anderson et al., eds., *The Foreign in International Crime Fiction*, 1). In the China mystery, the first categorical Other a reader meets is the mystery author, who is Other in the PRC, the plot setting. The authors are surely conscious of enacting their role as designated Other, a status thrust upon them by the Chinese state and further developed through self-Othering, sometimes nostalgic, as related in Chapter 5. Readers meanwhile are sensible of their own status as Others to China. Do they then identify with

26   Chapter 2

the authors as fellow-Others? Doubt those authors' perceptions of China because the authors are Others to China, value the authors' formal objectivity on those very grounds, or doubt authorial visions of China when they turn out to be not so different from the West? Answering these questions would require rafts of reader surveys and much reading between the lines of the answers. In this book we regard the texts and their production.

The Beginnings

The contemporary China mystery that is the subject of this book debuted in two separate coauthored novels: *A Death in China* (1984) by Carl Hiaasen (b. 1953) and Bill Montalbano (William D. Montalbano, 1940–1998) and *The China Lovers: A Novel of Murder and Treason* (1985) by David Bonavia (1940–1988) and John Byron (pen name of Roger Uren, b. 1947). All four authors were information specialists—three journalists and an intelligence officer. Such credentialing of the author would become another de facto genre characteristic of the China mystery. The pioneers might have generated literary influence, too, even if mediated by editors, agents, and the prior success of van Gulik: certainly from Bonavia to his mentee Dinah Lee Küng, and then perhaps Lisa See, who in 1997 published the first best seller in English featuring a PRC police hero—female, like Küng's sleuth. But the years after 1985 were not favored with additional China mysteries from the four progenitors. Bonavia suffered premature death. Hiaasen gained fame from thrillers all his own about crime and corruption in south Florida, but he never wrote about China again. That is unsurprising, since only Montalbano, his fellow journalist at the *Miami Herald,* had lived in China, as the Beijing bureau chief for Knight-Ridder newspapers, 1979–1981.[54] Montalbano did not write another China book, either. His later novels of murder and scandal draw on his postings to the Vatican and Latin America. Uren went on to conceive other books under his poetic pseudonym of Byron that were not crime fiction, beginning with one on Chinese erotic art that consciously followed in the footsteps of Robert van Gulik.[55]

In retrospect, the two pioneering China mysteries, with their heavy borrowings from spy, thriller, and adventure genres, look relatively distinct from others' works yet to come. They are full of high-level Chinese politics and its conflicts, foreign agents, Western journalists, visitors and expats, Chinese confidential informants, and the PRC's little-understood officials—with uniquely *rogue* Chinese officials as the murderers, perpetrating schemes wholly outside the knowledge of the bureaucracy. Interest in Chinese bureaucratic conflict and its political mandates in these early 1980s days, just barely post-Mao, overshadows

Birth and Anatomy of a Genre   27

procedural interest in the police. The Bonavia/Uren work has a PSB police hero, but Hiaasen/Montalbano seldom involves the PSB. One almost hears faint echoes from the PRC's own Mao-era thrillers, which likewise had to let conspiratorial imagination fill in for actual particularities of crime and investigation. Both of the Western coauthored novels have some short and punchy chapters and terse and catchy though not hardboiled dialogue. The styles are more suggestive of professional writers' mystery novels than the China mysteries to come a decade later. Both novels reference the recent 1983 hardliner crackdowns, as if the post-Mao reforms might not last. Montalbano recalled, in 1993: "[In 1981] I had left a serene, monochromatic China, a universe not only committed to an ideology but also palpably different from most of the rest of the world because of it. I returned to awesome vitality and dynamism, to riotous color and excitement by the bushel."[56]

A side puzzle is why Hiaasen's name comes first on the cover of *A Death in China,* though Montalbano, a dozen years his senior, was his mentor and surely the source of all China-related content. Critics agree that Montalbano had his own deft way with words, and that *A Death in China,* Hiaasen's third and last collaborative book before he set out as a mystery author by himself, does not reflect the humorous and satirical style for which his individually composed crime novels are known. The two prior novels of both authors, also by Hiaasen and Montalbano in that order, are about drug smuggling in south Florida. Perhaps the older journalist wanted to give his colleague a career boost, or recompense for plotlines and raw material about Miami and Key West Hiaasen provided in their earlier collaborations. In Florida, Hiaasen was the native; Montalbano was originally a New Yorker.

David Bonavia was the first resident Beijing correspondent for *The Times* of London, previously on the *Far Eastern Economic Review* staff while stringing for *The Times* in Hong Kong during the mid-1960s. The *Times* then posted him to Saigon and later Moscow, which expelled him in 1972 after he interviewed dissidents. That year he and his Australian-born wife Judy Bonavia, later known for her travel writing, moved to Beijing, then relocated to Hong Kong after 1976, David Bonavia's base once more for travel in and reporting on China for the *Far Eastern Economic Review.* His nonfiction books about Chinese life and politics in the early 1980s, most famously *The Chinese,* won acclaim and a place on college reading lists in those heady startup years of Deng Xiaoping's reforms.[57]

Roger Uren served Australia as a China watcher in Beijing, 1981–1984. He held diplomatic status in China and other countries through 1993, then transferred to Australia's Office of National Assessments as the chief intelligence analyst handling East Asian issues. The leaf before the title page of *The China Lovers*

28   Chapter 2

identifies "Byron" as "the pseudonym of a sinologist who is expert in the organization and activity of the Chinese police and security services." Uren's website now says he provided the concept and plot for the book, while Bonavia shaped the narrative through editing and addition of an "enormous amount of color."[58] In 2019 the Australian government arrested Uren for having taken home secret documents. Commentators surmised that he was gathering material for a new work, a spy novel![59]

Both coauthored mystery thrillers feature a hero who gets to the bottom of multiple crime cases while outwitting competing crime solvers and disrupters (bosses with their own motives and rival services—that is the spy thriller contribution); multiple murders, and smuggling; disguised and treacherous identities; and a few pages with chases, violence, and suggestions of sexual hookups, without graphic sex scenes. American art history professor Tom Stratton is the hero of *A Death in China*. On a trip with colleagues to Beijing, he must confront his dark past as a Vietnam War soldier who ran a 1971 black op for the CIA across the border into Guangxi that killed many Chinese. David Wang, a Shanghainese resident in the US since before the 1949 revolution in China, was Stratton's doctoral adviser and mentor after the war, at a bucolic college outside Cleveland like Oberlin or Wooster. He was Stratton's confessor and healer as the veteran strove to forget his violent past. In 1983, David Wang has come to China and been murdered by his brother, a PRC deputy minister of culture who poaches the newly unearthed terra-cotta warriors from outside Xi'an and smuggles them abroad in coffins meant to repatriate foreign tourists who died in China. His final intended ruse is to fake his own death using David's corpse, then emigrate, fleeing with David's passport before he can be arrested for corruption. The CIA and American journalists are active again in Beijing now, in the novel as in life. Will they help Stratton solve the crimes and escape from his predicament as archetypal "beset citizen," even after the deputy minister's private thugs kidnap and abuse him, or do Stratton's own fellow nationals have other plans?

Criminal Affairs Division Commander Li Chunlong is the hero investigator of *The China Lovers*. Patriotic but progressive and only in his late forties, he is a "rocket cadre" who lifted off to high office before it was his turn according to the rules of seniority. As in Qiu Xiaolong's Chief Inspector Chen novels yet to come, much of the tension here comes from higher-ups who want to stop the investigation. Comrade Li follows his persons of interest with stakeouts and interrogations. He has a subordinate as "Watson," to be his soundboard and periodically summarize the clues. As in many a classic plot, a petty thief in this one relieves a rich man's safe of valuable antique paintings, by Bada Shanren in this case, not realizing that documents he also took indicate that the KGB decades before used

Birth and Anatomy of a Genre   29

kompromat to "turn" the safe's owner, a high-level PRC diplomat and spy. And the thief stole these documents the very night that their subject was murdered in the next room. The smuggling ring that wanted the paintings has left a trail and Comrade Li puts together the pieces. He finds the fence, a minor princeling and frustrated petty official in the railway bureau; the fence's friend, another lesser princeling and also a CIA informant, whose father has access to important inside information as a big wheel in the Civil Aviation Administration of China; the girlfriend of the thief's tipster; a Kansan in her twenties named Bette Shroder who works for an American journalist and sleeps with various partners, including the fence; and a CIA operative named Shack who has his own taste for Chinese art prohibited for export, is as adept as anyone at breaking and entering, and has US visas to offer as bargaining chips. Upon hearing that the PSB has interrogated Shroder, Shack rushes to open his own secret investigations. (A snarky, sexist, and maybe Orientalist double meaning of "China lover" refers in the first instance to Shroder.) Although certain background aspects of the characters are necessarily doled out piecemeal to provide surprises later in the plot, Bonavia and Uren's novel—and some by other authors since—provide thumbnail social and career biographies of their characters, including their bureaucratic career résumés and fates during the Cultural Revolution, at the point in the text where the characters first appear. This practically mimics, consciously or unconsciously, a convention of China's several-century-old classic novels, which themselves took a cue from biographies in official histories.

The information dividends, in these pioneering novels and their successors, come at three levels. (1) The big picture: social forces, politics, and their unseemly interrelations, or "corruption." These forces can be dramatic, given the pace of change in reform China. But policy differences yield place to high-level struggles between factions. (2) At mid-levels: displays of investigative procedure and also daily life *as* procedure, which is rather laborious in 1980s China—telephoning, traveling, finding people, shopping, tailing, and bugging. Today these portraits can evoke nostalgia. (3) Eye-catching scenes from urban Chinese life—sights, sounds, and smells from the streets and cultural and social idiosyncrasies of the folk. Popular fiction often delights in mentioning famous artists and songs from highbrow and pop culture of the times. These two early China mysteries, however, seldom indulge in cultural name-dropping and spare the reader snippets from the *Daodejing* or Sunzi's *The Art of War*. The plots move too fast for that.

At the mid-levels, about how things get done, the journalist and intelligence authors are of course authoritative about where diplomats lived in those days, the kinds of excuses and rationales Chinese and foreign presses put forth when suppressing and manipulating news about embarrassing incidents, which Chinese

30   Chapter 2

laws one had to obey and which were optional, how bodies of tourists who died in China were handled (courtesy of Montalbano), and how one transited around Beijing in 1983–1985. Many successors in the genre would turn obsessive in telling which boulevards their crooks and cops travel to get to their destinations, and exactly where they have to transfer from one subway line to another, providing local color and establishing the authenticity of their geographical knowledge. It will be up to later novelists to deal with changing communications technology such as cell phones, and then to move the plot along by copying characters' text message conversations into the narrative.

At the third, grassroots level are the insights and tidbits for which Bonavia was celebrated: character sketches of diverse Chinese lives; bureaucratic architecture, basics of police organization, and official protocol; the omnipresence and effects in Chinese bureaucratic life of the Cultural Revolution and subsequent politics, including their impacts on subsequent interpersonal relations and promotions; Chinese hospitals; elevator operators performing surveillance; the bad service in local restaurants; official manipulation of crime statistics; at what hours the heat is turned on and the lights are turned off; China's attempt to stop the formation of a Foreign Correspondents' Club; hijackings on Chinese airlines; the inability of Japanese to master indefinite articles in English; the nature of psychological depression; and, oddest of all, a four-page disquisition spoken by an American Russian expert brought in to coach the CIA about the beauties of the Russian countryside and what he perceives as Chinese men's lust for Russian women as a case of "opposites attract." Most other bits of information are embedded in single sentences, integrated into Uren's intriguing plot seamlessly enough that one seldom feels in the classroom. Only later mysteries by others would entice a reader to hop on a plane to Beijing. Even so, the long pause to come before China mysteries caught fire may, in the end, reflect the difficulty of equaling the no-nonsense page-turning appeal of the two initial offerings.

The Difficult Years

The progress of the China mystery in the decade after *A Death in China* and *The China Lovers* was difficult—plagued by publishers' indifference, particularly in North America. The mood of Sino-Western relations went from ecstatic to disillusioned on June 4, 1989, and Asia-related mysteries as a whole languished in subsequent years.[60] Two authors, Dinah Lee Küng and Christopher West, nevertheless began in the 1990s to parlay their China knowledge into mystery writing. Küng penned what became a trilogy, with Claire Raymond, a journalist and Hong Kong bureau chief like the author, as the series hero. Only the second novel, *Left in the Care of* (retitled *The End of May Road*), enjoyed timely publication, in the banner year of 1997. It was Küng's prior mystery, begun in the early 1990s but long unpublished, that served as a bridge between the mystery writing of her prematurely deceased mentor David Bonavia and the China mysteries with themes from journalism of later authors.[61] Drafts of Küng's first two novels, beginning with *The Wardens of Punyu,* circulated in the 1990s in the publishing hive of New York. Küng also played a leading role there in human rights work, a major theme in the *Punyu* book, supporting her husband's work at the UN. Mystery Writers of America helped Küng workshop the manuscripts. Drafts went out to the publishing world, including the West Coast's "über-agent" Sandra Dijkstra. She helped Lisa See publish her successful 1995 history about See's Chinese American forebears, *On Gold Mountain,* then oversaw See's transition from journalist and historian to become the Western world's first best-selling China mystery novelist.

Meanwhile Christopher West was writing his "China Quartet," featuring the series sleuth Wang Anzhuang of the "Beijing Central Investigations Department." West enjoyed more initial success publishing his fiction than Küng. He, too, had a China interest, as student and travel writer. His pioneering China mysteries, appearing in 1994, 1996, 1997, and 2000, were favorably reviewed, though their impact was limited. West later turned to popular business and history writing unrelated to China. Küng, after writing her China mysteries, also turned to other genres, notably a social comedy novel, *A Visit from Voltaire.* Her China mysteries, including a thriller in her series written in 2004 and set in Tibet, were belatedly printed and digitized as a "Handover Trilogy" in 2011.

Christopher West and Dinah Lee Küng's contributions to the genre appear to embody some role reversals. Chris West, a self-described rebellious young man of the Sixties, gave up his doctoral studies and courses in Mandarin and Chinese philosophy for a 1985 solo backpacking trip. The initial result was a travelogue, his *Journey to the Middle Kingdom* (1991),[62] but West's subsequent "China Quartet" mysteries view China through the eyes of a Chinese policeman, whose viewpoint is narratologically native but foreign to the author and most of his readers.[63] West thus developed the PRC police procedural concept initiated in the Bonavia/Uren novel, evidently without having read that novel.[64] It was Bonavia's onetime colleague Küng who consciously carried on her former mentor's mission of turning news about China into mystery fiction. Her series investigator is relatively autobiographical and therefore, given the journalist's need always to avoid the Chinese police, a model "beset citizen" sleuth. Her books' narrative perspective is that of a China outsider—more like Montalbano's Stratton than Bonavia's Li Chunlong.

32   Chapter 2

Chris West's fictional series detective, Inspector Wang Anzhuang, is one of the most sympathetic Chinese cops in the literature. Born in a dirt-poor Shandong village about 1951, he enlisted in the People's Liberation Army (PLA). That kept him out of the Red Guards during the Cultural Revolution. Decorated for bravery in the quickly and deliberately "forgotten" inconclusive Sino-Vietnam War of 1979, in which his closest comrades perished, Wang came to Beijing to please his first wife. He was not cut out for a life of urban sophistication and social climbing; they divorced, and his rural enlisted-man's background paved his way to employment in the police force. Furthermore, his late father had been CCP secretary of the village where Anzhuang grew up. In attitudes, tastes, and interests, Wang Anzhuang looks like a rustic forerunner of the Shanghai Chief Inspector Chen that Qiu Xiaolong would soon create. Loyal to the CCP that hired him, even when he sees it making mistakes, Wang cares for his family and objectifies the very concept of justice by recalling the image of that word (*zhengyi*) as his father once wrote it on a scroll. He is not one to disdain tradition, whether he believes in all of it or not: divination, the *Yijing* (Book of Changes), local opera, local food, *qigong,* the classic Chinese novels, plus Sherlock Holmes. Only Qiu Xiaolong's Shanghainese poet-inspector can read Sherlock Holmes tales in the original, but Wang Anzhuang has the translations. He also collects the avant-garde 1980s literary monthly *October*—a Beijing counterpart of the literary magazines familiar to the far more Westernized Shanghai inspector.

In the first novel, Wang Anzhuang witnesses the mass political demonstrations in the spring of 1989. He is not sympathetic to them. Then a young woman protester gives him a flower. He sees troops fire on students at Muxidi days before the major incident there and tries to stop it. That instinctive call for restraint brings Wang political difficulty ever after, though he succeeds in reenrolling in the CCP (police officers had to resign and reapply for membership pending investigation in the post-massacre crackdown). At the end of West's debut novel, Wang meets Nurse Lin, a native Beijinger more Westernized than he who likes to be called Rosina. In the second novel she has become his wife and a recurring character for the mystery Quartet. She enjoys talking things out, so she is Wang's confidante, even a coinvestigator at times. Spousal participation is not officially approved, but Wang Anzhuang sometimes flouts the rules. He is not above breaking into the offices of rural officials and using a fake official ID.

West's plots are complicated, involving hidden murders and conflicting schemes to earn money in the new economy that provide multiple suspects for multiple crimes. In the first mystery, *Death of a Blue Lantern* (1994, plot set in 1991), Wang confronts two cases: the murder of a smuggler who never made it out of a classical *erhu* concert and the death of a Chief Security Officer at an

Birth and Anatomy of a Genre   33

archeological site. Wang discovers what links the crimes while fending off both the secret society[65] involved in smuggling and agents of "Internal Security," presumably the Ministry of State Security (MSS), who have been getting a cut of the smuggling profits. They know about Wang's vacillation regarding the 1989 protests and use that information against him.

Death of a Red Mandarin (1997), third in the Quartet, is mostly set in Hong Kong during the months before its handover from Britain to China. Zhang Fei, a senior PRC cadre who lives at the PRC government house in Stanley and is the red mandarin of the title, is the first murder victim, followed later on by his mistress, a prostitute. He was a sadist and a gambler whose job was looking into software piracy. Wang has lots of suspects, including the triads who set Zhang up with his girlfriend (and murdered her), not to mention a sleeper in the plot, the murderer of Zhang, an acquaintance with a revenge motive from years before when they both lived in Shanghai. The indefatigable Li Anzhuang, housed out in Kowloon rather than with the PRC big brass in Stanley, investigates software pirates, gaining entrance to their offices by going incognito as a "shabby mainlander" delivery man, and he knows a clue when he sees one (a lost button from a sleeve). With help from computer nerds in the Mainland and Hong Kong, he figures out coded numbers, which represent not only telephone numbers but also slots in the triad hierarchy (489 means Dragon Head, in life as in the novel), and Bible verse references that the murderer sent the victim as warnings. An honest if overcompensated British inspector cooperates, acknowledging that both sides in the coming handover tolerate triad activity. Wang Anzhuang must work around interference from Beijing propaganda chiefs, his own superior, and patronizing ethnically Chinese Hong Kong native officers. But the case is solved; the murderer, who really is a good person, escapes to Indonesia with help from the triads; and China officially pins the murder on nonexistent British agents. All in 195 pages.

In books two and four, Wang Anzhuang's family plays a role. *Death on Black Dragon River* (1996) brings the inspector and his wife on a visit to his home village in Shandong, within driving distance from Ji'nan. "Dirt-tracks, wheatfields, long, straight canals lined with poplars: the rural province of Shandong. The province where he'd grown up, the province he still regarded as home, as a bastion of good sense, kindness and continuity in contrast with the crazy, selfish, novelty-obsessed capital where [Wang] now worked" (15). It is, however, 1993, and prosperity and reconstruction are reaching the countryside even in Shandong. Yet historical debts from the Mao years are not forgotten, class prejudices have not entirely dissolved, and a present scandal looms. The self-styled reformist Party secretary has a plan to flood a local valley to build profitable fish farms

34   Chapter 2

without properly compensating injured parties who grow crops there, including Inspector Wang's brother. But the brother is an alcoholic. Other farmers, mostly impoverished to begin with and of historically bad class background, are up in arms and have organized against the secretary. They, and a family of petty crooks in town, are not even within the social milieu that West dramatizes as suspects-to-be at the welcoming banquet for the Wangs upon their "return home" and later at a memorial service for an unexpected murder victim—the Party secretary. Local wealth appears concentrated in the hands of the secretary's son, and a young lady from Shanghai's Fudan University doing social research on rural Shandong has an undisclosed past connection to the village. The murderer is finally revealed to be one of the walking wounded from history. Rosina uses psychology to talk him down from killing her and her husband, and a crosscutting plot is Rosina's attempt to help her husband's brother recover from his own psychological trauma and alcoholism. Christopher West claims a career interest in psychology; he took college courses on counselling in the 1990s and "was particularly intrigued by Transactional Analysis and the Karpman Drama Triangle," the subject of one of his later nonfiction books.[66] The climax to this novel appears to exemplify that interest.

West's final mystery, *The Third Messiah* (2000; plot set in 1999), is notable for its credible creation in fiction of a new-style Sino-Christian sect armed with a revivalist and evangelical message. The group is inspired by the visions of Hong Xiuquan (1814–1864) and his Taiping movement to establish a Heavenly Kingdom on earth. In this novel, a latter-day saint has established a thriving agricultural commune of God Worshippers outside Beijing. The collective rural life and spirit of self-sacrifice, giving everything to the charismatic leader (the living Messenger of Hong Xiuquan) following one's rebirth into a world apart from the meretricious society of Western commercial values—with a few adaptations from Chinese culture—is not wholly alien to the intended spirit of Mao's communes. In this novel, Rosina's younger sister Julie has proved psychologically ripe for conversion. She had lived at home with their parents and hated it. More Westernized even than Rosina, and more bourgeois, she clung to her fake designer handbag and cell phone, met her boyfriend at KFC, and pursued anything that took her away from the old people with their tai chi, decaying hutongs, and Peking Opera on TV. But the boyfriend jilted and humiliated Julie, preparing her psychologically for a conversion skillfully managed by a missionary. She runs away to the commune. It is up to Wang Anzhuang to rescue his sister-in-law from a guarded commune of believers that naturally fears the police even after the mysterious death of their leader. The policeman must meanwhile wrestle with his own complicated feelings about religion, modernizing Westernization,

Birth and Anatomy of a Genre   35

and even Chinese tradition, which is inherent in some of the cult's resort (like Hong Xiuquan's) to quasi-Daoist, imperial, and shamanistic trappings. West provides convincing portraits, too, of assorted cult members, the missionaries who prospect for vulnerable people like Julie, and a *qigong* master in the neighborhood who cashes in on superstitious belief through his own racket. Wang Anzhuang deplores this New Church of the Heavenly Kingdom, yet he feels nostalgia for the rural life and some sympathy for the new church's crusade to revive honest rural simplicity.

In West's mysteries, well-chosen and detailed information about Chinese life is seamlessly integrated into the narrative, along with documentary facts and observations of what people were reading, watching, and listening to in the 1980s and '90s. The police in his novels have arrest quotas and disagree about the propriety of accepting a free snack from a street vendor, which Wang himself rationalizes as furthering *guanxi* (networking). He carries a Tokarev 77 pistol and winces to hear mention of the selfless socialist hero Lei Feng. Young people praise their friends with a current neologism from the English, "cool." They call the police "dogs." Rosina laments society's lack of understanding of mental illness. And a CCP police cadre receives a Christmas card from his CCP police superior—an event more likely in 1999 than in later years. The locations are mostly fictional compared to later China mysteries by others. West abstracted the China he observed into a broad vision of China's ideals and lifestyles, old and new.

Dinah Lee Küng (born in Detroit; BA from UC Santa Cruz and MA in Asian Studies from UC Berkeley, 1972) began as a China journalist at the *South China Morning Post,* Hong Kong, 1974–1977, followed by stints in New York for Reuters, in London for the *Far Eastern Economic Review,* in Singapore, 1982–1983, and Hong Kong, 1983–1986, as correspondent for *The Economist, The International Herald Tribune, The Washington Post,* and National Public Radio. She was promoted to China Bureau Chief for *The Economist* in Hong Kong, before moving on to *Business Week,* 1988–1992, where she was Bureau Chief for China and Southeast Asia, 1990–1992, like Claire Raymond, the hero of her three China mysteries. The weekly whose Hong Kong branch Raymond heads is *Business World,* with headquarters in Rockefeller Center like its near-namesake. Küng retained vivid impressions of Maoist China from her first student visit, in a delegation led by Cambodia's Prince Norodom Sihanouk in 1972.[67]

Her turn to detective novel writing began as she transitioned from Hong Kong and its *Business Week* bureau in 1992 to join her husband, Peter Küng, who was newly assigned to New York as Head of Mission to the United Nations for the International Committee of the Red Cross. (Claire Raymond's Swiss lover in the first novel, who marries her at the end of the second, is a Red Cross executive

36   Chapter 2

named Xavier Vonalp, as similar to Peter in career postings as Claire is to Dinah.) Having won an Overseas Press Club Award in 1991 for Best Human Rights Reporting, about connections between prison labor abuses and international manufacturers, Küng decided her series would emphasize human rights problems. While still in Asia she had done most of the research for her first novel, *The Wardens of Punyu,* in visits to that district (usually called Panyu in Mandarin) south of Guangzhou. Robin Munro (1952–2021), director of Human Rights Watch in Hong Kong, provided sensitive materials on organ harvesting.

The plots of the Claire Raymond mysteries bear heavy international and cross-cultural ramifications, though only the first (and later the third in the series) are really about human rights. The first two novels begin with individual disappearances and deaths that lead into a morass of multicultural mystery. *The Wardens of Punyu,* whose setting is 1995 in the revised edition, opens with a visit to the *Business World* offices in Hong Kong by a PRC medical doctor on his way to American exile. He claims the PLA forced him to remove a woman's liver while she was alive and not even anesthetized. Next, Raymond must investigate the disappearance of two of her stringers, one of whom washes up dead on an isolated beach in the New Territories. It complicates the situation that he was dealing drugs from his authorized posting in Bangkok. Claire fails to see that the death makes *her* a murder suspect—to the Hong Kong police. The other reporter, a cocky, overpaid young man with a direct line to fellow males at the magazine's New York headquarters, has stumbled on to a computer factory outside Punyu that embodies a corrupt partnership of American investors and local PRC officials. The American investor, with his Chinese partners, purchased a reform-through-labor (*laogai*) plant, kept the inmates in that gulag without letting them know their sentences had been served, and told them they were learning cutting-edge skills in their production of his laptop made for export, the Lychee. If they protest or try to escape, they forfeit vital organs and their lives. The organs go to rich Chinese and Hong Kongers for transplant. Facilitating that outrage is another criminal partnership, with a medical school in Guangzhou. Its doctors perform vivisections in the factory. Raymond makes her own dangerous foray on to the factory grounds across the border in the PRC in search of the missing stringer. He is dead, too, murder number three, though the human organs' story involves much larger numbers than that.

Küng creates a variety of secondary characters with unusual multicultural backstories and she mixes in much "procedure." Jim McIntyre, a former lover from Claire's earlier days in New York, gives Claire tips about avoiding bugs in her hotel room, how to read official code on Chinese license plates, and the necessity of memorizing the telephone numbers of her sources. He sounds like he

Birth and Anatomy of a Genre   37

might be CIA. An interview with a fictional professor at the Sun Yat-sen University of Medical Sciences in Guangzhou (identified by journalists in life as a party to transplant abuses) provides a thumbnail history of Chinese transplanting and how it has been accelerated in recent times by the upsurge in prisoners from Strike Hard campaigns and the miracle immunosuppressant drug Cyclosporine A from Sandoz. A Chinese medical journal tells how long a removed liver will be suitable for transplant (8–10 minutes after heart arrest) and the necessity of putting prisoner donors on a high protein diet for six months prior to execution. In the US Consulate General, Raymond learns about the Black Star pistols recently favored by the PLA and People's Armed Police; Hong Kong had gotten serious about outlawing guns only in the last two years. As a journalist without papers for this project, Raymond knows enough to enter Guangzhou indirectly and inconspicuously via a small port nearby. Other, more extraneous but atmospheric information is proffered. Besides nostalgia for the old ferries and tales from the journalists' underground, favorite performing artists are mentioned: Filipina pianist Cecilia Licad playing Rachmaninoff, organist Kei Koito playing Bach, pianist Michiko Uchida playing Mozart.

Küng's second mystery opens with a small child found dead in a ditch. Soon a second toddler is kidnapped, and finally Claire's own newborn, all for no apparent reason. None of the families get a demand for ransom. The surprising international interest this time is the Filipina nannies who serve well-to-do or professional working mothers like Claire in Hong Kong's midlevel towers. Like the mothers, the nannies grow hysterical, not only from the damage to their reputations, but also from their unique charismatic and shamanistic spiritual gatherings, as well as fear that they may be sent home to the Philippines in six months, after July 1, 1997, when Hong Kong will be handed over to the People's Republic. They, too, are prisoners, of their own enclosed and isolated social group and its unrelenting fears, gossip, and ostracisms. Claire, for her part, is much more revealing in this novel of her inner thoughts: the discoveries of how motherhood has changed her and her worries that Xavier in the end will not want to marry her. The original title, *Left in the Care of,* suggests a metaphor for Hong Kong, which was about to be taken from its British foster mother and delivered into the care of a family whose claims to being the birth mother were problematic. In the third novel, *The Shadows of Shigatse,* Claire Raymond as journalist and sleuth accompanies her husband to Lhasa as part of his work to inspect UN-funded clinics. A second mission is to discover the mole who is betraying to Chinese police the identities of clinic patients secretly escaping to Nepal. Claire wants to spare those in flight from police rape, murder, and maiming, without derailing the international cooperation supporting the clinics. Moreover, Claire has yet

38   Chapter 2

another mission on the side, to look up the long-lost son of a Tibetan friend of her suave ex-boyfriend Jim. He is CIA, just as the reader suspected.

The Wardens of Punyu and *Left in the Care of* made several contributions to the coming subgenre as Küng's manuscripts circulated in the mystery fiction writers' world in the mid-1990s. Küng created an interesting cast of secondary characters and above all a credible recurring female detective as lead for a China mystery *series*. In the Punyu novel, Claire Raymond is the boss, overseeing breaking stories and taking responsibility for her wayward employees. The Hong Kong novel casts Claire Raymond in a more maternalistic role, for she is still on maternity leave. Filling in for her at the office is one Hopkirk Wells, whose name sounds hardly preppier than that of G. Harris Hillward, who works "Political and Econ" at the US Consulate and is an alumnus "of Groton, Princeton, and Georgetown." Claire still manages to coordinate the major sleuthing, in consultation with old colonial hands from Britain like a Mr. Alistair Evans-Smith. Otherwise, Claire Raymond is anathema to all political stakeholders, hence legitimately "beset."

The CIA's intervention in Tibet in the early 1950s is something Küng read about, but personal friendship lies behind her portrait of a recurring good Catholic priest character, Fr. Fresnay, a quirky Jesuit who celebrates mass in the New Territories when he is not on Mosque Road on the main island, helping edit a newsletter for professional China watchers (recognizable as the influential *China News Analysis,* founded in life by Rev. Lázló Ladány, SJ, 1914–1990). Fr. Fresnay turns up some leads in the first and third novels and keeps tabs on the Filipinas in the second, ministering to them and struggling to draw them away from their demons, much as his prototype, Rev. Yves Nalet, SJ, did in life.[68] Küng herself had done much of the research for her novels, and her plots suggest another formula of China mysteries to come. Given CCP control of the Chinese judiciary, which serves the captains of industry right or wrong, justice is best achieved by exposing problems to the Western press.

In life, Küng gave publishers a list of human rights stories she was prepared to address in mystery plots: tales involving the underground Catholic Church, state newspaper censorship, the post-Tiananmen underground railroad out of the PRC, repression of the Falun Gong, "business elites and prostitution rings," etc.[69] But such scenarios were not welcome in the 1990s. In shopping around her first novel, an American publisher told Ms. Küng there was little market for international mysteries, apart from cozies, which could be set in England; a novel about a crime in Vermont ought to seek a reading audience in—Vermont. (HarperCollins carved out an exception for Donna Leon's Venice mysteries in 1992.) Another firm doubted the credibility of someone like Mr. Vonalp, though he was

Birth and Anatomy of a Genre   39

modeled after the author's husband.[70] The gender of the author and her hero might have been unwelcome, too. Claire Raymond is a "boss lady."

Küng's second book did see print in 1997, from the prestigious Carroll and Graf, though that press had declined to publish her first, more "Chinese," Punyu tale. Many of the larger publishers were attempting to access the giant China reading market for their own products in the late 1990s and human rights topics were of course offensive to Chinese in power. Another problem was that the author, a blonde, was a poor fit for marketing the novel's multicultural sensibilities. Lisa See is a redhead who looks no more "Asian" than Dinah Lee Küng, but the Djikstra firm was behind See, and she had already cemented her cultural credentials with great éclat in her *On Gold Mountain: The One-Hundred-Year Odyssey of My Chinese American Family* (1995). The mystery Küng first published in a timely manner originally bore a title without a hint of a Chinese theme: *Left in the Care of: A Novel of Suspense*. Its cover art is dominated by the faces of two Caucasian women and a Caucasian child, with an image of a Chinese opera actor in the corner. The cover of a 1999 reprint by Replica Books has no China-related images at all, just a Caucasian mother and child.

Identity-as-authenticity was not over in the book industry. When Michel Imbert wrote his first Judge Li novel in 2004 (*Jaune camion*), his publisher printed Mi Jianxiu (who is fictitious) as author and Imbert as translator, to make the product seem *"plus vrai"* ("more authentic"). It sold 5,000 copies. Unhappy at the imposture, Imbert put out his second Judge Li mystery under his own name. It sold only 500—until the publisher repackaged that novel and some of the subsequent ones as works by Mi Jianxiu again. Was the publisher wrong?[71]

1997: The Year of the Handover and of the China Mystery

Nineteen ninety-seven was a watershed year. The handover of Hong Kong from Britain to China on July 1, whose anticipation had caused much global anxiety and emigration from Hong Kong, was uneventful. A bigger shock arrived on July 2. The Thai baht collapsed, ushering in what would be called the Asian Financial Crisis. But that, too, would pass, with China earning kudos for its handling of the global panic. In 1998, China diminished the role of state enterprises in its economy and changed the premier from Li Peng, "the butcher of Beijing," to the reformer Zhu Rongji, a fellow "Shanghai Gang" comrade of Jiang Zemin. When Jiang visited the US in October 1997, it was the first by a Chinese head of state in 12 years. The PRC was on a path to entry into the World Trade Organization in 2001, the final year of Jiang's official leadership of the Chinese

40   Chapter 2

Communist Party. Meanwhile, fire sales of state-owned enterprises, often to the Party bosses previously in charge of them, were bringing riches to insiders and misery to laid-off factory workers and pensioners. China's own publication industry, although more heavily monitored again since the late 1980s, saw an explosive and unforeseen rise of a new social-political exposé genre designated as "anticorruption literature," followed by media productions with the same theme, until the trend was closed down prior to a major Party congress in 2002.[72] Few plots about corrupt privatizations would be produced in China mysteries abroad. Much preferred were stories of egregious machinations by international capital manufacturing for export, as in *The Wardens of Punyu* and its successors. Investment in China was booming again.

And yet an end to this second honeymoon may have been foreshadowed, too. In the September 1997 CCP elections for the 15th Central Committee, two heavily promoted younger princelings failed to make it on to the Central Committee as expected, but got elected as alternates, with votes that were next-to-last and dead last in the total. Next-to-last was Bo Xilai, who a decade later would champion old Maoist rituals in his Chongqing bailiwick and come to be feared as a neo-Maoist aspirant to total national power. Bo, however, overreached, and his career crashed spectacularly. He ended up in prison, like his fellow princeling wife Gu Kailai, who was accused of murdering a British businessman. The case of Bo and Gu would inspire detective novels by Qiu Xiaolong, Lisa Brackmann, and Jan-Philipp Sendker.[73] The other princeling, the lowest vote-getter to squeeze by in 1997, would become a Chinese Communist strongman unprecedented since the days of Mao Zedong: Xi Jinping.

Meanwhile, across the waves, the PRC-themed police detective novel had finally arrived in what the publishing industry recognized as a successful, replicable form, with the appearance on January 1, 1997, of Lisa See's *Flower Net*. It had a female hero whose procedures were engaging to mystery lovers and who could star in a series: an intrepid native investigator in China's own Public Security (police) apparatus, Liu Hulan. Random House, when it took over publication of See's mysteries from HarperCollins, promoted the books on their covers as "Red Princess Mysteries."

In French, the first of Alban Yung's mystery novels, *Message COFACE à Pékin* (COFACE Message in Beijing), also appeared on January 1, 1997. Yung would go on to pen more China mysteries solved by sojourning French and native Chinese cops, with send-ups of French diplomats, visiting prime ministers, and French academic sycophants of the PRC regime. (France recognized the PRC in 1964, but there were ups and downs in the relationship, particularly after France sold arms to Taiwan in 1991; full diplomatic relations were suspended but resumed in

Birth and Anatomy of a Genre   41

1994.) Yung's novels are full of sparkling wit and have delighted a niche readership with their inside jokes and outrageous plots. Although they display much
interesting local color along with intriguing and humorous caricature (the objects of which are sometimes obscure to this reader), Yung's novels have yet to be
translated or become international best sellers.

Also arriving in 1997 were Dinah Lee Küng's first published novel (the
middle one in her series), Howard Goldblatt's translation from Chinese to English of Wang Shuo's *Playing for Thrills: A Mystery* (1989), and a movie, *Red
Corner*, starring Richard Gere and Bai Ling, a thriller about an American businessman wrongly tried for murder in China. Cinematic crime and legal thrillers about contemporary China would lack successors. Even this one was
produced in Hollywood, through ingenious use of sets and computer manipulation of two minutes' footage from China and 3,500 still shots, with a few
Chinese actors flown to L.A. to fill in. Top American critics panned the film's
stereotyping; the Chinese government was so enraged it withdrew Bai Ling's
citizenship; and Hollywood was headed into an era when substantial revenues
would come from PRC audiences, pending permissions from the Chinese government. Luckily for the mystery authors and their publishers, novels flew under the PRC's radar.[74]

Lisa See is another author who came from journalism, although not China
journalism. In her modest words: "I had worked as a journalist for many years
and had been the West Coast correspondent for *Publishers Weekly* for about eight
years when I started *On Gold Mountain*. . . . I also benefited from the success of
Amy Tan's *The Joy Luck Club*. Publishers were actively looking for more Chinese-
American stories."[75] She had some popular fiction-writing experience before
that, in 1985–1988, as "Monica Highland," coauthor of three novels. Two are set
in China, the other in California; all feature multicultural characters. Lisa See's
coauthors, publishing under their own names, were her mother, the noted novelist, literary critic, and UCLA English professor Carolyn See (1934–2016), and her
mother's partner, born in Shanghai to missionaries, the novelist, writer of China
memoirs, and UCLA literary scholar John Espey (1913–2000). Lisa See identifies
intensely as Chinese American; her online interviews and book talks emphasize
this as a fundamental premise of her life and writing, though she is also quick to
credit influence from her mother, whom she accompanied in her travels after a
divorce when Lisa was three. She also tells of a Japanese aunt and African American stepmother.[76] Lisa See felt particularly at home with her grandmother Stella
on her father's side—Caucasian yet by choice culturally Chinese—and Stella's
family. Lisa hung out at a Chinese antiques shop they ran, enjoyed family life
there, and insists that "I'm Chinese in my heart."[77]

42   Chapter 2

Lisa See's practice as a historian and archival researcher looms large in her early China mysteries, as in her subsequent, still more popular historical novels featuring Chinese women heroes. A page or two of acknowledgments, listing information sources along with those who helped with publication, and even pointing out which places and characters in the plot are real and which are fictitious, is common in the larger world of North American and British mystery and thriller fiction. (It is rare in Chinese-language mysteries published in the PRC.) Dinah Lee Küng's original 1997 edition of *Left in the Care of* offers a two-page bibliography of printed sources on Philippine history and medical knowledge, though neither she nor Bonavia before her had felt the need to cite current history sources in their novels. They had gathered much of the information themselves. Lisa See extended these precedents in the China mystery subgenre by going full throttle with citations in all three of her detective novels. They provide two- or three-page lists of people, book titles, even which libraries hold the books, along with indications of which plot elements are fact, fiction, or legend. See's first mystery even puts her acknowledgments in a foreword, as in an academic book, and her prior nonfiction family history, *On Gold Mountain*. Ordinarily such notes come in an afterword. Successor authors of China mysteries and thrillers have tended to follow her example, in more abbreviated form. Qiu Xiaolong and Diane Wei Liang are exceptions, although both of those authors have published partly or wholly autobiographical books on the side that suggest how their life experience inspired or ended up in their mystery fiction. No more than Küng does See recall having her own work cited by later mystery writers as an inspiration.[78]

See enjoyed "field experience" in the PRC. She accompanied her lawyer husband, Richard B. Kendall, to Beijing in 1994, where he represented Chinese interests combating financial fraud.[79] She met high-ranking Ministry of Public Security (MPS) officials, although, so far as we know, no female leader like her hero Liu Hulan. The police bigwigs, See recalls, "were covered in gold: big gold Rolexes, big gold rings, big gold necklaces and bracelets, because they were corrupt but they were up front about it. They were getting up to sing sappy love songs in these gorgeous tenor voices [at a karaoke bar], with the tears streaming down their faces. If you're a writer and you get to experience something like that, there's only one thing you can think: This is the best material and *I've* got it!"[80] See says she grew up in a Cantonese-speaking family and studied Mandarin for four years. The Mandarin had grown rusty by her book-writing years, but she studied it again in the 1990s and returned to China once or twice a year for research and to keep current.[81]

After See, the China-themed police procedural would continue to feature a series hero in multiple volumes that can be enjoyed wherever one begins reading

Birth and Anatomy of a Genre   43

in the series, accompanied by a consistent "series memory" from one volume to the next as in the mystery genre at large. The formulaic elements were gelling. On the crime-solving side: (1) A hero cop (judge, or other investigator for the state or CCP); (2) The hero's bureaucratic superior(s) and subordinates; (3) Colleagues, possibly including foreigners; (4) Procedure(s) for cracking the case, signing in, traveling, etc.; (5) Side interests, hobbies, and hobbyhorses, plus capsule Chinese history lessons; (6) Chinese cuisine (some critics see "food porn"), art, music, and other culture; (7) Family relations and human-interest angles and subplots; and (8) Devices such as alternating subplots and suspended action at the ends of chapters.

On the dark side: (1) The big, newsworthy offense(s): human rights abuses, iconic injustices, international outrages, or religious cult conspiracies; (2) Smaller crimes, including murders that lead investigators to the big, multi-actor offenses; (3) Clues left by the wrongdoers or their victims; (4) Intriguing diversions that sidetrack the investigations, as when guilty parties strike back; (5) Incidental social commentary; and (6) The villains at the top, revealed at the end.

Lisa See created a new kind of police hero who acknowledges that she is a highly entitled red princess but does not act like one. Her insights and quandaries propel See's three mysteries: *Flower Net* (1997), *The Interior* (1999), and *Dragon Bones* (2003).[82] The first and third were *New York Times* best sellers. The hero's father is Vice Minister of Public Security in the opening novel, the organ in which she serves; her mother, once a famous dancer, is presently confined to a wheelchair and suffering from dementia. Both parents came from wealth before the Communist revolution. In the spirit of the Mao era when their daughter was born (1956), the parents named her after a young woman martyr for the Communists, Liu Hulan (1932–1947). See's investigator embodies her predecessor's independence, bravery, and spirit of defiance.

The fictional Liu Hulan's social privilege and access to the apex of China's regular police (she is moreover an only child born before the one-child policy) lend a modicum of believability to her fearlessness and extraordinary license to investigate. Spirited away from the chaos of her country during the later years of the Cultural Revolution, she attended a boarding school in Connecticut as a teenager, then college and law school at USC and a stint at a California law firm where she met her future lover and husband. Her Beijing friends are mostly internationalized princelings like herself, including a fellow American law graduate who named himself Nixon Chen. Lisa See can thus provide her readers the attractions of plutography with Chinese characteristics (and the affinity for corruption that she saw among MPS figures in life), as well as the cultural

44   Chapter 2

contradictions between China and the US with their different concepts of law and of which kinds of evidence may be shared with the Chinese bureaucracy. The contradiction reaches its zenith at the end of the first novel, when the head villain in that narrative is revealed to be the Vice Minister of Public Security—Hulan's father.

Notable secondary characters include a dishonest Chinese American reporter in the second book who fabricates her own human rights stories and a colorful multinational cast of archeologists and adventurers in the third who make excellent suspects for murder. There are also recurring positive characters who are not colleagues in the service, more like those of Dinah Lee Küng than those of Qiu Xiaolong and Michel Imbert yet to come. A positive series figure is David Stark, a professional colleague and Liu's equal in human relations terms. In See's first novel he is an assistant US attorney in Los Angeles (the occupation of Richard Kendall prior to and a few years after his marriage to See). At the start of the second mystery, Stark opens a Beijing office for a big L.A. law firm (in life, Kendall was the head of his own law firm when See wrote her mysteries). Like Xavier Vonalp in Küng's novels, Stark is Liu Hulan's on-and-off boyfriend in the first two novels, and by the end of the second, her husband and the father of their ill-fated baby, born out of wedlock like Claire Raymond's. More than Vonalp (until Küng's third novel), Stark functions as Liu's coconspirator as well as sounding board; the beginning of See's second novel alternates between "Liu chapters" in Beijing and "Stark chapters" in L.A., until the two link up to work their cases together. The interplay between the two characters is a major dynamic of the novels, one that Qiu Xiaolong would occasionally adopt, using Chief Inspector Chen Cao and US Marshal Catherine Rohn.

Themes of major scandal come from the international news. In *Flower Net* (1997, with a contemporaneous plot), it is vivisection again, the cruel harvesting of bile, a prized Chinese medicine, from the gallbladders of live bears raised for that purpose in Sichuan. The son of the US ambassador was in on international smuggling of it; discovery of his corpse initiates the plot on page 3. Triads, already David Stark's bête noire in his L.A. investigations, handle distribution in the US, plus human smuggling, spectacularly exposed in an offshore smuggling ship mishap recalling the 1993 *Golden Venture* tragedy off Long Island. The feds go aboard and find the corpse of a Chinese princeling and made man, murdered with the same poison found in the ambassador's son, his partner in crime 6,000 miles away. Further intrigues, corrupt practices, and murders, as of an FBI agent in the US, lead to a final shootout at a "bear farm" hidden in Sichuan.

Birth and Anatomy of a Genre   45

As its title suggests, *The Interior,* See's second novel, explores misconduct outside the big cities, this time at a Sino-American joint venture toy factory in Shanxi province making action figures tied to a US cartoon television series. Management exploits and allows sexual abuse of the mostly female workforce and is plagued from within by intergenerational plotting about the future American control of the enterprise, which leads to a murder. A provincial governor is management's local partner, suggesting a tale of corruption, except that he is something of a red herring—he was framed for the murder. The big tragedy, held until the end and almost submerged in the intricacies of the plot, is that 176 young women perish at the factory in a Shanxi version of the Triangle Shirtwaist Fire. Liu Hulan had been rusticated to work nearby at the start of the Cultural Revolution, prior to her removal to America, so in the plot she goes undercover as a factory girl to get evidence on another murder that serves as opener. The novel ponders in the end not only the crimes but also the unbridgeable estrangement between the red princess and her old village friend, who stayed behind and is the mother of the opening victim. Rural Chinese women would figure again in See's later career as a historical novelist.

Multiple hot button topics from 1990s reportage likewise populate Lisa See's third novel, *Dragon Bones.* The major concerns are a mind-bending religious cult resembling the Falun Gong and the controversial, not yet finished, Three Gorges Dam. The time is 2002. Liu Hulan not only shares Beijing's animus toward the cult, she also bears it personal malice after an incident early in the plot. The cult's core believers are not in Beijing, but Hubei, near the dam, whose construction they hope to stop, and they fly a dangerous flag of nationalism, calling themselves an All-Patriotic Society destined to restore ancient values and greatness to China. Hulan and David, the investigators, are shocked to discover that an intellectual Chinese American software guru who has walked among them, unsuspected, is the cult's cloistered charismatic leader. The emblem and source of his cultic power, Hulan discovers, is an underground fungus colony (*Armillaria*) thought to be the world's largest living organism, a "swelling mold" and "living earth" that the cult links to Yu the Great, tamer of China's waters in mythological times. In See's update of the ancient myths, Yu fashioned a priceless *ruyi* scepter from it, a Chinese Holy Grail, which, if joined with nine tripods representing Yu the Great's map of empire, might unite the Chinese people and bestow authority to rule on any possessor—the PLA, for instance, or a cult leader with a will to power. Five cultish murders at the dam site, with amputations on the corpses suggesting the Five Punishments of ancient times, provide clues.

46   Chapter 2

See's crisscrossing subplots are absorbing, if improbable. A major attraction of her mysteries, as in her later novels, lies in the cultural and descriptive detail. Wrote one critic:

> Readers familiar with present-day Beijing, where a few warrenlike traditional neighborhoods still hold out against the onslaught of garish hotels and office buildings, will take delight in her local descriptions, from the ubiquitous street carts selling candied crab apples to the shining Mercedes-Benzes hooting their way through swarms of Flying Pigeon bicycles. She's particularly successful at conveying the sights and smells of Beijing's raw winters, when the air is "thick with coal smoke, exhaust and the freezing fog's lingering dampness."

The reviewer was more ambivalent to see the characters "continually providing us with thumbnail lectures on everything from the history of Chinese triads to the finer points of traditional medicine."[83] But See observes with a trained eye. *Flower Net* describes a Chinese man in Los Angeles squatting on his haunches: "He could have been on a street corner in any Chinese city" (198–199). See also veers ever-so-briefly into psychology, detailing characters' demeanors in different situations and the moods of David and Hulan as they converse. Liu Hulan knows when a Chinese man is discomfited because he is shorter than she. She also knows she must reprimand lower-ranking officers when they are rude, lest her own stature be diminished.

The Genre in Full

By the end of 2000, in the fourth year of the subgenre's rebirth, nine authors had published China mysteries (West, Küng, See, Yung, Mones, Rotenberg, May, Pattison, and Qiu), and all but West (who had already written four) would write more. Five authors had already written (and published, except for Küng) a second book in their series (West, Küng, See, Yung, May), and they were joined the next year by two other authors (Rotenberg, Pattison), plus Lee, though he and West would add no more to the subgenre. Except for Mones, who experimented with different kinds of rather beset heroes, and Lee, with his lone multicultural Chinese-language spy whodunit, all these authors created a series investigative hero, in most cases a Chinese police detective. (Küng's investigative journalist was the exception, and Yung's visiting French police detectives do steal the show from the locals.) The full panoply of China mysteries by 41 authors appears in three sequential lists in this book's Appendix. Chapters below occasionally will refer to May's fourth (his fourth *China* mystery), Pattison's eighth, etc.

The China mystery had become a trend and its first native author, Qiu Xiaolong, was set to become the flagship creator. Other new authors, both young and middle-aged, would enter the fray in the next 20 years. Creators of mystery series not wholly defined by China (by Sampson, Stone, Church, Hamilton, Flint) would also have their heroes come to the PRC once or more to fight crime, investigate it, or escape from it. Peter May, Eliot Pattison, and Lisa Brackman meanwhile created, besides their China mysteries, completely different series detectives or thriller heroes investigating crime in other times and on other continents.

Publication of novels in a series with recurring characters is its own generic draw; Laurie Langbauer traces the attraction back to nineteenth-century English novels of the "everyday," down through Sherlock Holmes tales.[84] Our contemporary China mystery series featuring a recurring hero tend to be loosely linked, with character and case-order consistency and sparse textual references to prior cases, like Dr. Watson reminding the reader of Holmes's previous triumphs.

Commercial editors and publishers helped shape the China mystery genre in multiple ways, in texts and paratexts. Qiu Xiaolong is no exception. His editor asked that his plots begin with a corpse.[85] *Death of a Red Heroine* opens thus: "The body was found at 4:40 p.m., on May 11, 1990, in Baili Canal, an out-of-way canal, about twenty miles west of Shanghai." It grabs the reader and sets a Chinese scene in the universal voice of a crime investigator. Qiu's subsequent works announce a murder on pages 5, 6, 3, and 3, respectively. An Yu's 2020 novel is not so generic—call it a quest novel haunted by multiple family mysteries—yet it, too, begins with a corpse on page 1. Face down in a bathtub.

Monetary return is not the only motivation to write and publish. At least three authors must have put up their own money to publish their mysteries, although they, too, may have dreamed of TV and movie rights one day. Success in the media has however been mostly limited to Qiu Xiaolong, and it has not necessarily been up to the expectations of his fans.[86] He has, however, created a character, Inspector Chen, whose name transcends the novels. (Chinese translations indicate that his given name, Cao, in Mandarin is "Chao," meaning "über" as in "Übermensch" ["super," as in "superman"]. And Chinese speakers would not neglect to address him as *Chief* Inspector.) The cult of this hero is nurtured by Cheniana books Qiu has authored and well-publicized international book tours, though not in the PRC.

Qiu Xiaolong is now the most prolific author of China mysteries as defined in this book. Yet he emerged as an accidental, even reluctant mystery writer. Prior to coming to the US, Qiu Xiaolong was an English-to-Chinese literary translator and two-way interpreter, an award-winning modernist poet, a member of the Chinese Writers Association (in the 1980s, when membership was quite prestigious), a

48   Chapter 2

postmodern literary critic, and assistant and then associate research professor at the Shanghai Academy of Social Sciences.[87] Funded by the Ford Foundation, Qiu Xiaolong came in 1988 as a resident visiting fellow to Washington University, St. Louis, to get material for a book on T. S. Eliot. (Eliot was born in St. Louis; Qiu's fictional inspector visits Eliot's hangouts during his two visits to the US, cites his name in awe, and recites his poems in the mysteries.) When in life the democracy movement came to Beijing, Shanghai, and other cities in 1989, Qiu, in America, showed sympathy with the demonstrators. Voice of America mentioned this, so after the crackdowns on the protests in China, he remained at the university; he earned a PhD in comparative literature in 1995, with a dissertation on "Love in Classical Chinese Literature: Cathayan Passions vs. Confucian Ethics." (Confucian ethics were the specialization of Inspector Chen's late father in the fiction, a professor; Confucian themes recur in Qiu's novels.) Even after the success of his first novel, Qiu was not a full-time mystery writer. He published his own poetry in both Chinese and English and translated classical Chinese poems, going on to edit three anthologies of them, including a *Treasury of Chinese Love Poems.* Readers of the Inspector Chen mysteries are treated to translated Chinese poems from antiquity, mostly from the Tang and Song, and Qiu's own original creations, represented in the novels as poems by the inspector.[88]

T. S. Eliot was fond of detective fiction, but that is not what led Qiu Xiaolong to write in the genre.[89] On a return trip to China in 1996, Qiu was astounded and impressed by how quickly it had changed. He felt he must "write a novel about the society in transition." Being new to fiction, he "thought of using a detective story as a ready-made framework, in which I might say what I want to say."[90] He had enjoyed Sherlock Holmes and Arsène Lupin novels in Chinese translation during his younger days, on the sly. In post-Mao times, when crime fiction was no longer banned, he preferred "social" police procedurals by Maj Sjöwall and Per Wahlöö. Qiu explained in 2015, "For a sociological attempt, a cop can be a very convenient agent, who can walk around the city, knock on people's doors, and raise all sorts of questions, though not necessarily all have the answers." His publisher liked his first manuscript and signed him to a three-book contract. "And then it turned into a series in spite of myself," Qiu says. He committed himself to an overt "sociological approach" and "smuggling poems into the popular genre of detective stories."[91] It may be his way of elevating the popular genre. Poems appear in China's classic novels, he often explains. The author has never been a policeman, though a friend of his was, and yet there is something of an alter ego of Qiu Xiaolong in his detective. Qiu speaks of writing under a mask.[92]

Diane Wei Liang, the other noted English-language mystery author of native PRC origin, might be considered another accidental writer of mystery fiction.

Birth and Anatomy of a Genre 49

With darker childhood experiences than Qiu Xiaolong's (she grew up in her parents' labor camp), she participated in the spring 1989 democracy movement in Beijing but was able to emigrate to the US and then the UK. She had a career as a college teacher in both those countries, then emerged as a media commentator on Chinese current events. Her life experience provided rich material for her first book, a novelistic memoir, *Lake with No Name: A True Story of Love and Conflict in Modern China* (2003, 2008). Some themes from that life enter the novels, whose hero is socially a rung below Lisa See's, but also well connected to China's elite.[93]

Most of Qiu Xiaolong's achievements in China have been inherited by his detective, a poet who cites lit crit theory and is an accomplished interpreter and literary translator. Inspector Chen is thus a distinctive and yet, given his background, believable intellectual cop, sharing the author's interests, tastes, and some but not all of his biography, including *not* having been a sent-down youth during the Cultural Revolution. (Chen did inherit a "bad class background" from his parents, like Qiu.) He is younger than his chief subordinate, true-blue Detective Yu, who becomes Chen's coinvestigator and confidant. Yu's father, "Old Hunter," and Yu's wife play those roles, too. Chen appears to be in his midthirties at the start of the series, though his exact age is vague, even in a CIA file on him faxed to Catherine Rohn in the second novel (150). Having been promoted to chief inspector so early in his career, Chen Cao is vulnerable as a "rocket cadre." And he is the archetypal character caught in the middle: between obedience and true public service, CCP truth and verifiable truth, orthodoxy and creativity, young and old, Red and expert, experience and innovation, bureaucracy and family. In his two novels with Rohn, he is caught between the values of China and America. Chen Cao's need to deal with pressures from all sides and his improbable yet persuasive multiculturalism enshrine the idealism and wishful thinking of the second honeymoon of China and the West.

3

China
Places and Problems

This chapter examines the places seen in a China mystery and the larger crimes depicted in them, besides the murders. Neither field is as diverse as one might expect, given the size of China and the importance of global connections in the mystery plots. Even with crime and alterity as major interests, visions of a second Sino-Western honeymoon—on mostly Western terms—prevail.

How China should be "represented" in any sort of writing is sensitive. Controversy about it rages among PRC and PRC-origin readers at home and abroad. In the Western academy, all writing with Asian settings comes under intense scrutiny from critical discourses of Orientalism, exoticism, image studies, and critiques of cultural appropriation, outsiders' gazes, Western imperialism, Cold War mindsets, global capitalism, and windows-on-the-world traits in world literature (differentiated from other pleasures of the text).[1] That most China mysteries as defined in this book are written and first published in English can also raise concerns about furthering this language's global hegemony and the effect of that on the global position of literature written in Chinese.[2] Writers of Chinese ethnic origins in any genre are meanwhile probed for self-Orientalism, assimilating, or documenting minority or immigrant consciousness instead of being "pure" creative writers, even while being asked by others to ratify "own voices" (fellow-ethnic) consciousness.[3] Euro-American crime fiction and film have a history of racism that once tantalized audiences with images of Fu Manchu and dragon ladies. The benevolent figure of Charlie Chan, too, embodies stereotypes and a reminder that Asian roles used to be played by Caucasians in the movies.[4] Crime fiction raises still other questions about male-gendered values and perspectives, a subject broached in Chapter 4.

The mysteries discussed in this book contain some reductive cultural explanations for unschooled readers, occasional stereotypes, peculiar observations, and small mistakes, as noted in this and other chapters. The works are no more socially realistic by literary critical standards or pervasively contemplative than most popular fiction. Yet they are worlds apart from "rising dragon" nonfiction books and the prejudices of mystery writers of the Victorian and Agatha

China: Places and Problems   51

Christie cohorts.[5] The murders, for instance, are multiple and suitably alarming, but not attributed to Chinese cultural alterity.[6] Usually that goes even for cruelty and torture perpetrated by the authoritarian regime, which is typically cast as colorlessly paranoid or bureaucratic.[7] With its roots in journalism, the China mystery plays on reader interest in transnational criminal conspiracies. The authors may feel reluctant to invent local tales of rape, wife beating, elder abuse, drug addiction, corrupt doctors, domestic human trafficking,[8] or ethnic intimidation. Murder is the generic crime. Perhaps fraud is the common crime most neglected.

Exoticism can evoke attraction or repulsion through racial, national, or cultural coding, and cultural appropriation sometimes undermines native agency, but the exotic can also inhere in topography, flora, fauna, fragrances, and cuisine, Victor Segalen reminds us. By my readings, overseas-produced China mysteries tend to emphasize panhuman social values.[9] Blandness can result; popular fiction clings to the familiar as well as the strange. Further, if Homi Bhabha were to ask China mystery authors, Do the native characters speak in their own voices? the authors might reply, Yes, but what if the archetypal cultural hybridity comes from characters hellbent on conventional "modernization" and assimilation to Western-origin commercial, consumerist, and aesthetic norms?[10]

Of comparative interest are the Commissario (Captain) Brunetti mysteries, more than 30 best sellers since 1992, which the American-born former academic Donna Leon writes in English and sets in Venice. She lived there for more than 30 years before moving just across the border to Switzerland in 2015, convenient for monthly return trips to her adopted home. With Leon's novels as her chief example, Eva Erdmann writes that global crime and detective novels interest "a potentially international audience" through "recourse to cultural stereotypes and clichés that are affirmatively used, ironically used or problematized" (22).[11] Epitomizing a type would be Commissario Brunetti himself, or Qiu Xiaolong's Chief Inspector Chen. Both heroes are fluent in English, burdened with celebrity cases, office politics, and the press, sometimes even wary of a nervous breakdown. One reads ancient Greek; the other, literary Chinese. One knows opera, the other writes poetry (their creators' respective passions). They constantly drink coffee, a convention with a long history in the genre. Chen is more the gourmet, except regarding coffee. He preceded Brunetti in investigating eco-scandals! In the China mysteries, national stereotypes are fodder indeed for irony and identity humor, often nationally self-deprecating, in works by "out-of-place" multicultural authors like Yung, Vittachi, and Flint. Cultural difference takes many forms. On first viewing her Commissario Brunetti tales as filmed in Venice for German television, what leapt out at Donna Leon was not the German

52   Chapter 3

speech, but that the actors were not touching each other in the Italian way, and their outfits and haircuts looked German.[12]

Erdmann notes, not necessarily approvingly, that Leon's novels sprinkle in elementary expressions from the Italian. China mysteries similarly insert Mandarin, Cantonese, and Tibetan words in Romanization, and some append a glossary or insert tone marks and/or actual Chinese characters in the text. Lisa Brackmann perfected the technique of letting a Romanization of a Mandarin phrase dangle on the page so the reader can guess the meaning from context. Confirmation of the English appears later. Brian Klingborg adds to his Romanizations of Sinitic and Burmese usages some thumbnail explanations of their nuances and etymologies. And Daniel Nieh, in his second Victor Li thriller set mostly in Mexico City, presents a complex mix of English, Spanish, Chinese in Romanization when it is spoken and in simplified characters when the hero encounters it in writing. Miswritten characters and rebuses of characters are reproduced graphically so the reader can interpret them as secret code. However, as the field of translation studies might put it, China mysteries and Italy mysteries[13] more often "domesticate" dialogue spoken by their Chinese and Italian characters than they "foreignize" it by inserting words transcribed from Chinese[14] or Italian. That is mostly saved for technical terms, exclamations, and ways of addressing family members, strangers, social superiors, and inferiors. Leon dramatizes characters who disobey linguistic norms in furtherance of their own snobbery, social leveling, or investigation. Some readers addicted to Italy or China mysteries will already know a few words of Italian or Mandarin. That may govern whether token bilingualism in the text brings comforts of familiarity (or, contrarily, the stimulation of exoticism), illusions of insight shared with the author, or impressions that authenticity has been purchased on the cheap. Leon speaks mostly Italian now, but remains "English dominant" in her thinking.[15] Dominance of the first language may affect Qiu Xiaolong, Ha Jin in his early works, and Xiaolu Guo. Their English prose occasionally draws on what appears to be Sinitic phrasing. Whether readers see a more consciously borrowed trope such as "like spring bamboo shoots after rain" as creative or clichéd may depend on whether they have encountered it previously, perhaps in translation, as Qiu himself is aware.[16] Tourism and the ubiquity of popular culture references to Italy and China around the world, superficial though they may be, have rendered those places (and their cuisines) less exotic than those of other locations—maybe including Sweden, Iceland, and Elmore Leonard's Detroit and Miami, his Djibouti, to be sure.

How, then, do place-related mystiques and delights, crimes, frights, taboos, and social problems figure in these mysteries? That the PRC now officially

China: Places and Problems   53

represents itself as a non-Western and increasingly counter-Western global model for political development, and also as an emblem of Han cultural and ethnic prowess, complicates the matter. *Not* complicating the China mysteries written abroad are recent scholarly and multicultural debates (abroad) about the definitions of "China" and "Chinese." Novels on the other hand are relatively free to reimagine China as something other than a bounded or unbounded nation, national cause, or threat.

China as the Crime Scene

The PRC is vast, but the focus of China mysteries is Beijing and Shanghai. Urban settings dominate crime fiction globally and historically, and these two Chinese cities appeal to established reader interest, but China mysteries tend to emphasize these cities' economic and material dynamism, in contrast to other places that have not kept up. To borrow Franco Moretti's words, one almost sees a "modern idyllic form" akin to the landscapes with factories and rail transit instead of "parks, rivers, country seats" seen in the novels of early industrial England.[17]

Eight out of ten of our China mysteries unfold in or are investigated from Beijing or Shanghai, not even including Eliot Pattison's ten novels about an exiled Beijing inspector solving crimes in Tibet. Familiarity and local pride must have made the four native PRC authors locate their novels' plots in their hometowns.[18] For the non-Chinese writers, those two megalopolises and Hong Kong were their original points of entry into China. Shanghai is so important to the Inspector Chen novels that the power-hungry neo-Maoist villains of Qiu Xiaolong's ninth mystery, thinly disguised representations of Bo Xilai and his wife Gu Kailai, are not used by the author to lure Chen Cao out to Chongqing, which Bo rendered globally notorious as his power base. Instead, the fictional villains' depredations are moved home to Shanghai, in a work titled *Shanghai Redemption!*[19]

China's fabled capital city dominates the genre. The site lends local color and a sense of history, but even here the focus is on reconstruction and its by-products.[20] The rest of China seems to be what got left behind. The detective heroes created by Lisa See and Diane Wei Liang work or have worked within the Ministry of Public Security itself, at the top of China's aboveground police hierarchy. Alban Yung's main protagonists are French security men who go in and out of their embassy and the capital's most authentic French bistros. Detectives in the Beijing municipal PSB are Christopher West's Wang Anzhuang, Peter May's Li Yan, and Peng Yetai, coinvestigator and friend of Michel Imbert's Judge Li.

54   Chapter 3

Catherine Sampson's native hero is a Beijing PI who struggles to investigate within the law. Eliot Pattison's Shan Tao Yun and Duncan Jepson's Senior Inspector Alex Soong solve crimes in Tibet and Hong Kong, respectively, but are forever marked by their earlier careers and investigative skills honed in Beijing; the locals find them suspicious on that account. Other novels set in Beijing include those of Nicole Mones, Shamini Flint, and Lisa Brackmann. Deborah and Joel Shlian, Lee Barckmann, Cheryl West Petty, and L. H. Draken draw on their past employment and studies in Beijing. The Beijing law professor He Jiahong, some of whose whodunits in Chinese have been translated into French and English, depicts a unique Beijing lawyer who does his own sleuthing. The younger authors Daniel Nieh and An Yu depict an ultramodern Beijing, and so does the veteran author Zhang Xinxin. An Yu's *Braised Pork* is relatively light on local color, yet the novel ventures into familiar "explain China" territory in Chapter 6, while the plot is still located in Beijing. It is the foreign journalists, students, and lone travelers, when they were finally allowed to travel all over China, who created many of the mysteries not so bound to Beijing or Shanghai.

Focus on authentic local detail follows the big-city Chinese police detectives abroad, for they travel there as often as to rural China to investigate crime: Houston, in Peter May's fourth China mystery; Vancouver, B.C., in David Rotenberg's fifth; St. Louis, birthplace of T. S. Eliot and home of Qiu Xiaolong, in Qiu's fourth; Myanmar jungles in Brian Klingborg's second. Shan Tao Yun is miraculously enabled by a somewhat rogue FBI agent to travel from Tibet to Seattle to help interrogate a billionaire software tycoon and criminal collector of Tibetan art. His lakeside mansion is not *quite* at Bill Gates's address. Alleys, subway stops, neighborhoods including Muslim quarters, malls, and restaurants in the Chinese and even the foreign cities, if not fictional, are all in the right locations and up to Golden Age whodunit standards, sometimes with a map included.[21] (Qiu Xiaolong however tends to move times and places around.) Hotel lobby décor and signature dishes of now-shuttered haute cuisine restaurants can be verified on archived web pages, and in the novels they may be served with a side of plutography, beginning in the parking lot. A pre-prandial aside in a thriller set in Hong Kong informs us that a Corvette C7 can travel 180 miles per hour and go from zero to sixty in less than four seconds (hemmed in by a 40 mph Hong Kong speed limit), and, somewhat related—but not too—that the Pagani Zonda of the detective's friend may not legally be driven in the US.[22] University settings tend to appear under pseudonyms, but most can be guessed from their attributes.

China in these works appears culturally and politically to be a "single chessboard," to recall a term from the Mao era, not so diverse. Tibet locales are the exception. In the hands of Küng, Pattison, and An Yu, Tibet is China's internal

China: Places and Problems   55

Other in the nation's age of triumphant material growth, much like the southwestern locales favored by PRC authors who write in Chinese. When development breaches Tibet in our novels composed overseas, the result is oppressive and exploitative. However, the authors do not depict China as a "civilizational state," culturally missionary; the major Tibet novels paint a picture of local culture being annihilated and supplanted by Han power more than Han culture.

Depicting China's other extraordinarily long and historically contested land frontiers are only James Church's *A Drop of Chinese Blood,* set in Yanji and Ulan Bator, Mongolia (Church says he has never visited Yanji, as he has Pyongyang) and Brian Klingborg's mysteries. The latter's hero, Inspector Lu Fei, is based in a fictitious and nondescript small town 70 kilometers from Harbin ("Raven Valley"), not near the Russian border (Lu is threatened with even worse exile to such a location), and the second novel sends Lu undercover across the Yunnan/Myanmar border. Klingborg's informational asides sum up rural, jungle, small-town, and second-tier-city locales with background information and aperçus that often apply to the whole nation. His China, during its rebirth, appears soiled and bleak.

In most China mysteries, the PRC's vast countryside comes into play as a place for under-the-radar malfeasance that stokes and feeds upon the new wealth of urban China. The choice of a Wuhan base of operations for a recurring (mostly benign) criminal-entrepreneurial family in the novels of Ian Hamilton appears arbitrary, even more than the other, more interesting places the globe-trotting Ava Lee visits. In *The Wild Beasts of Wuhan,* those include Denmark, Ireland, and the Faroe Islands. Her base of operations is the usual Hong Kong and Shanghai. Lisa Brackmann in *Hour of the Rat* offers detailed and noteworthy scenes of neighborhoods in Dali, Yunnan, and other cities of Southwest China, enriched by memories and follow-up visits.[23] The bemused journalist investigator in Paul Mason's *Rare Earth* finds himself in Inner Mongolia, where those elements are extracted, and so does Nicole Mones's first heroine, who goes there on the trail of the lost bones of Peking Man.

Lisa See early on drew attention to *The Interior,* as her second novel is titled. In the 1990s, Shanxi province, her location, still qualified as interior, and it is no less famous today for the kind of problematic mining and manufacturing that motivates her novel—it is just that a superhighway now links Taiyuan and Beijing.[24] Alban Yung locates the disturbing cultism that roils social order in his second China mystery way out west in Qinghai, whose environs also function convincingly as the place of exile for David Rotenberg's demoted cop hero in his second novel. Christopher West's Inspector Wang Anzhuang stands out because of his rural origins. Michel Imbert's Judge Li, also no princeling, knows Beijing's old hutongs by heart, but a novel about his rural homecoming takes him to a

56   Chapter 3

rowdy bar in a mining town in northern Jiangsu. He enters a fictional down-and-out Yangzi River port farther south, ca. 1982:

> Leaving the railway station, Li made his way across shredded plastic bags. It was a place of low-slung houses of brick blackened by grime, and broken glass windows; in the middle of the road, a mountain of cannibalized telephones as high as Mt. Tai, multicolored plastic sacks tied into bundles and tied under an awning, awaited recycling. Columns of black smoke arose from several places in the city center; the air stung his throat and irritated his eyes: under that gray sky, the city was a vision of an infernal realm. (*Lotus et bouches cousues*, 73–74)

For all their admiration of Tony Hillerman, the China mystery writers have created no non-Han, ethnic minority lead detectives, even in the Tibet novels, or equivalents of a French or Spanish tec born in Algiers, Tangier, or Barcelona. One looks in vain even for a Hakka Hong Konger. The main urban ethnic minorities depicted are Uyghurs, who figure as suspected petty criminals, true to a common Han Chinese prejudice. L. H. Draken's *Year of the Rabid Dragon* (2018) features a genocidal plot against that ethnic group.[25] Ethnic Koreans appear in novels by James Church and Cheryl West Petty, but the major villains, and Church's series hero, are North Korean nationals. Migrants from the provinces who come to Beijing and Shanghai for work appear in several novels' plots and figure as suspects for the police, but their miseries are seldom described with the level of attention accorded the Filipina nannies in Küng's Hong Kong novel, *The End of May Road*. However, in depicting how Shenzhen grew from a small congeries of villages into a giant city of migrants larger than Hong Kong itself, Jan-Philipp Sendker depicts migrants from far provinces reconstituting their home regional subcultures within the new big city (*Whispering Shadows*, 50ff, 123–124).

Michel Imbert's portraits of Beijing in the early post-Mao years provide rare impressions of grassroots people's courts. Beijing's good Judge Li oversees mundane cases of divorce, shirking at work, disputes between neighbors, and employee theft. Meanwhile, particular novels by Pattison, Imbert, Brookes, Liang, and others locate parts of their plots in a *laogai* camp, a gulag. Off-the-books detention (cf. "extraordinary rendition," but this is all within China), called "double detention" referring to time and place, recurs in works by Qiu Xiaolong, Eliot Pattison, and Lisa Brackmann. "He has been put under double detention" is rendered in Romanized Mandarin now as honorary English: "He's been *shuanggui*'d." It rhymes with waylaid.

China: Places and Problems   57

Zhongnanhai, "China's Kremlin," is, in the novels as in life, seldom open for inspection to nonresidents, yet it appears in a few plots. Inspector Chen is allowed inside to examine Chairman Mao's onetime home in a mystery with historical implications (*The Mao Case*); Michel Imbert's Judge Li goes in under escort to investigate in a case of missing documents (*Bleu Pékin*); a plot to invade Taiwan and stage a domestic coup d'état is hatched there in Alban Yung's *Message COFACE à Pékin*. Yung has a team of top-level Chinese and French operatives actually break into Zhongnanhai military barracks in *Touche pas aux pékins*. The Party and government inner sanctum yet remains imponderable, an abstract symbol of power.

China Reconstructs

Beijing and Shanghai serve together to put the China mystery's focus on China's newborn forces and its centers of wealth and power. "Creative destruction" in a quasi-capitalist direction appears unstoppable after the banner year of 1997, almost a force of nature rather than a result of political policy. A few novels mention premature deterioration in recent construction, but seldom empty high-rises or ghost towns indicating overdevelopment (except in Brackmann, *Dragon Day*, Ch. 24, and Sendker, *The Far Side of the Night*, 169–234).

"Shanghai must grow or die," pronounces a 1994–1995 conspiracy of businessmen who meet secretly in a power plant in Pudong, the brand-new metropolis and financial hub across the river from Shanghai's old city, in David Rotenberg's first novel, *The Shanghai Murders* (1998). The novel's time is six years before China entered the WTO, but already one year since the completion of Pudong's landmark Oriental Pearl Tower. Promoting entry of China into the WTO is precisely the goal of the conspiracy. The novel's hero, Zhong Fong, head of Shanghai Special Investigations, is only too familiar with the old Pudong from before the 1990s construction boom, when it was "an area of low, ancient homes and twining streets filled with sidewalk vendors and tiny shops," lacking sanitation and electricity, but hospitable to petty drug dealers and off-the-books abortionists. That included one who botched the operation on his wife when she fled there to end her pregnancy (13–14). The novel objectifies the district as *the* Pudong. "The Pudong grew even as [Zhong Fong] watched. The huge cranes of the planet's largest construction project, four times the size of even the dreams of Canary Wharf in London, pivoted and swung like gray metallic herons on an endless quest for food" (25). A 2002 French novel likens Pudong to Paris's skyscraper district. It is a "super-méga-hyper-La Défense" (Yung, *Touche pas aux pékins*, 142).

58   Chapter 3

Already in 2007, an ex-journalist character visiting Shanghai for the first time in years has to dig into the past to recall "his first trip to China: people wearing blue-gray uniforms, no cars on the streets, ration cards. Bicycles, bicycles everywhere. Faces full of suspicion and curiosity" (Sendker, *The Language of Solitude,* 261). A few years later, a Chinese American college student makes his own comparison as he views new "hordes of suave millennial Chinese" disporting themselves at Beijing's Capital Airport in 2014 (Nieh, *Beijing Payback,* 2019, 144). "When we came to visit as a family more than a decade ago, this massive terminal hadn't been built yet," he recalls. "The old one was filled with novice travelers listing around in a daze, squinting at signage, lugging giant plaid duffel bags made of cheap vinyl. Now the air is slightly clearer and the yuppies have cleaned up nicely. Their suitcases have four wheels; their sunglasses say Givenchy; they order without glancing at the menu at Burger King, at Yoshinoya, at Jackie Chan's Café." The speed of the transformation is one of its most salient features. In the eyes of an American forensic pathologist arriving in 2010, Beijing has "transformed itself from medieval to ultra-modern in the ten years" since her first visit (May, *The Ghost Marriage,* 458). When Catherine Sampson's *The Slaughter Pavilion* has a young Beijing woman visit London, the English city strikes her not as quaint but as old and dilapidated.

Pollution and traffic congestion are drawbacks of the rapid development, but like gout once upon a time, they are also emblems of wealth. Pollution is a subject of commentary in over 30 novels by my count. Already in the 1990s, visitors to Beijing acquire this first impression: "A pretty yellow cloud of pollution floated on the horizon, left of the aircraft, where Beijing ought to be." Moving indoors, then, at Ministry of Public Security headquarters: "The room was nothing other than a giant ashtray, with air so unbreathable that each breath irritated the throat. Smog had descended on the city, coating the windows with a thick and sticky film" (Yung, *Message COFACE à Pékin,* entries for October 25 and 27, 1996).

Even the unflappable and well-traveled Ava Lee is amazed at the traffic gridlock when she first sees Beijing (Hamilton, *The Goddess of Yantai,* 40). Road rage appears in a 2001 novel (May, *The Killing Room,* 329). In Wuhan, uniformed cops stand by while princelings beat up a bus driver who moves too slowly to suit them (Imbert, *La Mort en comprimés,* 130). As Beijing moves into the twenty-first century, transportation for police and judges (Imbert's Judge Li) transitions from bicycle to automobile. In *Chinese Whispers,* set in Beijing about 2003, Peter May writes:

[T]he municipal government . . . had issued an edict to every police station demanding a response time to all incidents of just twelve minutes,

China: Places and Problems   59

an edict well-nigh impossible to impose given the gridlock that seized up the city's road system for most of the day. Some stations had brought in motor scooters, but the municipal authority had refused to license them. And, almost as an afterthought, had also denied officers permission to attend incidents on bicycles. A return to the bike would be a retrograde step, they said. This was the *new* China. And so police officers sat in traffic jams, and average response times remained thirty minutes or longer. (17)

Only May's hero, the unsinkable Li Yan, still rides his bike so as to be first on the scene.

A native of Queens, New York, notes the synthesis of opposites and finds it basically good (Kjeldsen, *Tomorrow City*, location 1016):

There were so many different Shanghais, next to and on top of one another. There was the Shanghai of the past in the labyrinthine alleyways, *shíkùmén* architecture, and colonial relics of the bygone concession era, and there was the Shanghai of the present and future in the towering construction cranes, bustling markets, and ever-expanding skyline of Pudong. There were rich Westerners and locals in gleaming new Maseratis and Bentleys, and there were poor migrants pulling wooden carts and piled three or four or even five onto a single battery-powered moped. There were gated communities and luxury penthouse apartments rising high in the sky, and there were *cheng zhong cun* ["villages in the city"] made up of old shipping containers and corrugated-metal shacks that had no plumbing or electricity. Yet as disparate as it all seemed, it all came together somehow into one unified and dynamic system, inseparable and complementary parts of a whole, like the *yin yang*.

What next? A Beijing cabbie jokes with a French operative in 1999: "The latest urban legend is that a cosmonaut on the space station Mir passed along something he heard from his American comrades: China is now the only place on earth with empty housing projects that can be seen from the moon. In my opinion, that's more believable than the one about the Great Wall" (Yung, *Pas de mantra pour Pékin*, 46–47). Diane Wei Liang's detective Wang Mei sees dilapidated Beijing neighborhoods: "There was a frozen rubbish heap by the entrance to the courtyard. Someone had just thrown a few rotten cabbages on it." But these are the places left behind: "The scene reminded Mei of her childhood" (*Paper Butterfly*, 116–117).

60   Chapter 3

Crime in Fiction and in Life

Modern novels have social criticism. Mystery novels have crimes. Journalists' novels have scandals from the news. Novels set in China have pollution and corruption, and if written by a Chinese poet (Qiu Xiaolong), maybe a nonpoet (Cai Jun), or an author with graduate training in Chinese studies (Klingborg), poems. For all their embrace of China's economic progress, China mysteries written abroad still need murders: first-degree murders, multiple murders, serial murders. These are probably no more numerous than in recent crime novels written in the PRC, where the imperative is simply not to depict crime as occurring in a particular jurisdiction. Of course, afficionados do not read crime fiction that way, only officials do. In a mystery plot, multiple murders provide the sleuth clues to see a pattern and solve the case, reestablishing the image of order that characterizes the "real China." In life, the murder rate in China is low, even taking into account probable undercounting. Domestic violence and other kinds of assault are another matter. As in the mystery novel generally, the larger society can be "normalized" partly through contrast with the bizarre, ingenious, out-of-place crimes needing to be solved; in this, the China mysteries seldom disappoint.

Multiple murders thus occur in Küng's first mystery; all three of Lisa See's; Yung's first, second, and third; all five of Rotenberg's; all ten of Pattison's; all of May's, until his seventh; all ten of Imbert's except the first and eighth; Sampson's first; Brackmann's second and third; both novels in Klingborg's new series; and each of the PRC mysteries by Vittachi, Mankell, the Shlians, Stone, Church, Kjeldsen, Flint, Jepson, and Gapper. Many attempted murders occur besides the successful ones, plus massacres in Lee's and Mason's novels. Hamilton's mysteries set in Wuhan and Nanjing feature gangland slayings. Rotenberg, May, and Imbert are known for serial murder cases. Somewhat different are the works by Hiaasen/Montalbano, Bonavia/Uren, Christopher West, and Qiu Xiaolong. Their earliest novels start with a single murder leading to a larger scandal. (Qiu does have serial murders in his fifth, sixth, and tenth mysteries and multiple murders in his twelfth and thirteenth.) Küng's second novel and all of Mones's, Liang's, Zhang Xinxin's, and Brackmann's first are exceptional. Disappearances and other mysteries start the plot and keep it going for some time, with or without a murder later on. This can however lead, unexpectedly, to a trail of serial murders in the end (Klingborg's first).

How is murder accomplished in a country with so few guns in civilian hands? By knife, hatchet, poison or pathogen, explosive, strangulation, bludgeoning, push off a balcony or boat, perhaps a pistol hidden away after the Korean War. In

China: Places and Problems   61

a Chris West whodunit, Inspector Wang notices that a heavy bust of Karl Marx is missing from the office of a murdered village CCP secretary. His bashed-in skull shows ridges. Marx's sideburns were the point of contact!

Investigation of individual crimes against people or property then leads the detective or observer straight into larger scenarios of social dysfunction and malfeasance, a subject that is relatively sensitive in PRC domestic crime fiction, even for the writers who are current or former police and security cadres, allowed to write up cases they have solved themselves.[26] In works written abroad, the big pathologies can provide pervasive apprehension or be the big reveal at the end. The preeminent purveyor of the "social" China mystery is Qiu Xiaolong, with his big themes of bureaucratic infighting, official corruption, human smuggling, pollution, neo-Maoism—and in a future mystery, he says, COVID-19. Inspector Chen meanwhile comments sardonically, often in a remedial, even self-remedial spirit, on modern life and on how Chinese citizens view that life. Yet Qiu's plots are really driven by individual murders and quests, each mysterious in its own way; the preliminary title of Qiu's next offering is *Love and Murder in the Time of Covid,* and it involves suspicions of serial *murders* in a hospital ward. Being a scholar and poet at heart, the author also puts professors of Chinese literature and the personalities we study into his plots.[27] Critic Luo Hui sees Qiu's very poems, gourmet dishes, and adages as bearers of irony, even self-parody (50–55).

Noir and hard-boiled effects similarly join social themes to separate Diane Wei Liang's mysteries from Beijing cozy territory. Her female hero Wang Mei is an ex-cop private investigator no less, with procedures to match: trailing suspects herself, puzzling out connections from old photographs, and deceptively claiming official authority she no longer enjoys. Wang Mei walks the mean streets alone, beyond the Beijing West railway station: "Here, the narrow alleyways and courtyard houses of old Beijing had been replaced by reinforced concrete erected in the fifties and sixties when the government steamrolled the New Five-Year Plans. Now these buildings stood laced with time's decay. Soon they would be knocked down to make way for a new vision." Onward toward a shabby "hotel" district for migrant workers. "The night had become dangerous and cold. There were faint murmurs rustling behind old piles of furniture. Figures moved soundlessly in the shadows" (*The Eye of Jade,* 126). She reaches an alley that "smelled of both urine and food. On the right it was dark, walled in by small huts with tar roofs. At the base of the wall were piles of dirt, loose bricks, trash, and scrap metal from old woks or bicycles. Similar huts lined the left side of the alley, but these were front-facing, brightly lit, and noisy. They were the night cafés where most hotel guests came to spend their evenings" (128). A paraprosdokian

62   Chapter 3

indicates that Wang has discovered a body on a hotel room floor: "She had finally found Zhang Hong, but he was not going to answer any of her questions" (147).

Crimes in China mysteries of representative social significance in general originate from four sources, besides imagination: (1) Specific news items from China; (2) Scenarios of international import generalized from China news; (3) Theses, ethical interpretations (e.g., "corruption"), and advocacies; and (4) Personal experiences of the authors. Novels can and do mix these sources of inspiration, and they can be interrelated. Mining news sources is nearly indispensable for socially informed contemporary mysteries written abroad. Theses and sensational interpretations are eyeball catchers. Personal experience is foundational as material for most China mystery plots. This chapter will examine, in succession, the use of news items, if only as MacGuffins, Qiu Xiaolong's forte; fictionalization of recurring themes and problems in Sino-Western international news, a favorite practice of the journalists and sojourners in China; criminal themes that seem to have gone missing in the novels; and finally, overt theses in the mysteries. Autobiographical inspirations are saved for Chapters 4 and 5, about characterization and retrospection. The binder and leavening agent in all works, besides the generic imperatives of crime and investigation, is local color, information, or "culture." Noncriminal memes abound as plot hooks, too: Caucasian mummies in Xinjiang; the lost bones of Peking Man; dragon lore from the ancient state of Ba; fanciful hypothesized prehistoric links between Tibetan and Navajo culture; and surprises involving *fengshui* and Chinese medicine.[28]

True Crimes Transmuted in Qiu Xiaolong's Mysteries

For spinning out fictional plots from real criminal incidents, Qiu Xiaolong is the paragon, beginning with his debut novel, *Death of a Red Heroine* (2000). The corpse, on page one, belongs to an attractive woman in her mid-thirties, a National Model Worker and minor celebrity seen on Shanghai TV. The inspector unexpectedly discovers sexy lingerie in her apartment, caviar in her stomach, and clues to a tryst on romantic Mt. Huang. It develops that her male partner in romance, a man outed in mid-novel as one Wu Xiaoming, son of the Shanghai propaganda chief, had sponsored dancing and sex parties mixing his powerful male friends with women seeking to marry up. Wu then secretly photographed the women in flagrante delicto, to blackmail them at a later time. The Red Heroine discovered the photos and hatched her own counter-blackmail plot. She had to be eliminated.

Chief Inspector Chen solves the case in the end by having Wu's car searched. Its trunk yields a strand of the Red Heroine's hair. "Internal Security" then

China: Places and Problems   63

swoops in to arrest the culprit, not leaving it to the regular police to give credit to Chen Cao. That suits him fine. He would incur political problems in his career if he arrested "princelings" or *gaogan zidi*, which Qiu refers to throughout his series by the English acronym "HCC," for High Cadre's Child. A recurring motif in all Qiu's mysteries is conflict between the inspector and higher-ups who would quash an investigation to preserve the reputation of the Party, the same problem posed in the pioneering Chinese police procedural by Bonavia and Uren.

The perps in life were a gang of six princelings accused of tricking 51 women into attending dance parties from 1981 to 1984 and raping them. In 1986, before Qiu Xiaolong left for America, three of the accused were sentenced to death in a televised spectacle before 3,000 Shanghainese in a stadium. In the novel, the state pursues the crimes of sexual molestation and illicit photography not as an old-fashioned propaganda lesson about class warfare (murder of a proletarian hero), or about counterrevolutionary vengeance by perps who thought themselves protected by their inherited wealth and power (457). In Qiu Xiaolong's intended construction, the prosecution is a warning to the general public that the post-Mao sexual revolution and loosening-up generally can implicate them as carriers of decadent Western influence.[29] Chen Cao himself is the target of a secret accusation after he interviews a victim who ended up as a prostitute in China's decadent south. Why did he interrogate her on his own instead of hauling her into the local police bureau? Now it is the CCP that possesses an oppressive class nature: "[I]t was beyond Party Secretary Li [Chen Cao's superior], who lived in the high cadre residential building complex in west Huaihai Road, to understand how ordinary people like [the prostitute] were intimidated by the high cadres and their children. [She] would not have dared to say anything against Wu in the Guangzhou Police Bureau" (335–336).

Qiu's head villain is a composite figure whose name is vaguely reminiscent of two perps' in life, one of whom may actually have engaged in blackmail photography.[30] The author brought the time of the dance parties forward several years, from the early 1980s to 1990–1992 or later.[31] He added a murder case to the tale and made a fictional model worker the primary victim. And he usefully reminds or instructs his readers, in the narrative voice, that it was still "illegal for man and woman to share a hotel room without a marriage license" (451).

Thus does Qiu Xiaolong deftly work real events and unexpected themes of social change into his narrative, along with commentary on linguistic change, the dossier system, farmers' markets, the gap between state and private market prices, Shanghai housing and retirement perks for the politically privileged, and the names for literary theories, Chinese and Western. The explanations are not exhaustive, but concise, persistent, and perspicacious. And there are poems.

64   Chapter 3

When Red Is Black (2004, third mystery in the series) transforms another true-crime case, the shocking 1996 murder of the Shanghai writer Dai Houying in her home by an impoverished acquaintance whom she had been assisting.[32] The real-life victim was not famous enough to act as a hook or teaser, even for most native readers when the novel was published in Chinese translation in 2004. Qiu invented a clever revenge motive to make the murder of his fictional novelist look premeditated. She had written *romans à clef* during her years of post-Mao celebrity, as had Dai Houying in life, but the similarities would be recognized only by a literary scholar or fan of Dai Houying. For *The Mao Case* (2008, Qiu's sixth), the news trigger is a book well known in the West, a suitable hook for a Western reader interested in China: the 1994 publication of memoirs written in American exile by Mao Zedong's private physician, Li Zhisui, and other tell-all reminiscences.[33] In the novel, Chief Inspector Chen is delegated by the Minister of Public Security himself to investigate the granddaughter of a deceased movie star who had liaisons with Mao, another figure probably drawn from life but little known to readers abroad.[34] The granddaughter in the novel might want to write her own scandalous tell-all book.

A Loyal Character Dancer (2002, Qiu's second) opens with a corpse found in the Bund Park, hatcheted to death triad-style, but shifts in the next chapter to the loss of multiple lives on a human smuggling ship (here called the *Golden Hope* instead of the *Golden Venture;* in Lisa See's debut novel, it was the *Golden Peony*).[35] In Qiu's plot, as in the case in life, the crux is to assist prosecution in New York of a Taiwan syndicate head who runs human smuggling operations.[36] Inspector Chen must escort US Marshal Catherine Rohn to find the wife of a witness against the gang leader and get her on a plane to New York. But the wife goes missing in China. Qiu steers Chen and Rohn's search for her into coastal Fujian, wellspring of the illegal emigration enterprise, which informs the reader about root causes of a larger social malady, but the novel's action is even more energized by criminal gang rivalry in China, Chinese police corruption—in Fujian, not Shanghai—and differences in Chinese and American outlooks. Ms. Rohn is a potential love interest for Chen Cao and also his sparring partner in debates about China's one-child policy and the migrants' claims that it justifies grants of political asylum in the US. Yet the bigger political (and plot) obstacle is that the chief inspector's bosses want him to play tour guide to Inspector Rohn instead of helping solve what is after all mostly an American problem.

Two other Inspector Chen mysteries, *A Case of Two Cities* (2006; Qiu's fourth), and *Enigma of China* (debuted in 2012, in French; Qiu's eighth), deploy front-page Chinese news as a frame for "information," viz, how corruption is done in China. For the former novel, the antihero in life is a Fujian peasant

China: Places and Problems   65

turned entrepreneur, Lai Changxing, who smuggled US $6 billion of raw materials and industrial commodities into China in the 1990s, earning him nicknames like "Mr. Big," "China's Great Gatsby," and "the most wanted man in China."[37] Lai escaped to Canada and successfully fought extradition until 2011; his case was unresolved and well past the boiling point when Qiu Xiaolong wrote his mystery.

In the novel, the Central Discipline Inspection Commission in Beijing, which pursued the case in life (it had to send an army of hundreds to Fujian in a second wave to finish the job, since local police had tapped the central operatives' phones and foiled their first assault), gives Inspector Chen the special mission of investigating China's most corrupt man, one Xing Xing (as in Lai Chang*xing*). The time of the novel is about 2000 or 2001, so he is already on the lam in North America, like his counterpart in life—Canada in life, the US in the fiction. As in his other novels, Qiu Xiaolong has altered the particulars while retaining spicy details of the case. Xing Xing's base of operations is a fictitious town called Huayuan. (Lai's enterprises were the Yuanhua Group.) Xing Xing built a Red Tower, a pleasure palace where he corrupted venal officials with food, money, and women, which the CCP turned into an anticorruption tourist attraction after Xing absconded. That was precisely the strange fate of Lai Changxing's real Red Mansion in Xiamen. However, in the novel, Xing Xing is a Chinese official, not an entrepreneur. This strengthens Qiu Xiaolong's discourse of a China ruled by a corrupt communist bureaucracy, but precludes what might have been an interesting tale of China's new superrich, together with its sitting bureaucrats and continued absence of rule of law, ganging up to create something no communist leader could have foreseen: major organs of government and even the armed forces doing the bidding of a commoner paying for their services. As in Qiu's other novels, corruption lies not only in the larger scheme of things but also in the nitty-gritty of the social ethos. Inspector Chen himself is constantly tempted by offers of small, decadent perks.

Enigma of China is a frame for vignettes about corruption in the high-tech era. Ordinary Chinese citizens ("netizens") in life were deploying zoom functions to scour the internet for images of officials enjoying luxuries unaffordable on their salaries. The signature cases involved images of expensive wristwatches. In Qiu's novel, one Zhou Keng, corrupt director of the Shanghai Housing Development Committee, is outed instead by the pricey cigarettes he smokes.[38] Qiu had already created an avatar of the official he is modeled after, Zhou Zhengyi, in his fifth novel, *Red Mandarin Dress* (2007), about a real estate developer who rose from humble dumpling seller to become "the richest man in Shanghai." The later novel's enigma is that Zhou Keng is found hanged in the Moller Villa Hotel, a

66   Chapter 3

private mansion that became the fortified offices of the Shanghai headquarters of the Communist Youth League (in life, in Maoist times). In the novel it has been repurposed as a safe house and detention site for *shuanggui,* the off-the-books "double detention" of those the regime views as undesirables.[39] The mystery: Was Zhou Keng's demise murder or suicide? The cigarettes recall an accused official in a completely different scandal from life, Han Feng of the Guangxi Province Tobacco Monopoly Bureau. He had in 2007 written a scandalous diary of his sexual conquests, anonymously, but in early 2010 his authorship was outed by netizens who found clues online. That case is mentioned near the start of the novel to engage reader interest, a few pages after an advert to an even more notorious internet meme, "My father is Li Gang" (Qiu's novel revises that to read "My father is Zhang Gang"), but really both internet references are teasers.[40] The novel has some sex and blackmail, but, disappointingly perhaps, no pages from a licentious diary!

Much of the political interest that surrounds the Zhou case in the later novel is a competitive frenzy to settle the case between what outside news analysts called the "Shanghai Gang" locally in charge, represented in the novel by "Qiangyu" (that would be the Shanghai CCP head Chen Liangyu), and the head of the "Beijing Gang" (Hu Jintao, paramount leader of the PRC, former head of the Communist Youth League). In the novel, Beijing sends to Shanghai another team of investigators from the CCP Central Discipline Inspection Commission in Beijing. Both Beijing and Shanghai desire that the inherently suspicious death of the *shuanggui*'d man be attributed to suicide to protect the image of the Party, but it seems the Shanghai CCP had Zhou murdered because he had materials that might damage its local legitimacy and control. In life, Zhou Zhengyi was arrested for corrupt practices in 2003–2004 in what has generally been interpreted as a successful Beijing blow against Shanghai. Unfortunately for his reputation locally, Inspector Chen's success in solving the fictional criminal case to the satisfaction of Party Central can be seen as enabling victory by Beijing over Shanghai.

Qiu Xiaolong's disguised references to political conflicts in life "represent" China to popular readers, but he is also writing for others. Add up all his Sinological and personal allusions aimed at Chinese culture mavens and gratuitous metaphorical references to Chinese opera; his retrieval of forgotten but instructive cases from life and coded political references; embedding of his own original poems and translations of others' in the narrative; and thematic conceits of literary and crime investigations as metaphors and covers for each other (discussed in Chapter 5 below)—and one must suspect that Qiu is writing not just for his popular audience and fandom, but also for an insider audience of China

China: Places and Problems   67

specialists or would-be specialists who delight in the arcana. Qiu Xiaolong has injected into his popular mystery fiction the Chinese tradition of the "scholar novel" or "novel of erudition."[41] Leo Ou-fan Lee has, too. His detectives, spies, and smugglers send coded emails bearing covert metaphors from Chinese and French poetry, and also the *Rubaiyat* of Omar Khayyam. Alban Yung's mysteries embed other coded satirical references, to French diplomats and China experts. The smuggling in of information has a long history in the mystery novel, Chinese and Western.

China as Manufacturer for the World

Many of the generalized big crimes and pathologies discovered in the course of murder investigations in the other China mysteries dwell on China's export-led economic miracle. That subject is transnational, not necessarily related to Chinese cultural difference, and admits characters of foreign provenance familiar to both the authors and non-Chinese readers. Noxious factories, typically founded with Western capital (seldom from Japan, Taiwan, or Overseas Chinese[42]) and hidden in the densely populated countryside, combine Chinese and foreign actors as victims, as in Küng's original *The Wardens of Punyu*. Local officials tolerate whatever goes on that makes a profit, provides jobs, and maintains social order. Murders result. Urban China intrudes and saves the day in the form of inspectors, journalists, and out-of-place intruders, even investigators for NGOs. The Chinese employee victims are not likely exemplars of agency, but some dare to act as whistleblowers.

Collateral damage from a poorly run sweatshop can include pollution, human smuggling, thoughtless bioengineering, counterfeiting, and of course local corruption through payoffs, sinecures, money laundering, and other perks. Sometimes the hidden drama of a factory comes from an impending battle over its inheritance and continuity of ownership, usually on the Western side of a joint enterprise, seldom the side with Chinese, all-in-the-family management.

Küng's *The Wardens of Punyu* offers a prototype of the common dual social problem plot: malignant Sino-Western exploitation of laptop factories alternates with an even more horrific theme of involuntary organ transplants, both exposed almost by accident due to investigations of separate murder mysteries. Lisa See's influential *The Interior* (1999) then tells a tale of bad factory working conditions outside Taiyuan, Shanxi, interspersed with American father-son intrigue over a corporate takeover and final revelations that the factory is a cover for money laundering and embezzlement. See depicted these pathologies a decade

68   Chapter 3

before the suicides at Guangdong Foxconn plants producing Apple products became international news in 2010.[43]

John Gapper's exciting *The Ghost Shift* (2015) develops the same theme, set in a Dongguan electronics factory in the Pearl River Delta run by a Foxconn-like company, managed from Hong Kong (in life, it is Taiwan). It subcontracts to produce an iconic (and "addictive") Poppy line of smartphones and tablets for a firm based in Sunnyvale, California. The latter's founder, one Henry Martin, dropped out of college, did drugs, and sought enlightenment in India before returning home to Palo Alto. "Even a Chinese farmer without a mobile phone knew of Poppy's founder" (46; in life, Steve Jobs died in October 2011). As in life, the fictional subcontracting company has hung nets to catch jumpers, after 20 accomplished suicides by the novel's time of action in 2012. Some of the suicides are not so simple and therein lies the key to a second, more covert transgression: implantation of chips into select tablet computers that allows a PLA major general unauthorized backdoor access to their data. International adoption is yet another theme. A daring young Chinese American woman had infiltrated the errant factory for a Hong Kong workers' rights NGO, only to end up as a murder victim disguised as a suicide, in a case ultimately solved by her identical twin sister. The latter, a trainee for the Discipline Inspection Commission left behind in China after the girls were spirited out of Beijing following the 1989 massacre, is the perfect investigator in disguise. Henry Martin still likes communism when the scandal is over. China has problems, he admits. "But sometimes I wonder about moving over here. California's finished. It's got a terminal case of democracy. We're allowed to vote on everything, so nothing gets done" (297).

In *Shanghaied* (2009), Eric Stone depicts dystopian, squalid manufacturing outside Shanghai already in 1997. "Bad conditions, unsafe, maybe some indentured workers, kids" (25), "little more than mechanized versions of the workhouses you read about in Dickens" (114). Recruited on one-year contracts, the workers are virtual slaves until they get paid at the end of the year, minus the cost of their room and board, electricity use, a commission for the recruiter, and transportation fees (143–144). Counterpoint themes enter the picture again, notably smuggling—of counterfeit products, pharmaceuticals, and people, particularly to Mexico for maquiladora production or further smuggling north; prostitution; and money laundering.

Two novels from 2007 address outsourcing of manufacturing, which of course troubles only foreigners. In Catherine Sampson's *The Pool of Unease* (2007), Derek Sumner, the Beijing representative of Kelness, a Scottish steel mill, is found decapitated in that city. His rumored intention was to sell the plant to a Chinese businessman (Nelson Li, named after the admiral, adding insult to

China: Places and Problems   69

injury), for it to be dismantled and rebuilt in China (15–17). Readers of James Kynge's nonfiction *China Shakes the World* will recognize this scenario as Kynge's opening case study of European deindustrialization, about a Thyssen Krupp steel mill, onetime pride of Dortmund, which was moved to Suzhou. (Sampson's acknowledgments credit her old colleague Kynge, who had been the China Bureau Chief for the *Financial Times*.) Another Kelness scandal seemingly with origins in life is that the mill purchased scrap metal from Russia contaminated by radiation, which lowered the purchase price for Nelson Li.[44] Yet these are red herrings in the murder case. When British TV journalist Robin Ballantyne flies into Beijing for the story, she becomes a vehicle for exploring problems of press freedom and Chinese citizen anxieties in a time of social change, in chapters she narrates in the first person; alternating third-person chapters about her partner Song, an ex-cop reduced to tracking unfaithful husbands as a sub-rosa PI, reveal the vast disparities in wealth and power in reform China, whose new social classes are the homeless and the new rich.

Jan-Philipp Sendker's *Whispering Shadows* is a story, originally in German, about an American firm manufacturing car parts that moves from Wisconsin to Shenzhen to cut costs. It is now Cathay Heavy Metal, directed by Michael Owen, son of the firm's American patriarch, in collaboration with an ambitious and treacherous Chinese partner educated in the US who rationalizes his betrayals as revenge for American racism and condescension toward China. An alternating plot interest is another American father-son dispute about the future direction of the company, set off by the son's desire to sell Cathay Heavy Metal to a bigger company—which turns out to be a strategic asset of the Ministry of State Security (MSS). The ministry discovers too late Michael's Chinese partner's willingness to murder Michael to protect his own interest. Sendker's hero, German American ex-journalist Paul Leibovitz, is drawn into the case as the detective.

Pollution from China's new factories is a crime in itself and a motivation for secondary criminal cover-ups. Paul Leibovitz reappears as the hero in Sendker's second book in his series, *Language of Solitude* (2009). Paul discovers that the prevalence of disabilities in a rural locale of Yiwu, Zhejiang, is due to mercury poisoning akin to the Minamata disease. A factory manufacturing PVC is dumping its waste into a nearby lake. Family members of the disabled are temporarily detained for questioning when the scandal of this partly state-owned enterprise begins to surface, and that is a second official offense. Lisa Brackmann's *Hour of the Rat* (2013) has a substantial episode (Chs. 10–12) describing poisoning of the land at the infamous e-waste dump in Guiyu, Guangdong, and the role of children in the dangerous work of handling the toxic electronic detritus. The novel's account, in which sympathetic Chinese villagers rescue Brackmann's wounded

70   Chapter 3

American vet hero, Ellie McEnroe, was published after CBS's *60 Minutes* did an exposé in 2008, almost simultaneously with the Guiyu-inspired dystopian scenarios in Chen Qiufan's SF masterpiece, *Waste Tide* (2013; English tr., 2019).[45] Dual crimes in Brackmann's narrative are pollution and illegal bio-engineering, since Guiyu was chosen, in her fiction, as the perfect place to develop a GMO rice able to grow in toxic soil. Other subplots expose rural land seizures, desperate poverty, local tyranny, adulterated food, and GMOs generally, as well as the child labor. The major illegal seed-modifying company is a Sino-American joint venture. Some of the details of McEnroe's journey to China's Southwest, motivated by a search for the missing brother of an old army buddy of hers, come not only from Brackmann's own travels, but also a news story of an American ecoterrorist who in life fled to the same localities to escape the FBI.[46]

In *Don't Cry, Tai Lake* (2010; Qiu Xiaolong's seventh), when Inspector Chen Cao vacations in Wuxi, he happens upon a pollution case, one reported internationally after it caused a May 2007 algal bloom on Lake Tai that necessitated shutting down Wuxi's waterworks.[47] As Qiu's culinarily conscious writing notes, the lake was famous for a tasty local species of "white fish" and scenery commemorated by ancient poets. A second scandal must then be investigated: state suppression and criminalization of spreading information about pollution. The disseminator in the novel, known only as Jiang, represents the environmental activist Wu Lihong of life.[48]

When Chen Cao visits Wuxi, the algal bloom is in progress, but he learns about it only from a local young female environmental activist called Shanshan, whom he meets "by chance" (as in Xu Zhimo's 1926 love poem so titled, *"Ouran"* [258]). She emerges as another romantic interest and also as one of half-a-dozen murder suspects when Liu, manager of the grossly polluting No. 1 Chemical Factory, is murdered. Shanshan was covertly gathering evidence of his environmental malfeasance and giving it to Jiang, the Wu Lihong figure. As usual in a Qiu Xiaolong novel, the murder's the thing as far as the plot interest goes, but even so there are insights into other social problems—here, factory ownership. The second in command turns out to be the murderer of the manager, in league with the former's secretary, Mi or "Little" Mi (a pun on the Mandarin expression for "little secretary," which is itself a pun on "little honey," or mistress). The deputy manager knew that Liu had future plans that did not include him. Others who must be investigated include still more "little secretaries," since abandoned, and the victim's wife, who knew all about them and also has a son who wanted to inherit. Chen Cao solves the murder by getting Mi to confess, but Internal Security has got involved, and they, with their mission of punishing dissidents, must settle accounts with the "troublemaker" Jiang. His alleged crime is that he

China: Places and Problems   71

blackmailed the guilty polluters, taking money from them as a "consulting fee" (85). (Something similar was Wu Lihong's Achilles' heel.[49]) Chen Cao feels guilty about being unable to prevent that unjust conviction—of Shanshan's lover—but he must let it go.

Such themes recur in *Hold Your Breath, China* (first published in French, 2018; Qiu's tenth), a fictionalized tale inspired by journalist Chai Jing's globally famous 2015 viral video about air pollution, *Qiongding zhi xia* (Under the Dome).[50] In the novel, Chen Cao's lost love from the Lake Tai pollution case, Shanshan, plays the role of Chai Jing. The inspector is now tasked with finding dirt to discredit her. As in life, the video is officially taken down—after gaining 300 million views.[51] And yet this is only a secondary plot in the final, full-length novel. A longer and more intricate narrative details Detective Yu solving the serial murder of four people linked to problems of air pollution, or so they appear to the perpetrator. These murders, however, distract the reader from the other plot. They read like a second book.

Smuggling, Counterfeiting, and IP Theft

Smuggling, well suited to exploring exotic contraband, has inspired the China mystery since its beginnings in the 1980s novels of Hiaasen/Montalbano and Bonavia/Uren, then Lisa See's original best seller *Flower Net* (1997), down through Brian Klingborg's *Wild Prey* (2022), in which the presumed murder of a waitress who once served soups and stews made from endangered species like pangolins and tigers to rich diners up north in Harbin leads Inspector Lu Fei into Myanmar to uncover the whole sordid network.

Human smuggling evokes fascination, too, as the frame for Qiu Xiaolong's *A Loyal Character Dancer* (2002). Peter May's *Snakehead* (also 2002) provides a more detailed exposition, fantastic but multifarious and fact-laden in the telling. In May's saga, Colombians have smuggled 98 Chinese through Fujian, Colombia, and Mexico into Texas, where they suffocated in a truck—mass murder. Houston was home to America's fourth largest Chinatown and the hub of smuggling people in from China, May writes. The city also housed the world's biggest medical complex, the Texas Medical Center, already with 42 buildings when he visited. Local color is as interesting as in the author's China mysteries: menu specialties of a favorite Houston Tex-Mex grill; demographics and pathologies of Chinese human smuggling—there is said to be a one-out-of-three hepatitis B infection rate among the undocumented (59); old Soviet biowarfare exploits and more recent US deployment of herbicides in Colombia; and mechanics of the retractable roof of what was then called Enron Field, which is made to descend and crush a

72   Chapter 3

corrupt FBI agent in the nick of time. What steals the show is a biomedical revenge plot, in which migrants from Colombia are injected with flu-infected RNA, so that upon arrival in America they unwittingly spread disease.

A Mexican connection in human smuggling is also a major crosscutting offense in the Eric Stone novel about sweatshop factories and money laundering. Gangland criminals who smuggle Chinese to Europe and America are likewise the main bad guys in Alban Yung's *Touche pas aux pékins* (yet another China mystery published in 2002), along with Chinese police who cooperate with them. Among the felonies in Daniel Nieh's *Beijing Payback* (2019) is an anchor baby racket, which has a tie-in with money laundering, but the illegal immigration schemes are upstaged in the end by something more shocking: international smuggling of livers cut out of PRC prisoners for marketing in the US.

The goods smuggled in and out of China tend to be more interesting than the human contraband, who mostly enter the plots as corpses. The former includes objects of art, antiques, and relics besides the wildlife products. Seldom does one see plots involving opiates, meth, or fentanyl; foodstuffs, raw materials, precious metals, or currency. The exception is Leo Ou-fan Lee's detective-spy novel, *Dong-fang lieshou* (The Hunter of the East; 2001), which concerns the smuggling of arms and drugs into diverse Chinese cultural realms, mostly by a gang of Japanese. The smuggling of high-end bicycles to Tianjian for transshipment, and of other goods to a fake Special Economic Zone in Qingdao, seems like a low-profit, high-risk caper, almost antediluvian for the twenty-first century, but this plot in Michel Imbert's debut mystery, *Jaune camion* (2004), occurs in the bygone era of 1978. The novel's crosscutting crime, managed by the same crooks, is prostitution run out of the Beijing Hotel. The cases are related, run from the top. Judge Li exemplifies a rationale for dual investigations in fiction, and possibly in life. Says Deputy Brigade Chief Peng Yetai, "My friend Judge Li once told me that an investigation ought to be like reading a book. The writing is all there. It just needs to be deciphered. You can't read one chapter and skip all the rest" (142).

Stolen art objects and relics come straight from archeological digs, for smuggling to Hong Kong: temple statues from outside Beijing in Christopher West's *Death of a Blue Lantern* (1994), and from a location soon to be submerged when the Three Gorges Dam is finished, in Lisa See's *Dragon Bones* (2003). Antiques smuggled by a Canadian lawyer, including a Dunhuang manuscript he lights on fire (but this one is fake) in Rotenberg's *The Hua Shan Hospital Murders* (2003) provide another spectacle. An ancient stele targeted by East European and Middle Eastern expats, including a former Mossad agent and current members of the PLO mission in Beijing, is the object in Lee Barckmann's *Farewell the Dragon* (2007). Precious statues, paintings, and mandalas headed toward the Seattle

China: Places and Problems   73

collector of Tibetan art who does *not* live at Bill Gates's address are a concern in Eliot Pattison's *Beautiful Ghosts* (2004). As in life, countless other works of Tibetan temple statuary, loose-leaf books or *pecha,* and hanging paintings or *thangka* are variously cloned for sale as originals, destroyed, or spirited off to Beijing by Han officials in the other Pattison novels. A jade seal said to have belonged to Cao Cao, which survived the Cultural Revolution by having been taken from a Luoyang museum, is the eponymous object in Diane Wei Liang's *The Eye of Jade* (2008); whether that is the true sense of the code phrase "eye of jade" is part of the mystery.

Nicole Mones's *Lost in Translation* (1998) introduced the Chinese archeology mystery as its own sub-subgenre by way of a single American woman's help in the search for the lost bones of Peking Man. Most audacious of all is the theft and smuggling of the iconic Qin dynasty terra-cotta warriors in the founding Hiaasen/Montalbano mystery (1984) and Peter May's *The Fourth Sacrifice* (2000). The national and professional diversity of archeologists and smugglers provides a rich field of suspects, victims, and red herrings. Insights from Chinese art history and antiquarianism particularly illuminate Mones's second novel, *A Cup of Light* (2002), about counterfeiting and smuggling of real and fake antique Chinese pots. The hero detective, another single American woman, is an authenticator for an international auction house. At the center of the mystery is a purported exemplar of the Chicken Cup ware produced during the Ming dynasty Chenghua Emperor's reign. The main object is a fake of a fake, a copy of an item that never existed in life—a concrete realization of the "simulacrum" meme in Jean Baudrillard's cultural theory. Lead poisoning comes into this plot, too, through a concurrent investigation.

Rare and crafted objects turn reader attention to Chinese (or Tibetan) culture and history, but smuggling ivory *into* China is a surprise motive for murder in David Rotenberg's debut novel, *The Shanghai Murders* (1998). The smuggler, a well-liked African diplomat, is eliminated, and so is a crooked US Fish and Wildlife investigator, by a Taiwan-connected conspiracy of Shanghai businessmen. Deploying then a theme of reverse exoticism, Ian Hamilton's *The Wild Beasts of Wuhan* tells of forged *Western* paintings brought into the PRC for China's nouveau superrich. A collector in his Wuhan palace favors early twentieth-century Fauvists, the "wild beasts" in the book title.

Protected manufacture of fake and counterfeit products is its own subject. In Hamilton's Ava Lee series, a Shanghai triad boss manages eight factories in Jiangsu, employing more than 30,000 workers in the manufacture—going up the ladder of value through the years—of knockoff luxury clothes and handbags, CDs and DVDs, pirated Microsoft, Apple, Oracle, and HP software, and then

74   Chapter 3

iPods, iPhones, and iPads, plus products from Samsung and Nokia. The China assembly price for a fake iPhone is said to be less than seven dollars US in the early 2010s. Police tip off factory managers engaged in this "parallel manufacturing," who then lay out for confiscation waste items whose disposal is thereby obviated (*The King of Shanghai,* 74–75, 78–80, 175–176). Intersecting plots involve triad turf wars and bribery of officials. Triads can seem benign compared to the officials. When Ava Lee investigates an interlocking directorate of corporations in *The Princeling of Nanjing,* she constructs two detailed flow charts (reproduced in the novel and suitable for PowerPoint; 186, 426). They have 26 boxes representing 8 family members at the top and 18 shell companies and subsidiaries below. There is a seemingly obligatory foreign connection, too. One of the guilty parties is the chair of Britain's Conservative Party, known on TV for touting UK business and investment in China. Self-important French diplomats and blowhard go-easy-on-China Sinologists who advise them in Alban Yung's novels are just as bad. Consumer-assisted IP theft is Zhang Xinxin's topic in her novella *Haolaiwu tongjifan* (Hollywood Wanted; discussed below in Chapter 4). Zhang's Shanghai editor confirmed in 2020–2021 that the topic had become taboo in the PRC's own fiction.[52]

Biological and Medical Crimes

Biological conspiracies are vulnerable to Orientalist critiques, though such offenses are staples of crime fiction—and horror fiction. These involve the pathogens and organ harvesting previously mentioned, and medicines that violate IP or are fake. Also on display is ill-advised and even weaponized genetic manipulation of plants and animals. Gratuitous racist association of Chinese people with contagious diseases has gone on for more than two centuries, heightened again by the SARS, bird flu, and COVID epidemics and 2010s publicity about PRC breakthroughs in genetic engineering and cloning. Publicity about organ harvesting from Falun Gong detainees has inspired references by Shamini Flint (2013, pp. 210–214, 218) and perhaps Cheryl West Petty (*Beijing Abduction,* 2014, p. 200). A horrible vivisection scene with a Falun Gong girl is depicted in L. H. Draken's *Year of the Rabid Dragon* (2018, Chs. 49–52).

Perhaps from awareness of possible criticisms of Orientalism, the biomedical catastrophes in the China mysteries, like the other international scandals depicted, typically have origins outside the PRC, and the contagion plots often construct a causational wall of separation between the murders that must be investigated and the syndromes of biological malpractice. In Peter May's debut mystery with Detective Li Yan and forensic pathologist Margaret Campbell, *The*

China: Places and Problems   75

Firemaker (1999), a deadly GMO rice variety produced by an irresponsible US firm is the big reveal after serial murders have piled up that were actually done in "old-fashioned" ways. In the aforementioned *Snakehead* (2002, May's fourth), injection of the sleeper virus into hapless Chinese entering Texas is part of a Colombian plot to kill Americans. In *The Runner* (2003, May's fifth), the biggest secret to be discovered is secret performance-enhancing injections into Chinese athletes. A former East German athletic trainer and his Chinese partner have been experimenting with HERV (human endogenous retrovirus). May follows his passion, offering mini lectures on pathogens, anatomy, genetics, and the physiology of death. Still, the murder's the thing. As Detective Li and Dr. Campbell suspect, they have been called to investigate the work of a serial murderer, but the pathogen is not his weapon. The athletes have died from diverse schemes tailor-made for them, to *cover up* flaws in the biological experimentation that might have emerged later on and become more clearly incriminating if the deaths had had a uniform, medically identifiable cause. *Chinese Whispers* (2004, May's sixth) takes the reader down another biomedical rabbit hole, the controversial recording of brain responses called MERMER (memory and encoding related multifaceted electroencephalographic response), so-called brain fingerprinting. This questionable practice (duly doubted by the hero detectives) comes from an American, Lawrence Farwell, about whom May provides interesting information. A MERMER demonstration in the plot creates a "tell" that is understood only by a technician at the time, and this technician and all others who urge the Chinese police to adopt the method end up dead. The real plot motivator, again, is the murders: a psychopath is on the loose who has his own motives.

In *The Golden Mountain Murders* (2005), David Rotenberg's Detective Zhong Fong visits Anhui, site of the notorious AIDS epidemic in life caused by the return injection into rural blood donors of sera that had in the meantime been mixed and become infected. A package at the blood collection farm leads him to Vancouver, British Columbia, which is on the receiving end of shipments of still-clean Chinese blood. The trade is directed by white Canadians and corrupt Chinese associates.

Mysteries do not function well as science textbooks, as the great 1930s Chinese-language whodunit writer Cheng Xiaoqing once hoped they might.[53] There are moreover surprising cultural blind spots in the China mystery. Two novels about medical quests to promote human longevity overlook China's historical concern with longevity since ancient times, as among the Daoists. When David Rotenberg's *The Late Ching Murders* (2001) finds murder in a remote community in China's Northwest where people enjoy very long life spans, the big reveal is that American patent lawyers were going to appropriate and privatize their DNA.

76   Chapter 3

Rabbit in the Moon (2008), composed by the Sinophile medical doctors Deborah and Joel Shlian, dramatizes triple neo-Maoist, South Korean, and American conspiracies to steal an enlightened Chinese doctor's elixir of immortality.

The most eyebrow-raising plot is L. H. Draken's *Year of the Rabid Dragon* (2018), in which an inexplicable outbreak of rabies fills to capacity a central Beijing hospital. It leads an American freelance journalist to the discovery of secret government labs weaponizing a genetically altered rabies virus through CRISPR technology, to make it communicable and ultimately dangerous to a specific genetically predisposed population: Uyghurs.

For sheer horror, few plots can top Rotenberg's *Hua Shan Hospital Murders* (2003). Shanghai hospital wards that perform abortions (including Huashan, which in life is affiliated with Fudan University) are targeted for serial bombings by a mad Asian American, a convert to Manicheanism inflamed with anti-abortion sentiments nurtured by his upbringing in the US in a fundamentalist Christian household that adopted him from Asia. Manicheanism existed anciently in China but has had few adherents in modern times; the author may have picked that religion precisely because so few readers would raise objections.

Politics, the Legal System, and Other Subjects Seldom Highlighted

Politics appears at times in novels by Bonavia/Uren, Qiu Xiaolong, and Brian Klingborg, and in plots involving corruption and neo-Maoism in mysteries discussed below, but political and legal ideation is generally sparse in China mysteries, despite its interest for Western readers in other venues. Problems of the PRC legal system are raised explicitly in Qiu Xiaolong's later novels (discussed below in Chapter 5), and a few authors depict particular incidents of police misconduct, prison abuses, and torture.[54] Criminally faulty construction, necessarily approved by authorities, appears in one mystery.[55] Others evidence tolerance of organized crime (triads).[56] However, policy disputes and the grassroots citizen political protests that burgeoned in the countryside in recent years seldom appear.[57] Lisa Brackmann's mystery thrillers provide a rare mention of artistic dissidents. The gap between rich and poor, and city and country, is poignantly portrayed in a few works, though mostly with focus on nouveau riche entrepreneurs, criminals, and corrupt officials rather than on the poor. Murders occur in the frontline new factories capitalized by private entrepreneurs, seldom in the old state-owned enterprises that were being sold off in the 1990s.

Line conflicts between higher- and lower-ranking officers and interagency jurisdictional rivalry inspire many a plot in the West's procedurals, but seldom

China: Places and Problems   77

in the China mystery (and hardly ever in the PRC's own genre novels). When Imbert, May, Rotenberg, and Klingborg depict conflict and competition in the hierarchy, it is personal, not based in politics or even expressed politically. The man on top may be the villain whose role is to be exposed in a whodunit scenario, like Ministry of Public Security (MPS) brass in Lisa See's and Diane Wei Liang's respective debut novels, and Brian Klingborg's second. It is only Chief Inspector Chen who must listen to directives phrased in political jargon from his superiors. He has an extraordinary mandate to fight evil as he sees fit, like old Judge Bao and James Bond.

The theme of bureaucratic discord does emerge when über-cops tail Shanghai's Inspector Chen. They are "Internal Security," agents of the supersecret Ministry of State Security (MSS),[58] whose charge is counterespionage and anti-dissident work. In *The Mao Case,* Chen Cao gets to read political intelligence files from the MSS, but his mission from the MPS (from the minister himself) is to solve the case and forestall "tough measures" (torture) by the rival agency. That dynamic intensifies in Qiu's tenth and thirteenth mysteries. Pattison's seventh Tibet mystery, *Mandarin Gate,* introduces the People's Armed Police, whom the regular police regard as "thugs."

The euphemism or code expression "Internal Security" appeared previously in Chris West's first novel and is used also in Imbert's *En revenant de Tiananmen,* which refers to *la Sécurité d'État* (79) and seemingly to the same apparatus as *la Sécurité intérieure* (253). The MSS fights corruption (in Gapper), pursues Chinese who talk to MI6 (in Brookes), runs a factory (Sendker's first), and shows up in novels by Imbert, Mankell, Mason, Liang, and Klingborg.[59] Lisa Brackmann's Ellie McEnroe is followed and "invited to have a cup of tea" (a PRC euphemism for "come with us to a guesthouse without a name to be interrogated") by the separate Domestic Security Department (DSD) of the MPS.[60]

Other problems noticeably absent from China mysteries written abroad include drug addiction, juvenile delinquency, abuse and neglect of wives and seniors—family relations and the modern stresses affecting them generally—generational values conflicts, petty crime (mostly seen in Imbert's Judge Li novels set in 1978–1982; pickpocketing is a common police concern there), poverty, and rural migration. Peter May and Diane Wei Liang give some attention to the political origins of housing shortages of the old state allocation system, as did China's in-country writers who wrote about criminal inequities involved in their realist novels in the 1980s. But there are few scenarios of a husband stalking, beating, or murdering his wife or ex-wife, of a wife getting revenge on her husband, or a child striking back at his or her real, adoptive, or unexpectedly phony parents, as in global mysteries generally. John Gapper's *The Ghost Shift* has

78   Chapter 3

identical twins, a favorite plot device in the global mystery genre, but they never have a chance to conspire. At that, there are no mysteries about separated or missing children seeking their identity decades later. In fact, despite disturbing kidnappings in Küng's second mystery and Sendker's third, kidnapping for ransom, or to provide a bride or child for purchase (*guaimai*), is a minor theme in the China mysteries; murders to provide a corpse to join a deceased person in a ghost marriage is a more favored theme, for May (*The Ghost Marriage*), Imbert (*Lotus et bouches cousues*), and Klingborg (*Thief of Souls*).[61] Few crimes are motivated by romantic passion or inter-village feuds, or committed by homicidal hitchhikers. Amnesia and dementia do not appear; Chan Ho-Kei's *Second Sister* is unusual for its attention to identity theft. One has to look to China's domestic literature and popular fiction to see fraud and economic crimes like insurance scams and stock market swindles, as in He Jiahong's *Xing zhi zui* (Black Holes, lit., "Sex Crime"; 1996).

The big event noticeably absent from the mysteries is the spring 1989 democracy movement and subsequent massacre ("Tiananmen"; "June Fourth"), apart from some spot mentions, as in Christopher West's novels set relatively close in time to the event, and the major treatments in mysteries by Liang and Imbert discussed in this book's Chapter 5. A late narrative experiment embedded in Qiu Xiaolong's mixed-genre work *Inspector Chen and Me* (2018) depicts the hero cop having a "butterfly dream," of an alternate history for himself in which he sided with the students in 1989, lost his professional employment, and ended up as a streetside fortune-teller (99–150). Catherine Sampson, who as a young reporter covered the protests for *The Times* of London, recalls the massacre in her later articles, not her mysteries.[62] References in our many China mysteries to the 1976 Tiananmen and 1978–1979 Democracy Wall protests are even rarer, except in Imbert's *Jaune camion* (145) and *Bleu Pékin* (9). Those earlier protests against authority are nearly forgotten among the PRC's own citizenry.

Why is "Tiananmen" 1989, a turning point in Chinese history, so far in the background? Perhaps the writers and their publishers feared thematic overload after the plethora of revelatory eyewitness narratives, diaries, document dumps, and literary novels about Tiananmen that came into print after the incident.[63] Or they might have felt the mystery form, or their own insights, inadequate or undignified for commentary on such a subject. Also suspect is a spirit of "moving on" past the event; the China mystery, dominated by post-1989 plots, may even be a child of "Tiananmen," a child eager for separation from the parents. In Peter May's fifth China mystery, Li Yan, still riding a bike, nears "Tiananmen Square where the blood of the democracy protesters of eighty-nine seemed to have been washed away by the sea of radical economic change that had since swept the

China: Places and Problems   79

country" (*The Runner* [2003], 17–18). May's sixth and last full-length China mystery (2004) adds: "The Great Hall of the People . . . had been witness to the bloody events of 1989 when students demanding democracy were crushed under the wheels of army tanks. An event which had catapulted the Middle Kingdom headlong into such radical change it had produced not democracy, but instead the fastest growing economy in the world" (*Chinese Whispers*, 138–139). British journalist and media commentator Paul Mason's satirical noir thriller, *Rare Earth*, takes aim at a British television crew sent to the PRC in May 2009 to film a puff piece congratulating the country for its fight against environmental degradation. The journalists' mission is to balance negative press about "the bad China" that is expected to mark the "twentieth anniversary of the Tiananmen Square Massacre, or 'Events' as they'd agreed to call them. 'Let's do the issues that matter today—not twenty years ago,' their boss, Twyla had told them. That meant everything except torture, democracy and human rights"[64] (19).

Theses and Interpretations

The China mysteries' educational dividends lie mostly in the novels' street-level aperçus, random encounters, and attention-grabbing factoids. A major social thesis can distract from a mystery plot. But one can find a few theses among the China mysteries after all, beyond the works' common premise that culture, values, and ethics are basically panhuman. Of particular note is Henning Mankell's *The Man from Beijing* (2008). Its anti-capitalist and anticolonial thesis takes time to emerge, delayed and overshadowed as it is within a quadra-continental and dual-era plot. How modern-day China might figure into it is one of the initial mysteries. The title of the book, "Chinese" in the original Swedish and "The Man from Beijing" in the English translation, can be considered either a spoiler or a promise.

Mankell's sleuth here is not Wallander, but a similarly world-weary middle-aged woman judge of southern Sweden, Birgitta Roslin, who leaves her jurisdiction to investigate the mass murder of 19 mostly elderly Swedes in their village homes up north. She had a family connection there. The judge soon learns that other distant relatives of hers were hacked to death outside Reno, Nevada. Mid-novel the tale turns to two Chinese brothers oppressed by a Swedish American Roslin forebear in the 1860s as they labored to build the first US transcontinental railroad. A present-day PRC tycoon, the man from Beijing, acquired a diary written by one of them and has now plotted long-delayed revenge killings of descendants of the nineteenth-century oppressor. Subplots involve a false confession to the murders by a mentally disturbed Swede and a trip by Judge Roslin to

80   Chapter 3

Beijing, where she is tailed and mugged, but befriended by a powerful woman high in the CCP, a good, public-spirited socialist who hews to Maoism as it should be, uncorrupted. She is a Chinese New Left dialectical antithesis of the tycoon, her younger brother and himself a CCP adviser more in tune with the current quasi-capitalist line.

The full ideological lesson unfolds in Zimbabwe and in Mozambique, Mankell's second home.[65] The tycoon espouses Chinese neocolonialism in Africa, assisted by emigration there of Chinese peasants left behind by modernization, to forestall a new rural revolution in China that might overthrow nouveaux riches like him. He has his sister murdered, though her son saves Judge Roslin before he can kill her, too. The good son clarifies Mankell's thesis: Given the increasing capitalist-style wealth gap in China, the nation will either "be thrust back once more into hopeless chaos. Or fascist structures will become dominant." The battle is "the poor versus the rich, those without power versus those with it all" (444). The crisis is due not to residual leftism that props up the post-Mao dictatorship, but rather the new, "capitalist" reforms that maintain a power structure based on profits.

Mankell's support of a truer kind of CCP rule is exceptional among the authors, although distaste for a CCP elite addicted to self-enrichment is common in domestic and foreign nonfiction and fiction, including Paul Mason's raucously satiric descriptions of a gang of superrich red princess biker chicks following their bliss in Inner Mongolia in *Rare Earth*. The girls' Westernized boyfriends explain to a journalist their "love of Ayn Rand and Spotify; hatred of France, CNN and Amnesty International" (312). They love the Communist Party *because* it upholds their sybaritic lifestyles. Say the young ladies (in native English, which is not an anomaly, for they are all educated in foreign schools and speak good American slang; the author and the novel hero are British): "We're Communists till we die! . . . Listen—half of these girls been fucked-over by the Party: Chi had a dotcom fashion startup until some motherfucker in the Shanghai Party made a forced acquisition under threat of a wire fraud prosecution. But in the end Marxism is all-powerful because it is true! The CCP is essential to the peaceful transition to a market economy. The CCP will ensure social order from here to eternity" (104). Other observers, including social scientists, Qiu Xiaolong's inspector, and Rotenberg's police hero when he returns to Shanghai and sees that rickshaws have returned during his five years in detention, have voiced their own fears of capitalism returning in the name of reform (*The Lake Ching Murders*, 290).

Eliot Pattison's ten Shao Tao Yun novels might also be considered mysteries with a thesis, for they depict the deliberate extermination of Tibetan culture in

China: Places and Problems   81

its native region through systematic destruction and replacement activities directed by Han bureaucrats from Beijing. The mindless transformation of Tibet can moreover stand for reckless, bureaucratically directed development in all of China. Ex-Inspector Shan of Beijing, exiled to Tibet, warns a retired scientist installed in palatial retirement outside a sequestered PLA settlement of what will happen once the Chinese government discovers there is gold in his mountain locale.

> Not even the army will be able to stop what will happen then. Maybe it could have twenty or thirty years ago, but not today. Economic development is Beijing's new mantra. The first year or two they will just send survey teams. There will be helicopters coming and going overhead. Geologists will drill and blast. After that, they will build roads, with bulldozers and more dynamite. They'll assign a gulag crew to do the work for a year or two, maybe three or four hundred prisoners, so they'll probably build a prison camp right here at the village site. A new town will go up, built of metal and concrete. A depot, a garage, dormitories. Then the real work will begin. Scores of miners. More dormitories. Huge trucks to move the material as it is blasted loose. After they deplete the seams and have sluiced the dust in the streams, they'll pick a small valley in which to heap the soil they strip from the slopes, then spray it with sodium cyanide to leach out the ore. They won't stop until there is nothing left but bare, sterile rocks. Once they start, a Tibetan mountain lasts about a dozen years. (*Prayer of the Dragon*, 204)

In some 2010s China mysteries by others, a particular twenty-first-century and yet retrograde Chinese ideological tendency enters the plots as a major social malady: neo-Maoism. Its ascendency is exemplified in mass movement–style campaigns to fight crime and corruption, revive "red culture" and Maoist rituals, and cement local control by strong-man princelings aiming to acquire national power. Qiu Xiaolong's *Shanghai Redemption* fictionalizes the iconic case of Bo Xilai and his wife Gu Kailai, who was convicted of the murder of a British businessman (American in Qiu's mystery). Qiu's novel first appeared in French in 2014; translator Adélaïde Pralon's ingenious title for the book is *Dragon bleu, tigre blanc* (Blue Dragon, White Tiger), recalling Ang Lee's film *Crouching Tiger, Hidden Dragon* (2000) while suggesting hidden power of the husband and dangerous sexuality of the wife.

Similarly, the head villain in John Gapper's *The Ghost Shift* (2015), about the nefarious Guangdong province factory that makes Apple-style laptops

82   Chapter 3

implanted with secret software, is not the factory manager but the governing CCP secretary of all Guangdong, who speechifies using neo-Maoist rhetoric prior to his arrest. In Jan-Philipp Sendker's *The Far Side of the Night* (2017), another tyrannical strongman who rules a fictional Sichuan city not far from Bo Xilai's Chongqing opens the novel with like-minded vocabulary, during a program of "red" culture criticizing liberalizing trends. Deborah and Joel Shlians's novel, published in 2008 when Bo Xilai's "Chongqing model" was just getting started, already features a high-level plot to take power by reactionary neo-Maoist officials, but the conspiracy there is relatively remote from real events. Not so Lisa Brackmann's *Dragon Day* (2015), whose 2011 plot involves China's "rich and heinous" (187), including a young scion named Gugu. He summons up images of Bo Xilai's notorious playboy son Guagua, whose "charisma and seemingly fathomless pockets in life even led to the coinage of a new verb at Oxford [the young man's school between Harrow and Harvard], 'to Guagua,' meaning 'to seize power through smooth pleasantries, overwhelming financial might, and the uncertain knowledge of what will happen to your family if you fail to please.'"[66]

The elephant or dragon in the room—the ur-topic and explanatory concept of so many books of fiction and nonfiction about China—is corruption. The word appears not just in Qiu Xiaolong's but in practically all the China mysteries. Corruption is a syndrome and a potent word with ancient metaphorical roots in images of biological decomposition in Chinese (*fubai*) as in English. The concept is validated by references to it by China's leaders in anticorruption campaigns, and invalidated by those same campaigns when prosecutions are viewed simply as settling scores with political opponents. A problem of interface between the Chinese and Western concepts, aside from their shared naming of bribery, privatization of public assets, and nepotism as corruption, is the attribution of corruption in China to any "mistake" in policy implementation. Thus, the Chinese lumping together of "corruption, waste, and mismanagement," which under Western law and ethics would be deemed three separate problems.

In China as in the West, "corruption" can be a stand-in for simple abuse of power according to local norms, not the breaking of laws. In China it is an offense against the sovereign power, not against a legal code. Shan Tao Yun explains it to a Tibetan boss-of-his-village whose longtime protection by the CCP in Beijing is about to expire:

> "With such a difficult juggling act to perform perhaps you have not had time to catch up on Chinese history," Shan continued. "A pity, as you

China: Places and Problems   83

would soon learn that for centuries the most serious crime in China has been corruption. Murderers simply had their heads cut off. Sometimes they might even be allowed to buy their freedom. But those who stole from the emperor were always condemned to death by a thousand slices. . . ." (*Prayer of the Dragon*, 97)

In the PRC's own publishing industry, "anticorruption fiction" was a runaway best-selling genre with its own shelves in bookstores of the late 1990s, until 2002, when the genre was suppressed. For all their love of detail, the China mysteries written abroad have far less nitty-gritty than the native Chinese works about when to pay bribes and how much, how to privatize public property, divert funds from enterprise coffers, doctor the records, and deploy surveillance as a scare tactic for private ends.[67] In the China mysteries discussed in this book, bribery is the form of corruption most frequently depicted, as when neighborhood-level cops go about their work in the novels by West, Imbert, and Sendker (regarding Shenzhen). Judge Li's colleague, Deputy Chief Peng Yetai, has a reputation outstanding among his colleagues as one who does *not* take bribes (or beat up suspects, to get a confession); likewise, James Church's MSS inspector near the North Korean border. In Judge Li's central Beijing, even police clerks take bribes. They are offered to journalists as a matter of course in the narratives by Sampson and Mason. Gapper illustrates bribery to get through customs, and a subplot has one agent offering a bribe to another as entrapment, to hide the payer's corruption in other endeavors. Big money bribes to provincial officials protect illegal businesses in Brian Klingborg's mysteries. Shamini Flint's Inspector Singh and Ian Hamilton's forensic accountant Ava Lee (in *The Goddess of Yantai*) see bribery facilitating real estate transactions: payments not just to government officials but also to private enterprises such as realty assessment firms; likewise, when one wants information on big bank accounts (*The Princeling of Nanjing*). Back in Beijing, a beat cop explains corruption even as he runs his own racket to "protect" a neighborhood from development:

"Times have changed. . . . The days are gone when nobody had anything to their name. Since the reform, money rules, like it or not. There is collusion among the municipal officials, property developers, supply offices, and judicial authorities. Beijing is being transformed. It's up to us to participate in that transformation or perish. I'll talk to some people [who might solve your problem] I know, but I can't go to them with empty hands. If your committee can put together enough money, I can act." (*Fang Xiao dans la tourmente*, 101)

84   Chapter 3

A character is snared in an anticorruption sweep, legitimately or not, in An Yu's *Braised Pork,* and foreigners take bribes, too, in Lisa See's novels and Peter May's *Snakehead.* Casey Walker's *Last Days in Shanghai* (2014) offers the most pointed thematization of bribery. Funding the bribes is grand-theft peculation of public monies by an alcoholic mayor of Kaifeng. The novel's hero is Luke Slade, a twenty-four-year-old aide to a venal Congressman on the US side, one Leonard Fillmore, who represents San Diego and areas to the east. With the wonderment of a Jack Burden or a Nick Carraway, the young man learns of Fillmore's bribe taking, then finds himself inexplicably gifted with a briefcase of Benjamins passed on to him insouciantly by aides of the inattentive Kaifeng mayor, who must have mistaken him for his boss. He muses: "I felt the impossibility of my situation. Corruption filled my sight without shape or contour—a gray wall" (77). Walker's novel is not a comedy or even a tragedy, for Fillmore has none of the legendary magnetism of a Willie Stark or Jay Gatsby. He abuses Slade and is himself a figurehead for an eminence grise who funds him from the US side, a financier called Armand Lightfoot who wants Chinese money for a Sino-American joint venture to build an airport in the Imperial Valley. A Kaifeng cop who hates his larcenous mayor enters the plot and this is a noir thriller, with surveillance, chases, murders, and presumed murders. The corruption is mostly just background for power plays. Men in power on both sides of the Pacific are dirty, and law enforcement that would bring them down is not particularly idealistic, either.

And yet, corruption in most of these novels, like the other blots on Chinese development, is mostly just background music, mixed in with foreign and domestic tunes set to different beats. The big theme of China's turn-of-the-twenty-first-century anticorruption thrillers, namely grand-theft privatization of state-owned enterprises (SOEs), is missing from these mysteries penned abroad. SOEs, like government offices, represent the past, not the future. The interlocking directorates of knock-off factories in the Ava Lee novels, even when their creation, protection, and skimming come from provincial secretaries and governors (*The Princeling of Nanjing*), are creations of private capital. The knock-off producers are nimble, and they know what consumers will buy—therein lies their malignant power.

Corruption will not be solved by the Chinese justice system. No narrator or character voices confidence in it, not even Judge Li. The China mysteries do not delve critically into questions of legal reform and legal process until the later novels of Qiu Xiaolong. Eliot Pattison notes, as have social scientists, that trials are "conducted primarily for the people, to instruct them," not as instruments of justice.[68] This differentiates China mysteries written overseas from those written in Chinese in the PRC. In China's own generic crime fiction, the legal system must prevail and provide appropriate punishment as in China's traditional Great Judge narratives. In our novels written abroad, legal solutions are off the table for system-generated crimes and the court of public opinion comes into play as the last resort, and usually the foreign press. It has since the pioneering works of Hiaasen/Montalbano, Bonavia/Uren, Küng, and See. Brackman, in *Hour of the Rat*, Hamilton, in *The Princeling of Nanjing*, and Imbert, in *La Mort en comprimés* and *En revenant de Tiananmen*, construct plots and scenarios based on the same premise. Only Imbert's new cop protagonist, Lt. Ma of *Pékin de neige et de sang* (2018), contemplates getting justice using China's own journalists. And yet Bonavia/Uren and Küng, and particularly See, Mankell, Mason, and Jepson, have created very negative sketches of foreign journalists. In the PRC, distrust of the press runs as deep as distrust of the legal system. The favored instrument of "exposure" there is literature, not lowly, Party-controlled journalism. Embarrassment is what the CCP cannot abide, as Chief Inspector Chen Cao is always reminding the reader. When Chinese journalists are on the side of the angels, that is big news. It is to be celebrated, as in Qiu Xiaolong's *Hold Your Breath, China*.

The China mysteries offer a great deal of detail about Chinese places, more than China as a place, and about particular kinds of crimes, more than Chinese crime and corruption. The scenarios of Chinese material life and its mysteries tend to be site-specific, fragmentary, and begging for a conclusion, like clues to an unsolved murder. They also resemble the archetypal outsider's encounter with China and what makes it tick: it is seen only in pieces, on a need-to-know basis as determined by the ruling power.

4

Actors

Personas and Partners

Detective stories and crime thrillers are read for plot, not character development.[1] The China mystery is no exception, but many of its investigating or perpetually inquisitive heroes are memorable enough to carry a series. This chapter explores the types and characteristics of these and other characters—not so much as representations of particularities of Chinese culture, crime, or law enforcement, which are seldom deeply probed in the mysteries, but as emblems of human interaction. The two preceding chapters have observed how recurring plots and locations bind the China mysteries to particular places within a globalized world; this chapter maintains that characters in the plots bind the stories to human universals.

A common criticism of the China mysteries written abroad is that the characters do not seem written from a Chinese point of view. That is logical, but a more than superficial representation of police or even civilian mentality is hard to find in domestic PRC crime fiction. To steal a march on fictional inspectors who cherish the *Daodejing*: "Those who know don't speak; those who speak don't know." And a dramatic contest of good guys vs. bad guys is a proven formula in any country's popular fiction. A politically acceptable strategy in PRC crime fiction is to focus not on the place, "the people," or the police, but on the crimes, including the exploits of a perp so skilled at manipulating the workaday world that his life is one big picaresque adventure, as in the novels by Song Ying and Liu Zhenyun mentioned in Chapter 1. If not that, then the "psychology" of the criminal—aberrant psychology—like the existential detachment of the unmotivated killer in A Yi's *A Perfect Crime* (who recalls Camus' Meursault[2]). An author can have the crimes, often serial murders, be solved by a civilian genius crony of the police who possesses psychological profiling skills. The more outré a perp's behavior, the less it need be construed as a comment on social reality.

China mysteries written outside the PRC also feature some psychologically aberrant killers, notably in novels by Peter May, Qiu Xiaolong, and Brian Klingborg, but the offenders' psychologies are less interesting than the

Actors: Personas and Partners   87

outward manifestations of their fetishes. So far there is no Chinese Hannibal Lecter in the overseas-written repertory.[3] The detectives for their part are smart and upright, indeed "great," but not uncanny in their powers of perception. Cops like Zhong Fong, Li Yan, Shan Tao Yun, and Lu Fei are interesting due to constraints derived from their own personal tragedies, past missteps, or challenges to authority. Perpetually beset foreign civilian heroes like Robin Ballantyne, Paul Leibovitz, Ellie McEnroe, and Victor Li (from Sampson, Sendker, Brackmann, and Nieh, respectively) add interest to their series due to similar or even more severe vulnerabilities. All heroes of all upbringings, and most background characters, ultimately create scenes of benign moral universalism.

The Heroes: Heroic

Bumbling and dirty cops are numerous in the global mystery pantheon. So are talented civilians far more nettlesome or worrisome than the cocaine-injecting Holmes—some hard-boiled, others with a dragon tattoo. Nearly all the police heroes in our China-themed subgenre are portrayed sympathetically, not as oppressors, and they are dedicated to their job. So even are the comic foreign ones like Shamini Flint's Inspector Singh, and most of Alban Yung's French security men, though his diplomats and Sinologists can be very dense.[4] Almost as committed and resourceful are the Chinese cops' spouses, seconds in command, and *their* spouses. Yu Peiqin, Guangming's wife, goes undercover for Chief Inspector Chen when duty calls. Foreign civilian heroes whom the police might think do not belong in China are adversaries of evil, too, possessed of special talents or intuition.

The exceptional criminal cop hero in overseas-produced China mysteries is a Eurasian, the no. 2 Hong Kong anticorruption detective in Duncan Jepson's *Emperors Once More*. He is outed and defeated in the end by his partner, the PRC-born and -trained golden boy of the force, Alex Soong. Other top cops in the China mysteries are reduced to reproaching themselves for excessive smoking or coffee drinking, notably Li Yan and Chen Cao. Foreigners in lead roles can be cantankerous (Peter May's Dr. Margaret Campbell, though she soon plays a romantic Katharine Hepburn to Li Yan's Spencer Tracy), meddlesome (David Rotenberg's Geoffrey Hyland, who is Inspector Zhong Fong's onetime love rival), or medically fragile (Lisa Brackmann's injured female US war veteran Ellie McEnroe, who is also exceptional in having a menacing spouse). Still, no main protagonist, police or civilian, Chinese or foreign, takes bribes, gambles, or runs cover for triads. (Ian Hamilton's Ava Lee, a Canadian civilian, has

88   Chapter 4

clients who are "good triads," and she improves them. Daniel Nieh's Victor Li dabbles in crime at the start of his second thriller, but that is in the US.) Even among the journalist heroes, only Paul Mason's Brough fits the alcoholic stereotype, and it does not diminish his insight. One might call these characters—including most outside of law enforcement, even the foreigners and Vittachi's Feng Shui Detective—men and women with their own code, a little old-fashioned: not only latter-day Sherlocks, but also chivalrous Chinese-style knights-errant. That applies to the Hong Kong heroes of Leo Ou-fan Lee and Chan Ho-Kei, including their computer geeks and hacker heroes. Hero cops bend the law at times, but only on behalf of justice. In life, the Chinese public commonly disdains police officers as uneducated brutes and bullies. It is a common theme in Brian Klingborg's Inspector Lu Fei mysteries (also A Yi's), in which ordinary citizens at times push back against and even verbally abuse the police when they knock at the door.

Bad cops exist both above and below the novels' heroes, but police misconduct looks like a problem of individuals rather than general corruption; the bad cops' criminal conspiracy is the thing, a crime needing to be sleuthed out rather than a social problem. There are timeserving cops as wallpaper in Diane Wei Liang's *Paper Butterfly* and nasty, low-level recurring cop characters in Peng Yetai's Beijing precinct as depicted by Imbert, notably Peng's go-with-what-is-currently-accepted boss and a beat-'em-up Nightstick Zhang. Alban Yung and Michel Imbert have dreamed up some high-level coup planners in particular novels set in Zhongnanhai. The ex-father-in-law of Catherine Sampson's private eye character Song Ren is a rich, corrupt detective chief, with one Psycho Wang as his muscle, but the chief's malfeasance is discovered and he and his minion suffer pathetic ends. Likewise, a deputy police commissioner in Peter May's *Chinese Whispers* who assumed another man's identity in the Cultural Revolution, and yet another perfunctorily described commissioner in David Rotenberg's debut novel. Granted, sinister unidentified operatives are always tailing Chief Inspector Chen Cao, Zhong Fong, and several other good cops. Zhong is spied on by his own department. Chinese agents are naturally out to get Mai Martin (from Cheryl West Petty) because of her CIA husband, as are North Korean spies, who likewise trouble James Church's MSS Korean Chinese hero. Brackmann's Ellie McEnroe is stalked by a secret agent she calls "Creepy John," but he appears to like and sometimes protect her, and he resents the children of the rich and privileged. Pulling the strings at the top are civilians in most novels, less often generals: provincial CCP secretaries in Ian Hamilton's and John Gapper's mysteries, men with links to the Central Committee in Bonavia and Uren's pioneering procedural and Qiu Xiaolong's mysteries.

Resources to help an author get beyond stereotyping in the creation of Chinese police personalities include the many prototypes of sleuths in the global mystery genre and general impressions of law officers, including ethnically Chinese cops, at home. Peter May is one author who formed bonds with police in Beijing. He proffers generalizations about their methods, such as that they are less interested in motives than in building a case through relentless compilation of facts. As Li Yan's Uncle Yifu, celebrated former head of the Beijing PSB puts it, "the answer's always in the detail."[5] Michel Imbert and other authors observe that PRC society mobilizes nonprofessional human resources on behalf of "social stability" at the grass roots, still using the old Mao-era street and neighborhood committees from before the era of ubiquitous surveillance cameras. The stereotypes of these old organs are the same as in novels written in the PRC and in the minds of the Chinese public: assemblages of old-lady busybodies, nosy parkers, and timeservers. Law enforcement auxiliaries from the *Chengguan* or Urban Administrative and Law Enforcement Bureau likewise are the butt of negative comment. They are not under the PSB. In life, the public berates them for bullying and extorting money from street vendors and migrant workers.[6]

In 2001, Qiu Xiaolong was ambivalent about the goodness of Inspector Chen in his debut novel. The Great Detective formula clashed with his desired social messaging.

> Actually, Chen is not an ordinary Chinese. He is not even a hero, in my view. Of course, most Chinese cops are not heroes. You can see how low their social position is in my novel. Chen is above that, but in fact he is an antihero. . . . And Chen is in fact part of the HCCs' circle. To me he's not so pure—though maybe I'm committing what critics call the "intentional fallacy" when I say that. To me, in the end Chen does exactly the same as Wu Xiaoming, the criminal—Chen goes to bed with a female HCC, Ling, the daughter of a Politburo member. That's bourgeois decadence, but the cop gets away with it. I did not want him to be a morally irresistible character, as in so many Chinese novels with police heroes. Subconsciously, Chen himself is shocked by his behavior. At some level he may be attracted to Ling's power rather than to the woman herself, or her beauty. Maybe in my third novel I will make that point a little clearer. I've already written my second novel, a sequel to *Death of a Red Heroine,* with the same Chen Cao as the hero. I thought that perhaps he came off as too good in my first novel, more than I intended, so I told my editor that in sequels I would make him more morally repugnant. "Oh no!" the editor replied, "Don't do that!"[7]

90   Chapter 4

Chief Inspector Chen does express some self-doubt in his second novel, *A Loyal Character Dancer*. He wakes up one morning with a hangover and thinks, "How was he different from those depraved officials in Baoshen's case? Of course he had visited the club for his work, he rationalized" (204). (Chen had helped put away a corrupt vice mayor of Beijing called Baoshen, seemingly an avatar of Wang Baosen.[8])

About the loyal subordinate, Detective Yu Guangming, Qiu adds: "Since Chen is not a typical Chinese, I wanted another character to represent the ordinary Chinese, with all their problems, happinesses, and worries. Not someone who, like Chen, is fond of T. S. Eliot."[9] The same could be said of several other recurring secondary cop characters, including those from Michel Imbert, and some annoying toadies more given to naked ambition created by David Rotenberg. The interesting disclosure in Qiu's words is his sense of *duty* as a Chinese writer, realistically to represent *typical* Chinese working-class people. However, Yu Peiqin, Guangming's wife, is educated and has literary tastes. How did so many of these senior and salt-of-the-earth characters get to be intellectual, like Peter May's Mei Yuan, the street corner *jianbing* crêpe maker who looks out for Detective Li Yan, and the poet turned bookseller Qiao Bo, a recurring character in Qiu Xiaolong's mysteries? They were intellectuals until the Cultural Revolution, when Maoism made their type pay a price for their education. Apart from the dedicated malefactors and elevator operators, who are universally tagged as snitches, it is hard to find a recurring bad person among China's common-people urbanites in these novels. Then again, the hoi polloi is mostly faceless. The genre does not require more. And yet a frequent theme of the non-Chinese authors is the willingness of ordinary people in China to help those in distress.[10]

Devices of Characterization

Most contemporary China mysteries are narrated in the third person. This is common in mystery genres globally, including PRC mysteries written in Chinese, despite classic first-person narrators like C. Auguste Dupin's roommate, Dr. Watson, and Bao Lang (the recording observer of Huo Sang, Cheng Xiaoqing's 1930s "Holmes of the East"). The inner thoughts and figures of speech of Chinese police sleuths in the mysteries at issue in this book are not unlike ours, giving the reader a *sense* of realism through familiarity (the opposite of exoticism), along with reader-pleasing dry humor, irony, and double meanings specific to English. Thus, the police banter of Inspector Lu Fei's experience-tested boss, Chief Liang: "Killing a girl is too extreme, no matter which way you slice it. Her. It. You know what I mean" (*Thief of Souls,* 181). Klingborg's dialogues, on

Actors: Personas and Partners   91

the other hand, are also heavy on "foreignization" of the fictional speech, through insertion of Mandarin words in Romanization.

Police heroes in China mysteries tend to be neither hard-boiled nor malicious, even if some are observed lying to confuse a suspect, and they do not think their thoughts in political jargon, they just parrot it when necessary. In fact, not just the foreigner heroes, like May's Dr. Campbell and Rotenberg's Canadian drama coach, but even the Chinese cops see China to some extent as an outsider. Many are intellectual, able to trade tropes from world literature with foreign professors, Chinese ex-professors, and other walking wounded from the Cultural Revolution. Several cop heroes have resided in and/or had some education in the West (Liu Hulan, Alex Soong, Li Yan, Lu Fei; Shan Tao Yun learned English from his professor father). Or the Chinese hero may have enjoyed elite education in China. Chen Cao and Wang Mei got their original police jobs partly because of their good English. Other sophistication comes from having lived among more-than-urbane and cosmopolitan princelings, as enjoyed by Liu Hulan, Wang Mei, Zhong Fong's wife Fu Tsong, and Li Chunlong. Wang Anzhuang and Alex Soong have well-connected and artistic wives who are above them socially; An Yu's female hero, too, is an artist, with intellectual friends. Police officers, like other twenty-first-century Chinese, are already hybrid in culture and values, transitioning between socialism and postsocialism. Few major protagonists in our novels are ordinary lower-middle-class urbanite cops. Exceptions are Peng Yetai and his young subordinates, and Wang Anzhuang before he married.[11]

A few mysteries in the genre, such as Catherine Sampson's *The Pool of Unease,* are narrated wholly or partly in the first person, by the main protagonist, not a friend or self-appointed amanuensis. The narrator may or may not be of the author's nationality. A native Beijinger narrates some passages of Michel Imbert's *En revenant de Tiananmen.* The Korean Chinese hero, Major Bing Zong-yuan, relates James Church's *A Drop of Chinese Blood.* Conversely, Zhang Xinxin's narrator in *Haolaiwu tongjifan* (Hollywood Wanted) is a Chinese-speaking American male hired by Hollywood to go to China and infiltrate the film pirates. He begins the novel in the manner of *Moby Dick:* "Call me Luoma Suisu (When-in-Rome Do-as-the-Romans). I'm American, with a doctorate in philosophy. After graduation, I had to go back to the little town of my parents, to live in the room I thought I had left forever." As is more typical, the hero Sinologist in Imbert's *La Mort en comprimés* relates his infiltration of illicit PRC manufacturing in his native French, the author's language. Alban Yung's *Touche pas aux pékins* is likewise told by a Frenchman. Lisa Brackmann's three mystery thrillers are narrated in a knowing and distinctive voice by her American female hero, Lee Barckman's *Farewell the Dragon* is told by his alter ego, and Daniel Nieh's novels are told by a

92   Chapter 4

simpatico Chinese American male. Many chapters of Leo Ou-fan Lee's *Dongfang lieshou* (The Hunter of the East) are narrated in Chinese by that novel's Eurasian hero, who is as exceptionally multicultural and intellectual as the author. The final chapter of Chan Ho-Kei's *Yisan · liuqi* (The Borrowed) switches to narration in the first person by a native of Hong Kong who verbalizes in the same standard Chinese (Mandarin) as in the main narrative.

Rarely is the character of the major protagonist conveyed through intense introspection expressed out loud or through interior monologue, even in the first-person accounts, except for Lisa Brackmann's, which border on a confessional style, and Daniel Nieh's. Character in most of the works is revealed "transactionally," to use a word of our times. The heroes' ruminations are mostly not about themselves or society; they focus on suspects, motives, and details of their cases as they become known, typically in consultation with colleagues and other third parties.

Brian Klingborg's Inspector Lu Fei, a 2020s newcomer, is practically Inspector Chen 2.0, if not a pastiche. Lu is single-minded in pursuit of his murderer despite political pressures from above and corruption coming in laterally; eternally caught in between diverse competing social interests; constantly self-hydrating, though by beer and tea instead of coffee; and given to reciting ancient Chinese poems. (Lu's would-be sweetheart plugs Qiu Xiaolong's whodunits in the first Lu Fei novel, and also A Yi's modernist works.) Klingborg's narration is omniscient, but there is in effect a second omniscient voice that cuts in to tell the reader not only what the inspector is thinking but also how the reader should interpret it. Yet the reader gets to know and like Inspector Lu particularly from his one-liners, delivered even to superiors.

Dialogue is thus the medium by which the reader sizes up interpersonal relations. A little personal introspection is more prominent in the person of Chief Inspector Chen Cao than in the more endangered police heroes created by the other authors (including Pattison and Klingborg). That attention to the inner life may reflect Qiu Xiaolong's reservations about his hero. Chen's vulnerability and intellectualized self-doubt is surely one of his attractions to readers. In his fifth novel, he fears a nervous breakdown (*Red Mandarin Dress,* 129–130).

Narration in the Inspector Chen novels is however typically direct and economical, even prosaic, except when the inspector recites Chinese poetry or a nugget from Chinese philosophy. Catchphrases and adages recur as a lodestar for many authors' Chinese police heroes, usually handed down from previous generations (like "justice," the ideal of Wang Anzhuang's father, Daoist lessons from Shan Tao Yun's father, or Confucian wisdom from Chen Cao's; the fathers are deceased by the time of the plot). Sometimes the aphorisms convey narrative

Actors: Personas and Partners   93

pleasantries. Inspector Singh and his Beijing translator, ex-cop Li Jun, trade adages by Confucius, Deng Xiaoping, and Churchill, plus some they made up themselves, until it becomes a joke between them. Paul Leibovitz quotes Confucius to his Chinese girlfriend in Sendker's first China mystery; she feels obliged to remind him that "Even the Chinese philosophers get it wrong sometimes" (328).

Qiu Xiaolong's citations of Confucius are typically sober, but the example below from his debut novel is constrained by the hero's consciousness of self-irony, known from implied interior monologue. The addressee is Chen Cao's mother, and the source of legitimacy-from-authority is not just Confucius but Chen Cao's father. That triple complication is what keeps the passage safe from unintentionally self-satiric Charlie Chan territory:

> "I don't mean that, Mother. Still, if I can do something in my work to prevent one human being from being abused and killed by another, that's worth doing."
>
> He did not say anything more. There was no point elaborating on his defense, but he remembered what his father had once said to him. "A man is willing to die for the one who appreciates him, and a woman makes herself beautiful for the one who appreciates her." Another quotation from Confucius. Chen did not worship Confucius, but some of his sayings seemed to stick with him. (*Death of a Red Heroine*, 329)

Qiu Xiaolong dramatizes and even explains the existence of separate public and private personas among servants within the bureaucracy and thus, by extension, among all citizens in an authoritarian society. Party Secretary Li is Chief Inspector Chen's immediate superior and his original mentor. Effectively above Li is Commissar Zhang, who "did not think too well of Chen, and on several occasions had come close to labeling him a liberal" (51). Zhang is about to retire, which will render his power even harder to predict and avoid—his influence will transcend the world of explicit authority that is subject to rules. Chen Cao takes up a masked social role through deference to the commissar when he enters the conference room, and then observes and analyzes, in direct interior monologue—and ironically at that—how Secretary Li's second-level persona is leavened by a third-layer persona aware of the second. "That, Chen thought, was perhaps the secret of Li's success. Full of political nonsense, but not unaware of being so. So Li never forgot to add a few not-so-political words, words that made a little sense. That made Li somewhat different from other Party cadres" (53). Then it is Chen's turn to perform when the meeting begins. "'I've got your point, Comrade Party Secretary [Li].' Chen spoke for the first time 'With Comrade Commissar Zhang

94   Chapter 4

as our adviser, we will do our best and solve the case'" (53). After the meeting, Secretary Li assures Chen,

> "You have full authority as the head of the group."
> "So what shall we do about [Commissar Zhang]?"
> "Just keep him informed about the investigation."
> "Ah well, I see." Chen sighed.
> Chen saw only too clearly what he was in for: four or five calls from the commissar as a daily routine, not to mention the necessity of listening to Zhang's long lectures larded with quotations from Mao, Deng, or *The People's Daily,* and the necessity of suppressing frequent yawns.
> "It's not that bad. At least he is an incorruptible commissar."
> Depending on one's perspective, that was a good point—or a bad one.
> "It's in your interest, too, to work closely with a comrade of the older generation," the Party secretary concluded in a lowered voice. (54)

Both officers betray an inner persona. It is "voiced" (silently, though it is printed in the text) by Inspector Chen, whereas his boss's feelings must be deduced, even though clues to it are literally audible—but *sotto voce.*

Like nearly all the major Chinese police, judicial, and anticorruption officers in the novels (but not Qiu Xiaolong, the author, or for some reason his hero's latter-day ex-Harbin analogue—also born in Shanghai—Klingborg's Inspector Lu), Chen Cao is a CCP member. Secretary Li brought Chen into the Shanghai PSB, sponsored him for CCP membership, and even chose him to head up politically sensitive homicide investigations though Chen was a known intellectual and freethinker who had never walked a beat. The Party was seeking younger and more educated cadres for its police forces, and one explanation is that Li at first just wanted Chen Cao to translate an American police manual for him.[12] In the early novels, Li's warnings to Chen not to investigate sensitive subjects and people can be considered benign interventions to protect his young ward from "making a mistake." But as Inspector Chen persists in pursuing leads upward in the later novels, Secretary Li grows more distant and wary of his boy wonder, and not without reason. Chen has links to a Politburo member and he gets special assignments from Beijing.

Chapter 2 of this monograph noted Bonavia/Uren's early use of capsule biographies when a character is first introduced into the narrative, which can undermine the suspenseful piecemeal revelation of character in a mystery plot, but is common in old Chinese fiction and histories. Qiu Xiaolong's management of such biographies is an attraction of his narration: storytelling within the storytelling.

Actors: Personas and Partners   95

He provides mini human relations biographies for two minor characters who discover the corpse announced in the first sentence of his debut mystery. They will not be seen again, in this novel or any other so far. Passages such as these provide a sense of presence, contextual authenticity, and social history, despite their irrelevance to the case that develops—but that is not knowable at the start.

> The unusual trip had been suggested by Liu Guoliang, an old friend whom [Captain] Gao had not seen for twenty years. They had been high school buddies. After leaving school in the early sixties, Gao started to work in Shanghai, but Liu had gone to college in Beijing, and afterward, to a nuclear test center in Qinghai Province. During the Cultural Revolution they had lost touch. Now Liu had a project under review by an American company in Shanghai, and he had taken a day off to meet with Gao. (1)

The nuclear testing raises questions. Is it a red herring, since we never see Liu again? Preparation for a future novel that Qiu Xiaolong never wrote? Or is it there for its intrinsic intrigue? Most of Qiu's audience might not share a Chinese reader's curiosity about one point clarified here: how did these characters acquire the privilege of Shanghai residence? (They are natives.)

Enter Chief Inspector Chen, introduced through the eyes of a person outside the police force, and described entirely according to Chen's social past and relationships.

> In Lu's eyes, Chief Inspector Chen had fallen into Fortune's lap—or that of whatever god in Chinese mythology had brought him luck. Unlike most people of his generation, though an "educated youth" who had graduated from high school, Chen was not sent to the countryside "to be reeducated by poor and lower-middle peasants" in the early seventies. As an only child, he had been allowed to stay in the city where he had studied English on his own. At the end of the Cultural Revolution, Chen entered Beijing Foreign Language College with a high English score on the entrance examination and then obtained a job at the Shanghai Police Bureau. And now there was another demonstration of Chen's good luck. In an overpopulated city like Shanghai, with more than thirteen million people, the housing shortage was acute. Still, he had been assigned a private apartment. (10)

This is followed by a paragraph-long set-piece history of Shanghai's tight housing market and ten pages later, a thumbnail history of the reintroduction, post-Mao,

96   Chapter 4

of ballroom dancing in China (19–20). The backstory of Chen Cao's rise within the PSB is related a few pages later (24), soon followed by the story of how and why Chen decided to become a cop (31–32), after Detective Yu is introduced, again, not so much personally, as in regard to his having been passed over for promotion (30). Soon it is time for the character sketch of "Overseas Chinese Lu," who will figure in several novels to come.[13] He and the youngish inspector share culinary interests.

> It was in their high school years that Lu had gotten his nickname. Not just because Lu wore a Western-style jacket during the Cultural Revolution. More because Lu's father had owned a fur store before 1949, and thus was a capitalist. That made Lu a "black kid." In the late sixties, "Overseas Chinese" was by no means a positive term, for it could be used to depict somebody as politically unreliable, connected with the Western world, or associated with an extravagant bourgeois life style. . . . Lu befriended Chen, whose father was a "bourgeois professor," another "black kid." . . . After graduating from high school, as an educated youth Lu had been sent to the countryside. (33)

Thumbnail biography survives in Duncan Jepson's *Emperors Once More* (2014), though that novel's suspense depends very much on incomplete and misleading understanding of its most important characters.

> [Mrs. Chan's] husband had held a very good position in a *gweilo* [white foreigner]-owned plastics factory in the Po Kung Village on Kowloon side, a place later to become the epicenter of the terrible civil unrest in 1967. He was a senior project manager, which afforded him the means to live on Hong Kong Island and buy a home in the newly built apartment block in Happy Valley. Mrs. Chan had not wanted to work, as was the preference of most women born into her generation. Their views rested uncomfortably between the long-entrenched traditions of their parents, who had escaped to Hong Kong from lives of peasantry, poverty, war, and extreme politics in early twentieth-century China, and the more ambitious and emancipated generation that grew up in the emerging Asian economies of the late 1960s. (146)

There is even a capsule explanation of Alex and his wife, Jun, long after their marital spats have been dramatized for the reader as a running saga. This is just the first part:

[In college] Jun was the leader of her gang, and Alex had not been that thing [which the elite girls all want "and only one of them can get"]. True, he had a good family background, had never been purged, never sought the attention of the press, was not greedy or corrupt, was a first-class student and also a martial arts champion and skillful chess player. His family was well known in Beijing, but he was determined that after studying abroad he would go into law enforcement. This was generally considered to be an obscure ambition when there were pots of money to be made in business. (155)

Still in China's era of reform, judgment of character is inseparable from social background.

Relationships

Expression of the inner life, "subjectivity," initiative, and nonconformism are touchy subjects when Westerners depict them as occluded traits in Asia and attribute that to culture rather than society, raising the specter of Orientalism, or CCP nationalistic propaganda denounces such traits as bourgeois individualism and attributes them to Western selfishness. Bypassing the inner life tends to go with mystery and thriller genres, but in other Anglophone and Sinophone fiction, including popular writing, what kind of personal reflection is deep and what is trivial, marginal, or self-obsessed (as has been alleged of the PRC's quasi-autobiographical "pretty girl fiction")—not "lyrical in epic time," as David Derwei Wang puts it—is subject to differences in taste.[14]

The China mysteries produced overseas speak of Chinese "team playing" in opposition to "Western individualism," sometimes in eyebrow-raising terms,[15] though usually the advantage goes to the Chinese side. Scottish author Peter May's most overt simplifiers of Chinese culture tend to be American males, so they may be caricatures. American Bob Wade, a self-appointed Old China Hand, thus instructs newcomer Dr. Campbell at the police university where they are hired to lecture: the "biggest single difference—culturally" between China and the US is that "The Chinese focus on and reward group efforts, rather than individual ones. They're team players" (*The Firemaker,* 20). Campbell's native colleague and collaborator Detective Li Yan tends to agree about "the sublimation of the individual in favor of the collective good," citing both Daoism and a line Li has learned from John Donne ("no man is an island") (117). He is called out by his boss precisely for *not* being a team player, instead "firing off like a loose cannon, like some. . . . American cop" (372). Quips a freelance American journalist,

98   Chapter 4

then, in May's third mystery, *The Killing Room,* giving more unsolicited advice to Dr. Campbell: "'Hey, you're in China now,' he said. 'No such thing as the individual'" (89). An angry Chinese plotting revenge against the Westerners' imperialism in Duncan Jepson's mystery believes, "In them individualism is rampant, every little ego needing to be satisfied" (*Emperors Once More,* 325).

Michel Imbert in his visions of Beijing at the turn of the 1980s has a believable account of a lawyer trying to exculpate his client on the grounds that she was unduly influenced by *égoïsme* that ran amok under the influence of China's Cultural Revolution leaders, the Gang of Four (*Lotus et bouches cousues,* 14–15). Diane Wei Liang's hero Wang Mei, described by a friend as a "loner" unsuited for "collective action," ironically is called "selfish" by her far more acquisitive sister. Mei's family considers her borderline antisocial for not helping them join the gold rush for material goods.[16] In a previous career, Liang, the writer, coauthored an article on "Group Versus Individual Training" for a social psychology bulletin.[17] Few characters in the China mysteries, including the heroes, ponder where they are situated in China by ethnicity, social class, or political stance.

And yet, Chinese police heroes in the genre are women and men of initiative—daring, brave, headstrong, in fact prone to be loose cannons, beginning with Liu Hulan, if not Li Chunlong before her. Not all their actions are ordered by superiors. Some fictional cops really do try to imitate American cops seen on TV (Rotenberg, *The Shanghai Murders,* 156). Li Yan and Zhong Fong break regulations and have relations with American women. Li Yan even has a child with Margaret Campbell, hoping they may someday be given permission to marry. Shan Tao Yun investigates without authorization and before having even got official release from *laogai.* Granted, it does not serve the purpose of suspense fiction to focus on Chinese police officers' getting directions from their superiors, unless it heightens the sense that they are treading on forbidden ground or entering into rivalry with law enforcement competitors. Offbeat ordinary Chinese civilians with their own obsessions pop up in the China mysteries: cat rescuers and ecologists in Lisa Brackmann's *Hour of the Rat,* and a man in Imbert's *Bleu Pékin* who got from Marvel comics the idea that he can be Spider-Man and also lob a Molotov cocktail at the police. That the Chinese protagonists are so aware of their separate public and private personas accentuates their individualistic aura. A Tibetan intellectual tells Shan Tao Yun: "We're all actors, with different audiences for each mask we wear, each life we lead" (*Bones of the Earth,* 267). Then again, all such words in this subgenre are spoken by an idealized figure created by a Western or Westernized imagination.

Family is less important in these mysteries than might be expected in the Chinese context. Many of the heroes are unattached. Family is not a frequent

Actors: Personas and Partners   99

motivator of simmering, long premeditated crimes, either, as it is so often in global crime fiction. Chapter 3 noted father-son struggles for control of enterprises, but those are within foreign families from Montana and Wisconsin. These China mysteries are not "ethnic literature" from the Anglophone market that delights in exploits, customs, and intergenerational conflicts in large, extended, ethnically distinctive families. Lisa Brackmann's *Dragon Day* is the exceptional work built on family conflict in China. It has deadly consequences. That is within the billionaire class, and the evil son in that case is a criminal sexual deviant.

Only the rich have big families; the time of the action in a China mystery is usually a decade or more since the one-child policy was introduced in 1979. A colorful adaptation to the decline of arranged marriages is the Shanghai marriage market in People's Park depicted by Qiu Xiaolong, where oldsters persist in seeking mates for their unmarried only children by taping descriptions of them onto colorful umbrellas to catch the attention of other old parents.[18]

Married police heroes with families have their spouse and one child, a small child, in a nuclear family, truncated at the top. One or more parents of the hero may have met their end during the earlier political struggles; a surviving parent lives separately, apart from even the filially pious Chen Cao, Wang Mei, and Liu Hulan. The younger generation's *sense* of duty is the point. Wang Mei has a complex relationship with her mother, who wishes she would find a man and marry, and that is also the major subject of Chen Cao's conversations with his mother, but one hardly gets to know her. Siblings seldom enter the plots except as foils or dissenters. Ex-investigator Shan Tao Yun, exiled to Tibet, sees his long-lost son, now a criminal in adulthood, stationed in a reform-through-labor camp nearby (in Eliot Pattison's fourth and subsequent novels[19]), and he feels guilt for not having been filial to his own father.[20] A complex relationship between a Chinese father and his adult son is seldom dramatized in the mysteries, and Shan's of course is far from typical. (Qiu Xiaolong's *Becoming Inspector Chen* movingly relates children's latter-day resentment of their parents for having brought them up in a family "destined" to be persecuted. Even Chen Cao feels such "secret resentment" [117].) The female heroes likewise must face life without guidance from older generations. Liu Hulan, a red princess, is almost alone, having to rely on the protection of colleagues and her lover rather than her natal family once her father's treachery is uncovered. An old childhood friend, a peasant woman from her past, knows the policewoman better than she knows herself. Hulan has the audacity to chide the friend for her traditional family values. She replies, "It is sad, Hulan. . . . You were always running away; . . . even then you ran away from the truth of you" (*The Interior,* 183). The family circumstances depicted by

100   Chapter 4

Peter May's and David Rotenberg's leading characters are among the most complex, and their personal stories are suspenseful, if convoluted. Both men have been suspects in the murder of their own family members (likewise, Sampson's Robin Ballantyne).

An Yu in *Braised Pork* and many other authors tell further sad if incidental tales of the Chinese family as cruel and heartless. When the husband of An Yu's hero suddenly dies, her in-laws disown her and slander her as having cursed her husband (but not murdered him, after he drowned in a bathtub!), reflecting a traditional belief. Her friends and parents, too, have inhabited a world of divorce, she finally learns. A reviewer of *Braised Pork* has called it "an engrossing portrait of isolation."[21] Song Ren's self-enriched in-laws inhabit an even more dismal world of family relations in Catherine Sampson's novels.

The tragedy of Rotenberg's Zhong Fong is another outcome of the one-child policy, combined with the traditional preference for male children. Zhong's debut novel, *The Shanghai Murders,* unfolds about 1994–1995.[22] Four years before, Zhong's famous actress and drama teacher wife Fu Tsong had plunged into a recently poured concrete foundation for a high-rise, taking her newly aborted female fetus with her. Everything happened in Pudong, China's future financial center, which in those years was rebuilding itself up and out, hoping for deliverance from its reputation as a seedy backwater with "quacks and mountebanks" (14) ready to provide backroom abortions to suit the new one-child policy. Fu Tsong jumped into the abyss or slipped, just as Zhong Fong laid hands on her after a wild pursuit. The scene was however vulnerable to a more sinister interpretation when witnessed by another cop on the force.

What about sex? Zhong Fong's unintended and candid revelation of dismay at the thought that his first wife's pregnancy might not bear him a son emerges while the two are making love. But Rotenberg eschews lengthy or descriptive sex scenes, despite several opportunities. Brevity and deemphasis on the physicality of sex is the norm in the China mystery, despite temptations, erotic dreams, and short allusions to sex in the works of Qiu Xiaolong, Jan-Philipp Sendker, Lisa See, Dinah Lee Küng, Peter May (who reduced sex scenes in his revisions), Brian Klingborg, and others who have created male-female coinvestigators, beginning in the founding novel by Hiaasen and Montalbano (in which sex is only hinted at). More graphic sex scenes as by the doctors Shlian and Cheryl West Petty are distracting. Lee Barkmann's at least appear in the context of the tale of a young man's exploration of his sexuality. Sex hardly exists in Pattison's Tibet mysteries. Most gripping, from Lisa Brackmann, is Ellie McEnroe's puzzlement over and well-motivated fear of the spy who (maybe) loves her and stalks her, "Creepy John."

Actors: Personas and Partners 101

The novels acknowledge sexual interactions that must still be hidden in PRC society, such as homosexuality, extramarital affairs, and prostitution. Ray Stark's work partner Wen Lei Yue and Ava Lee in her series are lesbian, but their sexuality is seldom on display. Major male gay heroes do not play important roles, apart from mostly offstage murder victims like Ou-Yang in Imbert's *En revenant de Tiananmen* and Toudique in Yung's *Touche pas aux pékins*.[23] A gay bar and its owner play a role in Klingborg's mysteries, without much reflection on gay identity. Femmes fatales—favorites in prerevolutionary Chinese highbrow fiction and Western genre fiction—are scarce, too. Perhaps the entertainer "K-girls" who tempt Inspector Chen qualify.

Violence? The China mystery genre mostly avoids action for action's sake. It is not the authors' forte. The authors have researched their weapons, genetics, and human anatomical weak points, but this reader found dramatized fight scenes confusing and even boring compared to the authors' complex mental maps of social relations and escape routes—routes between cities and neighborhoods, not between rooms in offices and apartments traversed during fights. Daniel Nieh's *Take No Names* has exciting action scenes, but they take place outside of China. A few heroes are known for specific martial arts disciplines (Ava Lee, Zhong Fong, Lu Fei, Gapper's Song Mei). The authors do not try their readers' patience or appeal to exoticism with esoteric names of particular fighting postures and strikes. Succinct, judiciously infrequent, and exciting scenes of violence are served up by Ian Hamilton, Peter May (in *Snakehead*), Leo Ou-fan Lee, Kirk Kjeldsen, and Brian Klingborg. In any case, the fight scenes have little to say about character in or out of the Chinese context.

Gender Relations and Feminism

In the China mysteries written outside of China, gender relations and inequalities are frequently dramatized, explained, and criticized, typically in modern Western feminist terms, but these relations seldom become a sustained focus of attention or chief motivator of the action, even of the murders. However, women authors were instrumental in founding the contemporary China mystery and they have made major contributions ever since: Küng, See, Mones, Sampson, Liang, Brackmann, Flint, Zhang Xinxin, and An Yu. All their mysteries here, except for Zhang's and Flint's, put a canny, observant, and sympathetic female in the lead. Male authors have created Dr. Margaret Campbell, Ava Lee, Judge Birgitta Roslin, Song Ping (who bravely goes undercover as a factory girl to explore worker suicides in Gapper's *The Ghost Shift*), Au Nga-Yee (the real hero in Chan Ho-Kei's *Second Sister*), even the computer ghost Natasha, who turns out

102   Chapter 4

to be a young Chinese American woman in Leo Lee's *The Hunter of the East*. Still, most female heroes, if Chinese, are well connected and sleuth from a position of entitlement. That does make their success in a man's world more believable. From their privileged position, they inhabit a relatively gender-blind society, as "utopian models of female agency" (in the words of Sally Munt, *Murder by the Book,* 6, regarding women detectives since their nineteenth-century origins). Strong Tibetan women who are not elite appear in Küng's and Pattison's mysteries.

Critical studies of gender relations in life flourished again inside China after the post-Mao opening-up in the late 1970s, along with pushback against Western-origin critiques of Chinese gender relations,[24] about the same time that feminist detective novels gained popularity in the West thanks to authors like Sue Grafton and Sara Paretsky; lesbian sleuths also entered global crime fiction (Horsley, 250). Women have authored detective fiction since the pioneering works of Seeley Regester (1866) and Anna Katharine Green (1878), most famously during the genre's interwar Golden Age, but the genre was not considered "serious," notes John G. Cawelti (6). Literary historians generally associate the classic genre, notably the works of Agatha Christie and her colleagues, with conservative values and an ethos of restoring traditional social order.[25] Machismo in 1940s hard-boiled and noir works hardly advanced new ideas about gender. In the 1980s, critical feminist perspectives entered the PRC's own literary fiction, including Zhang Xinxin's, and even the newly revived generic fiction of crime and detection, though Chinese publishers insisted that the latter was mostly by, for, and of males. Since the 1990s, Japan has seen a "boom" in "women's detective fiction,"[26] but China, far less.[27] Depiction of feminism as a cause is scarce in the overseas-created China mysteries; unsurprisingly, the works evidence no familiarity with recent feminist, gender-crossing, and Japanese-style Boys' Love trends (male homoerotic attraction narratives popular with female readers) in China's own twenty-first-century criticism and popular literature (a kind of social dissent that can fly under the CCP radar; Walsh, 70–85). In *A Loyal Character Dancer* (157), Inspector Chen mentions Didi McCall of *Hunter* to Inspector Catherine Rohn: "That was one of the few American TV series available to us in the early eighties. Officer McCall was a huge hit here." Chen's next observation diminishes any feminist implications of the first. "In the window of the Shanghai First Department Store, I once saw a sleeveless silk pajama top called the McCall Top. It was because the female detective wore such a seductive top in one episode."[28]

Several factors may account for the lack of self-conscious feminism in spirit or content in the China mysteries written abroad. A full-bore feminist or

Actors: Personas and Partners   103

postfeminist novel would be a thesis novel, and, the last chapter argued, theses do not go naturally with mystery fiction. Küng, Mones, and Brackmann have written crossovers and social or comic novels wholly or partly outside the genre. Zhang Xinxin has always written primarily outside the mystery field, in Chinese. Authors of China mysteries must span cultures as well as genders. Non-Chinese authors must worry about cultural bias, misunderstanding China, and catering to an Orientalist vision of Chinese women needing to be delivered from the oppression of their own culture.

Lisa See's mother, Carolyn See (1934–2016), is commonly regarded as a feminist writer, and some academic papers analyze Lisa See's fiction as feminist.[29] But that appreciation has mostly been trained on her historical fiction, beginning with *Snow Flower and the Secret Fan* (2005), "the book that transformed her from a mystery writer with a modest sales record to bestselling author"; in 2011 Lisa See said, of Wayne Wang's film adaptation of that book, "it is about female friendship, about these binds that hold us together as women."[30] Most reviewers find that characterization apt for much of See's subsequent creativity. In popular fiction, however, it tends to pigeonhole her writing as "women's literature" marketed to non-feminist female readers.[31] See's later novels have generally escaped scrutiny as generic "ethnic fiction," too, though they follow a pattern of exploring Chinese sisterhood by discovering family secrets, a path trod by the Japanese Chinese American author Gail Tsukiyama. Tsukiyama for her part thinks of the characters in her first novel, *Women of the Silk* (1991), as "early Chinese feminists."[32]

In her mysteries, See's criticism of gender inequality comes mostly from dramatizations, accompanied by running commentary, of interpersonal relations generally in Chinese daily life. The negative implications for women are most visible in the middle novel, *The Interior* (1999), in which relations between Liu Hulan and a companion of her youth, now the mother of the first murder victim, presage those in See's historical novels. The reader hears a rural police captain call the victim, one of his citizens, a loose woman (66). And Liu Hulan's boss and David Stark talk over Liu's head about whether she should pursue an investigation while pregnant (126–128). At the end, when the awful Knight factory at the center of the plot finally comes under scrutiny, summary sociology diverts the plot into a nonfiction mode (382).

> Community groups, a reorganized board of directors, as well as a consortium of international watchdog organizations would carry out inspections. (This one action, if it was to be believed, wiped out half of Knight's workforce. Peanut and so many others had been sent "home," meaning

104   Chapter 4

that they'd simply moved on to other factories with less discriminating owners.) . . .

Chinese woman migrant workers were changing the face of the country-side. Unlike their male counterparts, these women either sent their earnings home to their peasant families, increasing the household income by forty percent, or were saving their salaries so they might return to their villages to open little businesses. It was estimated that women who'd returned from foreign factories owned nearly half of all shops and cafés in rural villages. Suddenly Chinese peasant girls were seen by their families as leaders of social and economic change; as a result, in the last calendar year female infanticide had dropped for the first time in recorded history. As a Ford Foundation scholar noted, female migrant workers were the single most important element transforming Chinese society.

In recent global crime fiction, but not China mysteries, female heroes appear in mass-market hybrid genres designated as "detective romance," "romantic suspense," and "female noir." Apart from occasional queer themes, most of these works however suggest stereotype as much as female empowerment.[33] Sex, romance, and erotic yearning are minor themes in the China mystery anyway. Beth Driscoll conjures up a picture of a larger, mainstream twenty-first-century middlebrow reading culture epitomized by a largely female book club world. It is commercial, middle-class, "reverential" (paying homage to high literary values), mediated (by mass media institutional influencers), emotionally engaging, recreational yet earnest (serious, not flippant), and "both female and feminized. It is female, because it is often produced and disseminated and overwhelmingly consumed by women."[34] (29) This brings us back to Lisa See. Each of her novels comes with Book Club Questions online. Yet See's works are seldom called middlebrow. They are heavily researched, the work of a popularizing historian of China (and more recently, Japan), suitable as nonfiction "China book" staples for *library* reading clubs. The titles of See's historical tales even clarify that they are fiction, for example, *Shanghai Girls: A Novel*. *Crime* fiction is outside the sentimental, "feminized" middlebrow, and Driscoll has little to say about it. Perhaps the crux is that crime and mystery novels, being so overtly and self-sustainingly generic (by name), cannot easily gain social admission to high culture.

Creation of a dominant female detective hero can still be seen as a feminist project on first principles. Dinah Lee Küng's hero Claire Raymond and Lisa See's Liu Hulan have male partners, but the women are professionally in charge. In See's debut mystery, *Flower Net,* there is a balancing, even an alternation of case discoveries, first by Hulan, then by David. The chief impediments facing Claire Raymond, Liu Hulan, Margaret Campbell, Robin Ballantyne, even Ellie McEnroe, come from the Chinese government more than male colleagues and partners.

Diane Wei Liang's hero Wang Mei is more independent in spirit and life goals than Liu Hulan, though not as self-directed and self-confident as Ava Lee. She spent her childhood in a labor camp with her parents, but in the post-Mao era has opportunities to amass wealth, power, and fame, the objectives of her sister, which Mei spurns. Yet the feminist implications of her career success are overshadowed by the professional one: Mei is a de facto private investigator, a role not yet legally authorized (she calls herself an information consultant). She has her own office and hires a male as her assistant, who makes tea for her. He is however a social inferior, a rural migrant from Henan whom she hired partly as an act of social altruism. It can however be counted as feminist criticism that Liang depicts male voyeurism in the slums and molestation in an office elevator. And Wang Mei left the MPS because her boss asked her to have a tryst with a government minister so as to facilitate his own promotion. That she is also oppressed by the expectations of her mother and sister, who want her married so as to boost the prestige of the family, does not contradict feminist critique.

Conspicuous among female heroes created by male authors is Ava Lee, the dashing and ingenious yet outwardly and even inwardly very businesslike lesbian Chinese Canadian forensics accountant created by Ian Hamilton. Wikipedia makes a point of saying that "the novels have been embraced by the Chinese Canadian community and by lesbian readers."[35] Ava Lee comes from wealth, is thirty-something, slim and pretty in her Brooks Brothers suits, also stylishly dressed when at leisure and out on the town. Her sexual preference is irrelevant.

Solitary Heroes and Associations Beyond the Understanding of the Bureaucracy

Family relationships yield to crime-related work imperatives in a mystery narrative; it goes with the genre in the Western style. The unencumbered lone wolf protagonist is iconic not just in mysteries, but also in American Westerns, spy novels, historical novels, thrillers, master criminal sagas, sports novels, sometimes even war and disaster novels—and romances, with their female heroes. Women sleuths in the global mystery genre are often single or spiritual loners intermittently married. The popular Chinese martial-arts novel, on the other hand (more than the contemporary PRC forensic crime novel in the Western-derived mold), like the classic Chinese novel from centuries before, tends

106   Chapter 4

toward multiple heroes. In the China mysteries written overseas, apart from Peter May's, Qiu Xiaolong's, Duncan Jepson's, and Brian Klingborg's, one rarely gets to look in on police hierarchy and teamwork unless and until an over-the-line free spirit is called out by a superior officer. There may be clashing personalities, but the different styles represent character *types*. And in the overseas-composed China mystery, most of "the masses," including the crime victims, are faceless. They do not narrate the story, nor does the murderer; the narration is not avant-garde. Meanwhile, few actors are suspended between good and bad, or what the old Mao-era critics used to deride in native PRC fiction as "characters in the middle."

Taking the place in the China mystery of independent amateur sleuths in the classic Western tradition, besides the loose-cannon and "thinking cops"—since private eyes can scarcely function in the PRC—are lone eagle foreign amateurs. They naturally are "beset" outsiders, even if they have a PRC work unit, like Dr. Campbell and the teachers or consultant heroes, interlopers, and mischief makers created by the Shlians, Lee Barckmann, Cheryl West Petty, and L. H. Draken, who tend to reflect China sojourns of their authors. Some heroes have come to China to learn from its culture, hide from enemies back home, or "find themselves" or their fortune. The most interesting characters, emphasized below, interact with the PRC on assignments of their own devising. It is of course the mission of the journalists to go looking for trouble. The heroes are not "tough guys" and some are women. Most find themselves beset simultaneously by The Danger—from criminal and official actors, assuming those are separate; by China's geographic enormity; and by unresolved problems from their own past. Here the mystery rejoins the larger formula of the quest novel. The resolution or transcendence the hero seeks may be articulated as justice, but it may also be for a more abstract or spiritual medicine to soothe old wounds of the self and of humanity. These are the characters that lend their mysteries fair claim to having crossed over into the literary novel.

An exemplary figure is Lisa Brackmann's Ellie McEnroe. Formerly a medic attached to the US Army during the Iraq War, in China she survives by her wits, despite a painful leg injury, PTSD, and a malevolent, ex-army, not-yet-ex-husband who does black ops for a CIA front or Blackwater-type mercenary organization, evidently with at least passive acquiescence of the Chinese government, since they, too, want to combat "Islamic terrorism" (read Uyghurs). Brackmann's first mystery alternates flashbacks to her traumas in Iraq with online conversations among avatars of unidentified artists, dissidents, freethinkers—and government spies—in an online video game called the *Great Community* (*Datong*, as known to the Chinese ancients and Kang Youwei). Later novels are told by

Actors: Personas and Partners   107

McEnroe in a confessional style. She faces The Danger, from whatever disguised organizations are tracking her; having to deal with the enormity of China, when she takes on, in her second novel, a missing person case involving the problematic brother of an old war buddy, which lets her see crimes against the environment in China's southlands and her own personal demons. In the third novel, a Chinese billionaire gives McEnroe a real detective case, investigating an American movie-business friend who latched on to his playboy son, the "Gugu" mentioned in the previous chapter. McEnroe is utterly without affectation or feelings of superiority, even as she drops acerbic and supportable opinions on, for instance, China's much-vaunted *maotai* liquor: "pretty foul, as befitting something that comes in what looks like a Drano bottle" (*Rock Paper Tiger*, 329).

Jan-Philipp Sendker's hero Paul Leibovitz is a lost soul. The son of a Brooklyn Jew who went to Germany and married a Social Democrat, Paul was bullied when his parents moved back to America. His tragedy now, as a retired journalist living as a hermit on Lamma Island, Hong Kong, is the loss of his only son, Jason, to leukemia, three years before the opening of *Whispering Shadows*. Divorced and racked with obsessive, unearned guilt, his chief connection with humanity is travel agent Christine Wu, a single mother whose background as a refugee from the PRC is actually grimmer than Paul's. Leibovitz slowly comes out of his shell in the course of three mystery novels, with help from Christine and his friend the Sichuanese Shenzhen cop, the challenge of crime cases thrust upon him by fate, then the need to survive during forays into the PRC. First is the case of Michael Owen, the outsourcer who entered a business partnership without understanding his Chinese partner, or even his father, the original heavy metals industrialist in Wisconsin. In the second novel, in which Minamata disease is discovered to be stealthily murdering farmers in Christine's old village in the Mainland, her more upwardly mobile relatives in Shanghai likewise attract attention from The Danger: the CCP, which like the MSS in the first novel cannot abide news of a scandal. The device of alternating subplots in the first novel is particularly ingenious in this one. Alternate chapters printed in italics and spoken in an anonymous and mysteriously unguessable voice begin the novel with the phrase "I've ended up in hell"; ultimately these meditative passages are revealed to be the thoughts of a stricken relative in the village struggling to escape a coma. Her thoughts become a metaphor for Paul's self-induced isolation, which is gradually being breached by enmeshment in others' tragedies. The enormity of China joins The Danger in the third novel. In a moment of carelessness, Paul leaves his precious second-born son, now four years old, to use a restroom, and the child is kidnapped by the local all-powerful tyrant, a neo-Maoist. Paul and Christine recover their son, but their trek through poverty-stricken villages and new ghost

108   Chapter 4

towns toward safety in the US Embassy in Beijing is long and suspenseful, framed by vivid descriptions of Chinese society. Sympathetic farmers help the couple stay invisible to the authorities.

Nicole Mones's three self-reliant and talented single American woman heroes (a translator for an archeologist, an antiques specialist for an auction house, and a writer for an American food magazine) have their own disabilities and real or potential family traumas to overcome. Guilt and self-doubt will not allow the hero of *Lost in Translation* to live in the US, where her father, a segregationist congressman from Texas, made her famous during her childhood as his "little girl," whom he said on TV he would never force to sit in school next to a "colored boy." Yet loyalty to her father years later causes her to break off a wedding engagement to a Chinese man, which the congressman back home opposes on racial grounds. She loves China, its people, and its culture, but they are her psychological crutch to escape an unhappy past and a rootless future. As an odd form of penance, she performs Daoist last rites for the mother of the man she did not wed, as if to make the Chinese line her substitute ancestors.

Daniel Nieh's Chinese American hero Victor Li in *Beijing Payback* and Mankell's Swedish judge Birgitta Roslin discover new things not just about their ancestors but themselves as they pursue crime cases. Brendan Lavin, a baker and two-time juvenile offender from Astoria, Queens, goes to Shanghai on the lam in Kirk Kjeldsen's *Tomorrow City,* to escape not just the law but also his vile former associates. He marries a Chinese woman and starts up another bakery, until 12 years later when the Queens outlaws find him and blackmail him into helping with a Shanghai jewelry store heist. Kjeldsen's tight and breathless prose follows Brendan through another escape, the taking of his wife and child as hostages, and finally their rescue and his escape this time to Phnom Penh, his next "tomorrow city." His wife and daughter disappear from view, so he donates his profits to a local orphanage and AIDS clinic. He would be a knight-errant if he could, and he has survival skills, but it is crime that pursues *him.*

Chan Ho-Kei's *Second Sister* features an ingenious configuration of dual loners. Au Nga-Yee is a woman librarian from a poor working family in Hong Kong who strives intrepidly, even hires an investigator with her life savings, to bring justice to those who slandered her fifteen-year-old sister through anonymous online posts. Shame caused the teenager to jump to her death from a balcony. Au Nga-Yee teams up, almost involuntarily, with a computer genius called "N," for nemesis. It is never clear whether he is at root a knight-errant or a clever criminal. Identity, the nature of gossip, human nature, and the vulnerability of modern youth become topics of contemplation in a Japanese-mystery manner, but the two heroes living in their almost antiseptic isolation, one a sympathetic

Actors: Personas and Partners   109

everywoman of the poorer social stratum, the other a master manipulator, reconstitute a traditional murder mystery whose interest is focused on surprises and misdirection of the reader in the plot.

The ultimate loner and man on the outs is Eliot Pattison's Shan Tao Yun, who is no amateur but no longer in uniform—indeed, he is effectively a criminal in his first six novels. Of Han nationality, Shan Tao Yun was once the Inspector General of a "Ministry of the Economy"; 15 years prior to the opening novel, *The Skull Mantra,* he exposed a giant automobile smuggling case in Hainan (in life, such a case broke in 1985), but his success in this and another major corruption case had consequences for Shan as "the last honest man in Beijing" (23). He was exiled to a gulag in Tibet by a cryptic one-page memo. In an extraordinary early exchange, Col. Tan of the PLA, military governor of a fictional county called Lhadrung and captain of its many gulags, summarizes it thus: "Only a single page for you, prisoner Shan. . . . Here by special invitation of a member of the Politburo. Minister of the Economy Qin. Old Qin of the Eighth Route Army. Sole survivor of Mao's appointees. Sentence indefinite. Criminal conspiracy. Nothing more. Conspiracy. . . . What was it? . . . Conspiracy to assassinate? Conspiracy to embezzle state funds? To bed the Minister's wife? To steal his cabbages? Why does Qin not trust us with that information?" (20).

The first novel, unfolding ca. 1999, finds Shan a prisoner assigned to a People's 404th Construction Brigade supervised by the PLA, building a road up into the mountains. He explains his old life in Beijing to the colonel: "I was never a prosecutor. . . . I collected evidence" (25). Besides his insights into corruption, accounting, resource development, PLA base deployments, and human motivation, Shan has every clever street detective's training in forensics, firearms, lines of sight, first aid, and so forth. And so he is released as a sort of ex-con, without any papers to authorize his freedom, and yet not the object of an all-points bulletin. For some years into the twenty-first century he is a nomad, solving cases while helping and traveling with former fellow inmates and lama friends Lokesh and Gendun, who lead him on a path of Tibetan spirituality. In the final novels, after Shan has absolved Col. Tan of a trumped-up murder charge in the sixth, the two men begin to form bonds of grudging mutual sympathy, largely based on shared distrust of Beijing. Col. Tan finally makes Shan a district constable. Shan is a modern-day knight-errant, and a former outlaw at that.

Shan and his lama companions discover other troubled souls on their journeys, as well as underground lamaseries still unknown to the Han, archeological treasures in danger of demolition, ancient murals, legendary species of medicinal plants, and hidden temples with iconographic puzzles and amulets from Buddhism and the ancient, pre-Buddhist Bon religion of Tibet. There are

110   Chapter 4

murders to be investigated or forestalled, encounters with hidden colonies of Russian freebooters and smugglers, an Oklahoma cowboy who is a retired American diplomat, a Shangri-La of folks descended from British soldiers of the 1903–1904 Younghusband expedition, slippery US mining interests, and Tibetan assassins (*purbas*) who have pledged their lives to protect the monks. In many novels a Han official at the top will seek to exploit the Tibetans and their cultural artifacts for profit, perhaps in opposition to another Han official living in Tibet against his or her will and even more menacing, but who in the end, like "the good Nazi," comes to regret the violence being done to an entire people and helps Shan escape with his life. The displaced foreigner characters serve as curiosities, murder victims, or coinvestigators.

Shan Tao Yun recites Tibetan prayers, recognizes Bon gods and devils he encounters on cave walls, and wears a *gau* (miniature altar) around his neck. He knows the mudras (Buddhist religious hand gestures) and when to perform them, instructing the reader. (Temples and lamaseries in the novels, standing or destroyed, are often composites; named gods and images of them come from the actual Bon religion.) Even some of the roving Americans and hidden Russians he meets are transformed by Tibetan Buddhism. All are heroic loners, not just the displaced cowboy, in a land as vast and unpredictable as the old American West.

Improbable Collaborations

When colorfully insubordinate heroes join forces, that is the generic sweet spot of buddy cops, sleuthing duos, and comic pairs. Judge Li with Peng Yetai and Alex Soong with Mike De Suza not only have each other's backs (until De Suza reveals himself as a traitor), they are fellow spirits or *zhiji*, an archetype long celebrated also in Chinese fiction of all genres, as in life. The China mysteries do not have the traditional CCP kind of duo, of paired operatives who supervise each other's ideological loyalty—except figuratively, perhaps, in the person of De Suza. He not only protects Soong from danger, he is the guardian of Soong's morality, reminding him not to stray from his marriage vows. Series sleuths who are fully multicultural as individuals are sparse in the China mystery, apart from the jetsetter Ava Lee and Daniel Nieh's amateur explorer Victor Li.[36]

At the comic end of the buddy cop spectrum are odd couples. Shamini Flint's Inspector Singh is odd on his own merits. On call to apply his genius from Bali to England and many Asian places in-between, he is overweight, slightly arrogant, and ridiculous looking enough to foreign nationals in his white sneakers and turban (he is a non-practicing Sikh) to be known abroad as "the curry cop" and "poppadum policeman." As a Singaporean national of minority ethnicity, he is

Actors: Personas and Partners   111

already "on to" the Chinese, and he does not even care for their food or tea. By nationality he is just the person to investigate corruption in China—particularly when the major perps are Singaporean developers, led by the husband of the First Secretary of the Singaporean Mission in Beijing. Singh in China has a companion who doubles as a foil: a down-at-the-heels ex-cop, Li Jun, his interpreter and soon-to-be coinvestigator. Little did Li know that his nephew, now deputy head of the Beijing PSB, is the Singaporean developers' chief Chinese coconspirator. (The uncle made his name arresting a corrupt capitalist named Wong Kar Wai.[37]) Li Jun had had to retire from the force years earlier because of a murder investigation that incriminated a princeling (138); news leaked to the press, so the HCC (high cadre's child) had to be prosecuted. The term "HCC" is Qiu Xiaolong's usage and was his alone until Flint used it. She must have read the Inspector Chen novels and felt moved to do a partly comic takeoff on them.

Flint's humor and irony are mild compared to Hong Kong author Nury Vittachi's, whose imitation of different ethnicities' habits of speech are nonstop farcical, as are his send-ups of local ethnic customs of all kinds, particularly magical and religious beliefs. His detective C. F. Wong claims to solve mysteries using *fengshui,* yet always comes to the right conclusion through perfectly logical reasoning to which all other parties are oblivious. He consorts with and even presides over comically self-important multicultural shamans and self-declared paranormals, ghostbusters, healers, and so forth, who are not so much a collective or "Shanghai Union of Industrial Mystics" (the title of his social-satire mystery set in China), or even a crime-fighting team as they would like to think of themselves, as a comic variation on a Harry Potterish universe hidden within adult Southeast Asian culture. Much linguistic humor comes from Wong's attempts to understand his teenage Australian assistant and ward, one Joyce McQuinnie. While everyone else speaks Singlish and other dialects, she speaks a highly Americanized pop-culture-influenced global English teenagerese. She does help solve cases. Like Wong, she does not let conventional ideas of "reality" blind her to what goes on.

Alban Yung pokes fun at French diplomacy, Sinophilia, sexism, and expat society—it is hard to say whether French culinary advocacies and idiosyncrasies are satirized or celebrated—including *entartement,* or politically motivated pie throwing with French characteristics. His French operatives and cutups, exasperated with what they regard as French diplomacy's obsequiousness to China, have organized a FIPEP, or Fédération Internationale Pour l'Extermination des Pandas.[38] Among Yung's most notable duos are orgiastic French cops and civilian yoga enthusiasts who link up with Daphne, a high-ranking Chinese policewoman skilled in martial arts, massage, and other bodily pleasurings.

112   Chapter 4

A special feature of China mysteries written overseas, compared to those written and published in the PRC, is the pairing, contrasting, and sparring of serious crime-fighting partners across cultural-national and gender divides— sometimes both, simultaneously. This can heighten the drama and provide a venue for social-cultural commentary, though binary contrasts invite stereo-types. Orientalist critiques raise the question: Do Western-origin characters dominate Asian-origin characters in these boundary-crossing relationships, and is that reinforced by the Western hero being male, dominating an Asian female second investigator?

Not as a rule. In this subgenre, as in PRC life and its own mystery fiction, the Chinese hero is necessarily in command and certainly not inferior intellectually or in knowledge of ways of the world. Liu Hulan takes charge over David Stark, Li Yan over Dr. Margaret Campbell, Zhong Fong over Geoffrey Hyland, and Chen Cao over Catherine Rohn (in China). French cops and ex-security men in Alban Yung's mysteries are exceptions, but they operate in a world of their own and provide social satire of the French in China.

More than in the PRC's own crime fiction, the hero may well be female, and, as mentioned above, in these mysteries, her lead role is not diminished by a male partner. Thus: Claire Raymond over Xavier Vonalp, Liu Hulan over David Stark, and Robin Ballantyne over Song Ren. (Ballantyne has a foreign passport, but is vulnerable as a journalist operating outside PRC law; she is buttressed by her talented and savvy female translator-helper, Blue, who in *The Slaughter Pavilion* visits London and helps solve a crime there.) Several other male-female pairings are equal, with the police power of the male equaled or even overshadowed by the superior education of the female: Lin Xiangyu (Rosina), wife of Wang An-zhuang; Fu Tsong, the highborn actress and deceased spouse of Zhong Fong, whose memory forever disturbs that troubled cop; and Yu Peiqin, educated wife of Inspector Chen's subordinate, Detective Yu. More traditional (and realistic) male dominance appears in the mysteries of Leo Ou-fan Lee and Chan Ho-Kei, though Lee's Natasha is the cultural equal of Pierre, and Chan's Au Nga-Yee of *Second Sister* is intelligent and far more likable than "N."

There remains a subtler question of whether Western characters feel superior to the Chinese characters they encounter. The material superiority of the urban West over twentieth-century China that Western characters and narrators observe in the earlier novels is relatively objective; it is reversed in mysteries of the twenty-first century, which depict the Westerners admiring China's material development. Race-, gender-, and culture-based superiority complexes are generally in abeyance when so many Western characters are "beset," as the authors pursue Sinophilic and purposely educational missions through heroes showing

Actors: Personas and Partners   113

off their superiority over "Old China Hand" characters who are objects of satire. The more complex Western characters have their own physical and psychological disabilities to overcome. The obdurate Margaret Campbell, something of a Western *non*-China-Hand stereotype—and American—is gradually reformed by being integrated into a new Chinese family, originally as a substitute mother for Li Yan's niece, who was abandoned by her own mother. Paul Leibovitz, too, is drawn into the mysteries of Christine Wu's lost family in Zhejiang and haltingly seeks salvation in his own new family. Claire Raymond, Robin Ballantyne, Ellie McEnroe, Paul Leibovitz, Ray Sharp (from Eric Stone), Philip Mangan (Adam Brookes), go to the aid of China's underdogs—Tibetans, Beijing's poor and homeless, China's rural poor, local social and eco-activists, factory workers, and ex-con whistleblowers. The Falun Gong is aided by Toronto lawyer Robert Cowens in David Rotenberg's *The Golden Mountain Murders*. Yet the foreign heroes are assisted, if not upstaged, by altruistic Chinese sympathizers, collaborators, and outright saviors, who intervene just as Mencius predicted they would if they saw a child about to fall down a well. One could conclude, more circumspectly, that the authors purvey a utopian vision of bidirectional colorblindness. Racist characters, like an INS agent named Hrycyk that Peter May depicts in Houston, Texas, are in the minority, so to speak. And yet, the foreigner good-guy characters, though they are flawed—in part because they are flawed—are inevitably more interesting than the Chinese cops.

Chief Inspector Chen Cao and US Marshal Catherine Rohn are a particularly intriguing pair of intellectual cops. They disagree on some political issues, but by mid-novel of *A Loyal Character Dancer,* they are ready for self-satirizing mock political exchanges.

> "I would like to stand here for a while." [Rohn] added mischievously, "Stuck on the wall like a snail to use your simile."
>
> "Whatever our distinguished guest prefers," Chen said. "Perhaps more like a brick in the wall. A brick in the socialist wall. As a metaphor, that was more popular during the socialist education movement." (160)

A Keller Entertainment Group pitch deck (promo) has proposed a TV series called *Inspector Chen and Me,* in which Chen Cao and Catherine Rohn might be recast as a gun-wielding, swashbuckling, spy-thriller-type couple, with Rohn as "the female Jack Ryan of the CIA." "Inspector Chen, the quirky poet and Chief Inspector of the Shanghai Police Bureau joins forces with sexy and tough CIA agent, Catherine Rohn, to fight corruption and terrorism in a weekly battle that takes them from Shanghai to Los Angeles and back again." They have "polarized

114   Chapter 4

agendas and opposite work ethics." The TV producers take our point about cop buddies: "What is it about paired detectives that can carry a series for years and years?"[39]

Citizen association and character itself are finally annihilated in Zhang Xinxin's *Haolaiwu tongjifan* (Hollywood Wanted, 2015, rev. 2021). Personality is replaced by ersatz identities in a breathless parade of the new Chinese society's forgotten little people in the cities—peddlers, misfits, menial workers, computer hackers, and programmers (*manong*, or "coding peons"). These identity-impoverished folks have renamed themselves after their favorite pirated films, movie stars, and action figures, most of them foreign, in their new avocations as underground pirate DVD copiers and self-appointed subtitle translators. They try to see themselves as heroes, as a "Fansub Gang" on a mission to divvy up pilfered movie video segments and write Chinese subtitles for them as quickly as possible to spread the joy online ("fansub" is short for media subtitling by fans, without authorization). Not only that, this gang films a selfie movie about their "profession" called *Hollywood Wanted* (that is, "On Hollywood's Most Wanted List"). It is an action flick, with the pirates, fans, and little people as the stars. They dramatize themselves fending off raids by law enforcement or fake law enforcement, assaults and attempted murders by enforcers, mafias, corrupt Oscars voters, and rival gangs and gate-crashers who want a piece of the action—the Flash Mobsters, Lookie Loos, Crowd Sorcerers, and ID Appropriationistas. The first-person narrator of this chaos is the aforementioned American Chinese philosophy student hired by Hollywood to infiltrate such activities and get them closed down. It is *mise en abyme*: the selfie movie predicts and more or less previews real events, notably a raid in early 2021.[40] The work also has the sort of farcical social commentary, surrealism, and absurdism for which Zhang Xinxin has been famous since her 1980s days as an avant-garde theater director in Beijing. Everybody, beginning with the undercover American sent by Hollywood as a spy, is continually photographing everyone else with their movie cameras, camcorders, and cell phones. Meanwhile their mobile screens get taken over by multiplying spam-demic flash messages that put into the public domain IP that was meant to stay proprietary, including the name of the fansub/flash mob's selfie film intended for their glorious coming-out. Zhang Xinxin calls into question distinctions among life, staged life, and onscreen presence; the fixity of identity; and whether community or the law should regulate what is socially acceptable. The detective story frame remains, but the work is a high-speed fantasy meditation, with cinema-style crosscutting in its very depictions of the amateur filmmaking, about the distracted and simulated quality of global screen-directed modern life.

How Fixed or Knowable *Is* Character?

By extradiegetic logic, series heroes should age and change within their series. Do they? Not much, even as the heroes and their associates experience promotions, demotions, marriage, childbirth, family reunions and disunions, travel abroad, success in founding new enterprises (Ava Lee), and death in the family, perhaps followed by the beloved's reincarnation as a mule or goat (in Pattison's Tibet novels). Ellie McEnroe, Li Yan, and Shan Tao Yun and his son Shan Ko are exceptions to the fixity of character. Ko is reformed and turns his life around with help from the lamas, like his father before him, and the father himself becomes perceptibly more prayerful in the later novels. The heroes of Chan Ho-Kei's *The Borrowed* age, but only on the outside. Any good cop may come to fear for his job security in time, notably Chief Inspector Chen,[41] but Chen's ethic and outlook change little. The heroes' series consistency maintains their seeming objectivity as observers of China, even as it undermines the theoretical realism of their observational perspectives.

How might character amid cultural difference be more deeply probed in these novels? A provocative questioning of human universality is advanced by Catherine Sampson. Her private investigator Song Ren recalls to his assistant, Wolf, how Robin Ballantyne felt about being unable to understand a particular conversation in Chinese.

> "When she arrived she told me she doesn't think it matters, because I can translate for her, and she thinks people are pretty much the same all over the world."
>
> Wolf was stunned into silence by this philosophy, but Song remembered the connection that he had felt with the foreign woman in the restaurant, that moment when they had looked at each other with mutual recognition.
>
> "Is that possible?" Song asked Blue after a moment. (*The Pool of Unease*, 221)

A similar skepticism about human universals is voiced in Jan-Philipp Sendker's *Whispering Shadows*. Paul Leibovitz converses, late in the novel, with the mother of Michael Owen; she had asked Paul to track down her missing son, the one who tried to change Chinese partners in midstream.

> "[Michael] tried to learn Mandarin. He read a couple of books about China and was convinced that America and China were not so dissimilar

116   Chapter 4

despite all the differences. Sometimes we really fought about that. We're in China here, not in Wisconsin, I told him. And he always said the same thing back. 'Darling, that doesn't matter. In the end we all dream the American dream.' I told him he was wrong, that we would dream the Chinese dream, but he only laughed and said that it was the same as the American dream, just in different colors. He was quite convinced of that." (217)

But Michael is dead because he did not understand his environment.

The mystery authors as a whole, who view themselves as having a deeper understanding of China than Michael Owen, his mother, or most spy novel writers and Old China Hands, appear devoted to human universalism. The black box in which human personality is confined, whether Chinese or foreign, can be viewed as a plot strength or a weakness. Likewise, indications of social and historical change, the subject of the next chapter.

5

Retrospection
History and Nostalgia

History in and around the contemporary China mystery is this chapter's topic. Joining most novels' relative distancing of their plots from overt political themes, noted in Chapter 3, is a certain reticence, surely related, about modern history. Even despite the instructional bent of so many works, the past comes up mostly in local-color asides: about the origins of Hong Kong's Happy Valley Racetrack; how colonial-era edifices became CCP headquarters after the revolution; how Mao's air raid tunnels were once repurposed as underground Beijing commercial space.[1]

It is not a criticism to say that the China mystery does not "nostalgically fetishize the past," as mysteries set in Europe's classical, medieval, and world war eras allegedly do.[2] Nor does this fit the imperial-era whodunits by Robert van Gulik and Elsa Hart, though it might describe PRC print, online, and media narratives that feature a Great Magistrate and draw on interest in combat, legend, and spectacle. In Qiu Xiaolong's thirteenth mystery, Inspector Chen prepares to write his own Judge Dee mystery and do better than PRC television producers of action series about him, sticking closer to the facts.

A historically minded reader will notice a wide temporal moat surrounding the China mysteries discussed in this book, separating them not just from the first half of the twentieth century, but also most of the second half, after the communist revolution. I know of just one mystery dedicated to the Mao years, 1949–1976—Michel Imbert's *Les disparus du laogaï* (2015)—and only nine set in the years following, 1976–1989.[3] Most China mysteries are definitively post-"Tiananmen," bearing a self-consciously up-to-date look. The time of the plot can usually be pegged to within a year or two, not long before the time of publication. The action then goes quickly. A murder might be solved within days, in chapters designated, in effect, "Day One," "That Afternoon," and "The Next Day." Even serial murders arrive in rapid succession.

Reconstructing the past is in principle fundamental to narrative art, particularly crime fiction, Peter Brooks reminds us, using Russian Formalist terminology: "Narrative always makes the implicit claim to be in a state of repetition, as a

118   Chapter 5

going over again of a ground already covered: a *sjužet* repeating the *fabula,* as the detective retraces the tracks of the criminal."[4] *Sjužet* is the plot put before the reader; *fabula* is the fictional events behind the story in their original order "as they happened." Viktor Shklovsky cited detective fiction to make the point in his *Theory of Prose* (1925), during the genre's Golden Age.

Crime investigation's similarities with historical research became a meme (we might say today) after 1969, when the professional historian Robin W. Winks chose "The Historian as Detective" for the title of his edited book on historical methodology. The phrase even entered the title of a New Literary Criticism article about a William Faulkner novel.[5] Josephine Tey's celebrated *The Daughter of Time* (1951) had already thematized the reinvestigation of a very cold case using historical research: the 1483 killing of the two little princes in the Tower of London, a crime usually pinned on Richard III. Tey's customary series hero, Scotland Yard Inspector Alan Grant, researches the murders while laid up in the hospital. Winks, a detective fiction aficionado, at first derided the novel's historical methodology, but later retracted his criticism and put *The Daughter of Time* on his long list of "Favorite Mystery Books."[6]

For contemplation and revision of Chinese modern history, one had best turn to highbrow fiction written in Chinese in the PRC beginning in the 1980s, when noted Chinese writers questioned the very nature of historical understanding.[7] Progressive writers of the era asked that literature *ganyu shenghuo* or "delve into life," even "intervene in life," reassessing and overturning past "verdicts" on historical events still affecting the present. Among our China mysteries written overseas, one finds a professional China historian named Marc Bernart as the hero in Michel Imbert's *La Mort en comprimés* (Death in Capsule, 2008). Before departing his home in Paris to do research on the Chinese Communist Party's history in its Beijing archives, Imbert's fictional hero encounters an old college schoolmate, Paul Castignac, who chose a career in China-related journalism instead of academic Sinology. Paul has a big story to discuss and comes to Marc's place for dinner. While Marc is in the bathroom, Chinese agents break into his apartment and throw his friend off the balcony. That makes Marc a murder suspect, so he expedites his trip to China in a variation of the suspect-as-detective scenario. There he finds Paul's informant, a red princess employed at the Ministry of Health. Bernart and his new friend solve the murder of Castignac by uncovering the big scandal whose threatened exposure provoked it. It was all about Sino-French production of a lethal counterfeit medicine. (More deaths.) Bernart sees the product being packaged by child labor in a school. Yet these crimes are in the near past, not the Yan'an, wartime, or foundational socialist eras that might have interested the hero

Retrospection: History and Nostalgia   119

professionally. The plot is engrossing, but the historical research angle is akin to a MacGuffin.

The China mysteries at issue in this book do not aim to revise Chinese history, not even the history of the revolution. The works discussed below are exceptional, but here, too, the weight of the past comes into view mostly through cold cases that resurface alongside current cases, crimes of delayed revenge, and topical social phenomena that appear revivalist. One plot by Qiu Xiaolong discussed below, unique in our China mysteries but having precedents in earlier Chinese fiction (such as Wu Jingzi's 1750 masterpiece, *Rulin waishi* or *The Scholars*), unfolds in an ancient dynasty so as to mirror, symbolically, Chinese rule-of-law in the present. Also worthy of historical contemplation is the fact that Qiu and the majority of authors discussed in this book belong to a particular generation (my own) stunned by the "living history" they have seen: the concerted building at home and attempted export abroad of Maoism, followed by the dismantling of it in China. Few of the fictional protagonists seem to age or change much during their series, but they and their creators do sometimes feel a twinge of nostalgia after all, when bearing witness to the breakneck transformation of China. Let us begin with irruptions of historic unrest within this otherwise pacific and very "presentist" popular genre.

The Beijing Spring of 1989 and the 1967 Turmoil in Hong Kong: The Unmentionable Past as Consequential History or Mere Plot Point?

A handful of China mysteries contain flashbacks to "Tiananmen" or "June Fourth," 1989, which is within some readers' living memory but may be considered history now that the PRC has practically erased accounts of it from the public record. The China mysteries mostly bypass the *mass* killings and context of the times. The murders in the novels are fictional, personal, and puzzling, reflecting the prime imperative of the mystery genre. In life, Beijing just before June Fourth witnessed surprisingly broad protest parades and unusual kinds of public solidarity. Bicycles and pedestrians yielded the right of way. Citizens donated free lunches, taxi rides, and other services. That background does not appear in the mystery plots, although some recall the student hunger strike and protesters' disagreements over strategy. The subsequent taboo on discussion of "Tiananmen" within the PRC however opens up new possibilities for exceptional investigation in a mystery novel. A detective hero who knows about those days can have an inside track for solving old and new crimes related to 1989, but the hero must hold this knowledge inside, keep it secret, lest insights into the past get the hero

120   Chapter 5

accused as a political offender. The overseas reader and the detective share special historical knowledge that in PRC society must not be known.

Two exemplary works create a metamystery—about how the novel's prologue might be related to "Tiananmen"—that goes beyond the main murder mystery that follows, without however entering the generic historical mystery territory of recreating the world of Beijing in 1989. Current time in Diane Wei Liang's *Paper Butterfly* (2008) is 1998 and in Michel Imbert's *En revenant de Tiananmen* (2013) the summer of 2008, just before the Beijing Olympics. The novel is outside the Judge Li series.

Liang's prologue is set in an East Wind *laogai* camp, a Reform-through-Labor setting in Gansu province, December 1989. It concerns a prisoner 3424 named Lin, with a grandpa who cannot write to him. That is helpful in connecting 3424 to the narrative that follows, but only after the plot is far along.

Imbert's prologue dramatizes protesters in Beijing's Chongwen district lying down in the street to block a convoy of jeeps. A boy in a white shirt enters a hair salon with an army officer who beats up a person inside. The officer drags both out. The boy in the white shirt is forced to drive a jeep over the protesters, making a bloody mess of them. The book title is a first-class spoiler about the setting, but that only intensifies curiosity about who the opening characters are and what they might have to do with "Tiananmen."

Each novel has a hero sleuth of sorts, although only Wang Mei, Diane Wei Liang's ex-cop turned extralegal PI, is a professional detective, and she must share reader sympathy with Lin, who years after the prologue has finally been released from *laogai*. Brief images of the Beijing Spring of 1989 recur in the main narratives as flashbacks in the minds of the novels' respective investigators: Wang Mei in Liang's novel, and an artist named Han Zuo in Imbert's. Han Zuo has flashbacks to his own post-massacre incarceration.

In 1989, Wang Mei had just joined the MPS and was sympathetic to the democracy protests. A Peking University classmate persuaded her to stay away, lest she be suspected as a police infiltrator. *Paper Butterfly* uses the device of dual narrative lines told in alternating chapters. The first stream of action relates Wang Mei's investigation of a 1998 murder. The second stream in Chapter Two depicts ex-con Lin's difficult journey home to Beijing from Gansu, destitute, during the months before. In the Wang Mei stream of action, a Beijing music production mogul hires her to find his star songstress, Kaili, who went missing prior to her heavily promoted performance at the annual New Year's gala. Several people are queried and Kaili turns up, dead. Wang Mei continues investigating after finding old love letters to Kaili from one "L," dated 1989. The couple were fellow student demonstrators in the square. The reader begins to suspect that "L"

Retrospection: History and Nostalgia   121

must be Lin, or "Little Gansu" as his new neighbors in Beijing's makeshift housing at the shuttered Dashanzi factory know him now. He finally reached Beijing, just before the gala, easily located his former love in her dressing room after a rehearsal, and brought her back to Dashanzi for a tryst. But she knew they could never have a life together now. So they quarreled. She fell to her death, by accident. In present time there is the kidnapping of a child, the one child of Lin's childhood friend and subsequent betrayer, followed by a climactic scene of Lin's arrest as the kidnapper. Lin's grandpa has just died, too, and there is a touch of ghost interest. The paper butterflies the old man once made as Manchu funerary emblems—long taboo and almost forgotten in the years of socialism—show up overnight on the doorsteps of neighbors in the Lins' old hutong. Guilty-feeling neighbors panic, suspecting supernatural retribution. For Wang Mei, the butterflies are a trail of clues leading back to Lin and the hutong with the troubled hidden history.

Han Zuo, Imbert's hero, inquisitor, and constant first-person narrator, is a modernist artist who also lives at Dashanzi. Fa Lina, his long-lost love from the spring of protest, long since married to another and already widowed, turns up unexpectedly to give Han a warning. They have both served time in *laogai* and not met since. In 1989, their group had a charismatic leader, the initiator of the hunger strike, one Zhung Zihong (fictional), a long-incarcerated current candidate for the Nobel Peace Prize. Han Zuo, Fa Lina, and six others who once belonged to Zhung's inner circle have by now all been allowed to return to Beijing. The others include Big Wang, who in 2008 is a police archivist, evidently for the MSS—he says his connection to the dissidents was never discovered; Bei Hua, another artist, now a gangster and pitiful but still dangerous drug addict; Duang San, a construction worker who saved Han's life on June Fourth; some other figures reduced to humbler circumstances; and Ou-Yang Hong, a former literature student with a checkered past—well enough connected in '89 to have avoided much time in prison, and who married up, into the family of a high cadre, became a businessman, then experienced divorce and disgrace. Now the MPS says Ou-Yang was murdered prior to his ostensible suicide jump off a balcony. His corpse had stab wounds. Meanwhile the heroic Zhung has just been released from *laogai*, in time to please the human-rights-obsessed Western media prior to the Olympics. With help from the alarmed and suspicious Han Zuo, who fears for the safety of all his old associates, the long-separated former comrades-in-protest are located and summoned to meetings in an abandoned factory near the art colony—by Big Wang. He says they must deal with pending police investigations as a united front. Perhaps the CCP has released the famous dissident Zhung so it can put him away again, this time for the murder of the equally troublesome

122   Chapter 5

Ou-Yang. Ou-Yang was gay and had jilted his lover, an actor and a dandy named Kong Lan. But Kong is a red herring suspect, Han Zuo and Fa Lina conclude midway through the plot, during sleuthing that takes them well outside their hard-won rehabilitated lives as ex-cons. Bei Hua, the gangster, was seen arguing with Ou-Yang the night of his death. Or maybe Zhung did kill Ou-Yang, as vengeance, if the latter was the informer. Ou-Yang was always taking photographs. Who within the group *was* the informer?

As Wang predicted, the aboveground police (Public Security) proceed to interrogate everyone. The suspects and their possible motives are so numerous that Han's father, a retired policeman, favors the reader in mid-novel with a classic whodunit-style summation of all the possible crime permutations (145–146). He has inside knowledge: the MSS wants the MPS to pin the murder on Zhung. Most of the former protesters do not know that Bei Hua, the future gangster, had an identical twin brother. Ou-Yang had infiltrated Zhung's group in 1989 to pursue Bei Hua after Bei's twin spurned Ou-Yang. And Zhung has a sister in Shanghai, an adversary possessing old photos. The twin is long dead, and soon Bei Hua is, too, presumably assassinated by the MSS. It turns out that Big Wang was the traitor within the Zhung coterie. The real crime now, in the eyes of the Party and state, is the appearance online of photos from 1989 and 2008. One shows Bei Hua running over protesters in a jeep in 1989, as dramatized in the preface (the price for saving his twin from the PLA; they had run him in during a roundup of gay men). A more important photo implicates a bigshot on the Olympics committee as a protester of 1989. Zhung is released without trial. Han Zuo and Duang locate Kong again and drag him to Duang's construction site. Kong is not so innocent after all. He stole Ou-Yang's photos and posted them online. It was the revenge of a jilted lover. He falls to his death at the construction site.

Imprisonment after Tiananmen has left scars and fears that motivate the hero of another Imbert novel, *Fang Xiao dans la tourmente* (2016), set in 1992. And the protest movement appears again in Imbert's *Pékin de neige et de sang* (2018), set in 2015. The protests are not dramatized there, but they enter the dreams and daydreams of a new detective hero, Lt. Ma Gong, a divorced and regretful father, something of a Chinese Wallander. Ma was at police academy in 1989, a class or two behind Wang Mei so to speak. He joined the protests. When in 2015 a construction worker named Sun Jie is murdered by a Uyghur gang for hire, Lt. Ma recognizes him as a geology student who memorialized Hu Yaobang in 1989 with an enormous specimen of realgar from Hunan, the former leader's native province. Subsequently fingered as a protester, Sun was unable to continue in a white-collar career. Soon another geologist is murdered, a university professor. Lt. Ma begins to investigate the links and learns of a crooked Phoenix

Company that builds dams and residential housing on unsafe landfill; Sun was bulldozing at one of the construction sites and his past training awakened him to the danger. He went to the Anticorruption Bureau, little knowing that Phoenix had protection from a high minister. His murder, the professor's, and that of the head of Sun's construction company once Ma closes in on the scandal, are the result. Lt. Ma's own chief is on the Phoenix payroll, so Ma has to fear for his life. When Phoenix is finally exposed in the Chinese press, the good cop is revisited by the spirit of 1989 and its faith that corruption can be overcome. However, during the investigation, he dared not let his superiors know how he could so cleverly derive a clue from 1989.

The upshot: these "Tiananmen whodunits" epitomize the China mysteries' approach to mystery writing, with all their strengths in plotting and limitations for the reader who is tantalized by historical questions. Historical novels, from *Ivanhoe* to works by Yan Lianke, have dramatized largely or entirely fictional events. But in the China mysteries, the trails of causation and outcomes prized by history buffs usually arise only in regard to unique fictional crimes perpetrated by a few singular individuals. The crimes may be symbolic, but it is not clear of what. The reader living abroad simply fills in certain untold events in conspiratorial collaboration with the author. No mystery contemplates what happened on the night of June 3–4 or why, as do notable nongeneric literary works in Chinese, English, and French from the Chinese diaspora.[8] In a mystery, tracing events to the past either helps the detective solve the crimes at issue or it gets in the way. And unlike history, the narrative will have a beginning, middle, and end.

This narrative demand is evident also in an ingenious plot made up of multiple slices of life from Hong Kong's past in Chan Ho-Kei's globally acclaimed police procedural, *Yisan · liuqi* (The Borrowed; lit., "13 · 67") (2014). This novel, too, offers no clear historical thesis or omen, even metaphorically, as do literary novels by Hong Kong writers Xi Xi and Dung Kai-cheung. Yet the climax at the end of Chan's novel falls in 1967, amid a relatively taboo historical incident in Hong Kong discourse: local spillover from the PRC's Cultural Revolution.

The work was published in Taiwan, which reproduces the expat provenance of other novels discussed in this book, but Chan is a native Hong Konger who fondly describes his beloved city. The six chapters of his novel run backwards, from 2013 to 2003, 1997, 1989, 1977, and 1967 in succession. In life, leftists staged riots in 1967 and planted real and fake bombs throughout Hong Kong in sympathy with the turmoil in the Mainland. A few events from history are mentioned in Chan's plot, including a particularly tragic 1967 bomb planting that killed an eight-year-old and her toddler brother (482).[9] It turned public opinion against the leftists.

124   Chapter 5

The focus of each chapter in the novel, however, is a particular crime to be investigated that fits its times, but not ostentatiously so. The first murder, in 2013, is solved through the trickery of getting suspects to believe in high-tech brain-wave-reading technology that has yet to be invented; the final, 1967 chapter depicts civilians and cops distracted by the riots and terrorism. Continuity comes in the persons of the detectives. At the start, in 2013, the police hero who will be encountered in the later, flashback chapters, Supt. Kwan Chun-dok, is retired and on his deathbed, in a coma. His protégé, Sonny Lok, cons a hospital room full of suspects into thinking that the old man is sending him decodable brain signals. Sonny will appear again in later plots, beginning in 1989. He gradually ages and is promoted, considering the novel read backwards. The year 1967 is the narrative climax and also a historical point of origin.

The narration is very procedural, with attention to the cops' personal and command relationships, unlike most of the other mysteries discussed in this book. Types of weapons are detailed, how long it takes the characters to go up and down the stairs or on elevators, and, in the final chapter, to cross the harbor by ferry—as in European classics of the 1930s that dealt in railroad timetables, or like-minded PRC whodunits of the post-Mao years (which Chan may have read, in addition to translations of Japanese whodunits). What endears Chan to his Hong Kong and Hong Kong–origin émigré readers is his fine authentic detail regarding "old" Hong Kong locations and social types. That local color summons up nostalgia, for Hong Kong, too, has changed a great deal in recent decades. *The Borrowed* follows causes and effects—in the world of criminals and their crimes, and of police officers, as mentee matures into mentor—but it does not illustrate trans-generational causes and effects in social history.

The Borrowed thus has a single, spot mention of the 1989 democracy demonstrations in the Mainland, on the last page of its May 1989 chapter. The 1997 chapter takes place one month before the handover of Hong Kong to the PRC. The public mood is tense, but the case Kwan and Sonny must solve is an apolitical crime of acid splashing. Mainlanders are among the perps, which may be symbolic or socially knowing, except that the Mainlanders are a distraction from the central crime. The head malefactor is a cunning Hong Kong criminal who arranges to be splashed on his own face to escape detection following his jailbreak.

Mao-Era Blood Debts

Other nationwide post-1949 mass movements led to persecutions and murders. The PRC's own writers after 1978 published fiction in Chinese for their standard mass audience describing historical miscarriages of justice, torture, killings, and

Retrospection: History and Nostalgia   125

grain theft that led to starvation during political mobilizations. Stories calling for a "reversal of verdicts" from those years were christened "scar literature" and "literature of reflection." In the China mysteries written outside the PRC, as in general fiction written in-country, the Cultural Revolution in particular has left scars on many a fictional character. But the consequences are depicted as mostly individual.

The Cultural Revolution is a distant background theme in Christopher West's *Death on Black Dragon River,* Michel Imbert's *Fang Xiao dans la tourmente,* Adam Brookes's *Night Heron,* several mysteries by Peter May and Jan-Philipp Sendker, and Qiu Xiaolong's sketches about the old Shanghai neighborhood where Inspector Chen grew up. Crimes committed in 1970 by a cruel *laogai* camp boss resurface to haunt the head man in Imbert's aptly named *Rouge Karma* (Red Karma, 2005). In most of these novels, traumas of the Mao years, including persecutions that led to suicide, are closeted in the past, available only in the memories of those who were there. As in life, the tragedies are further hidden behind a generation gap. However, those who have been rusticated or persecuted together can feel bonds of comradeship after rehabilitation: Judge Li and Peng Yetai, for instance, or Shan Tao Yun and his lama friends, who first met each other post-Mao, in *laogai.* If the protagonists were Red Guards together, they can on the other hand collaborate in post-Mao times as criminals, like Victor Li's father and his former associates in Daniel Nieh's *Beijing Payback.*

Past violence provides historical motivation in Qiu Xiaolong's novels, too, and yet the Cultural Revolution as a social movement is still a black box, mostly a motivator of individual crimes. In Qiu's fifth novel, *Red Mandarin Dress* (2007), a girl called Jasmine has been murdered and her corpse laid out for the police to find in a red "mandarin dress" (*qipao* or *cheongsam*). Revenge from the Cultural Revolution years might be the motive, for the victim's father in his younger days was a hated bully in a pitiless Red Guard faction. Old styles of dress were considered bourgeois at the time. But the Cultural Revolution connection seems misleading when two more corpses turn up, also posed in red mandarin dresses. The new victims were in the sex trade (Jasmine was not) and no peculiarities in their pasts are connected to the Cultural Revolution. The dresses are retro yet ambiguously so, Chen learns from an expert on Chinese costume, a poet-scholar named Shen Wenchang (cf. Shen Congwen in life), who lives in Shanghai in this novel and is Chen's old friend. Factoids about fashion, the dress's politics and generational appeal, and the history of particular materials and sewing skills that are of forensic, historical, and cultural interest lead to more clues and edification for the reader. The red dress turns out to be a fetish, whose mystery the chief inspector penetrates thanks to his knowledge of Western psychology and old Chinese

126   Chapter 5

literature. He sees that the three murders (and then a fourth, of a young police-woman regrettably used as bait) point to a psychosis born of the Oedipus Complex, here joined with Chinese cultural demonization of women, a theme Chen has studied in China's old literature. Knowledge of the Cultural Revolution does help him solve the case. He reasons that the Oedipal tendencies of the murderer emerged when he saw his mother in bed with a man from a rival Red Guard faction. Moreover, the graveyard where the policewoman's corpse was dumped, also in a red dress, was a locale notorious in the violent 1960s. Yet everything about that decade is a diversion from discovering both the murderer and his motive, which is politically significant, since it is rooted in present-day corruption. The psychotic murderer is a lawyer opposing the crooked real estate magnate modeled on Zhou Zhengyi noted in this book's Chapter 3. The murderer was too clever by half when he adopted a pseudonym punning on a name from *Dream of the Red Chamber*, whose deciphering was child's play for the poet-inspector. This novel even has an alternating plotline, about Chen Cao's research for an MA in Chinese literature. It introduces an explicit theme of the literary scholar as detective.

Qiu Xiaolong's next novel, *The Mao Case* (2008), addresses the personality cult of Mao Zedong and his affairs with young women. Chinese society in this case is rather special: movie stars and jetsetters from the early socialist years and their descendants (like those in Nien Cheng's *Life and Death in Shanghai*), and more recently, 1990s oddballs called "Old Dicks," a phrase explained as Shanghai dialect for the British idea of "Old Sticks" (39). The current ones belong to the pampered fringes of the reborn rich class: entrepreneurs and descendants of old wealth who have had some of their property returned and now like to dance, party, and enjoy retro culture from Shanghai's prerevolutionary days. The novel is not really a murder mystery. There are two murders to be solved, and a third in plain sight at the very end, but the first two come so late that they seem like misdirection in the plot. The murderer first appears only on page 243, which is hardly kosher in any fair-play whodunit. The main mystery is not "whodunit," but what happened to a heretofore unpublicized object of Mao memorabilia that might be embarrassing to the Party if it were smuggled abroad and made public.

The object of the quest is like a Holy Grail in a Dan Brown mystery; its very existence can be questioned. It could be calligraphy in Mao's hand, an undiscovered poem to a wife or lover (Chen Cao knows Mao poems that mention two of his wives), or perhaps a new tell-all memoir, this one based on Mao's affair with a Shanghai movie star, now long deceased because she was persecuted to death in the Cultural Revolution (like Shangguan Yunzhu). The inspector knows all the recent memoirs, including the one by Mao's physician disclosing how the chairman abused young women. Jiao, the granddaughter and now sole descendant of the 1950s film idol, might be keeping the undefined object, so the police must examine her past, her mother's, and that of *her* mother, the star. Each woman had lovers, who must be investigated, too, as well as Mr. Xie, a painting tutor and owner of a mansion where the Old Dicks like to congregate, dance with young women including Jiao, and discuss modern and retro culture amongst themselves. So this is a quest mystery in the form of a police procedural, not a thriller based on decoding iconography (the ken of Lisa See, Eliot Pattison, and Duncan Jepson). Inspector Chen goes undercover as a poet, a serendipitous second identity for him, to get to know the Old Dicks, Xie (who might be the very one to smuggle documents or memoirs overseas), and Jiao herself, whose house is full of Mao memorabilia and who studies painting with Xie. The murderer, however, is someone else, another psychopath, this one with a Mao fetish. The inspector finds what must be the hidden object, a scroll, but he does not unfurl it to find out exactly what it is! Is he, too, subconsciously afraid of *lèse majesté,* even now that the chairman is dead? That is indeed a large historical theme, irrespective of the plot's plausibility.

A mass movement further in the past and more forgotten than the Cultural Revolution, though it mobilized more sectors of Chinese society and killed tens of millions of citizens through starvation and malnutrition, is the Great Leap Forward of 1958–1960. This tragedy gets mostly sporadic mentions in the mysteries,[10] but the historically minded Michel Imbert memorializes it at length in his *La diplomatie du panda* (2019). The main narrative starts in Chapter Two, in 1982. Four corpses turn up in separate Beijing locations. Imbert brings back his original series detectives, Judge Li and Peng Yetai, to investigate. The historically salient aspect is how the victims were murdered—by starvation.[11]

The narrative begins with Imbert's practiced device of an enigmatic first chapter, set in July 1960, with unnamed characters in an unnamed place. It turns out to be a fictional town outside Nanchang, Jiangxi province. In the Beijing police procedural that follows, the four 1982 murders are the main case. A subplot involves the senseless slaughter of two giant pandas at the Beijing Zoo, whose livers were extracted. Why is another mystery, until they are cooked and served up by a high-ranking Chinese diplomat and Politburo member at a dinner attended by the US ambassador and an American journalist, to damage Sino-US relations and their panda diplomacy. Offended by US reporting and diplomacy regarding the disputed Diaoyutai/Senkaku Islands, the diplomat had ordered evisceration of two pandas promised to the US as diplomatic gifts. Other subplots, about wife beating and crooked cops, are more routine for the good judge.

128   Chapter 5

The police identify the serial murder victims by analyzing lists of missing persons, passing around photos (Judge Li travels to Jiangxi), and checking out a meeting in Beijing where the victims were last seen. The dead turn out to be former Jiangxi cadres, all CCP members who migrated to Beijing and found good official work. They are among the anonymous people from Chapter One. The starvation tortures of 1982 are revenge, carried out by a conspiracy of younger Jiangxi migrant workers including descendants of those who died in 1960. And the leader of the 1982 executions is the selfsame Jiangxi leader and murderer of humans in 1960, and also the Beijing pandas in 1982. He changed his name and made a new career in the Foreign Ministry. His ironic yet credible legal comeuppance is that he is convicted not for his crimes against humans, but against pandas.

One other novel by Imbert, *Les disparus du laogaï* (2010), is not only the exceptional work that unfolds during the Mao years and thus feels like true historical detective fiction; it also illustrates the difficulty of keeping a mystery going when historical and social spectacle is sufficient to overwhelm it—including, in this work, a scene of cannibalism in a *laogai* camp and a mass uprising by the inmates that gets many of them killed. The first half of the novel unfolds almost entirely within that forced labor setting. Two wrongly convicted inmates, Liu Mahu and Yang Zaokuai, with their immediate taskmaster, a rare cadre with a conscience nicknamed Duckbill Wu, join forces sub rosa in a quite unusual investigative and surveillance trio. That begins when grain goes missing from storage during a famine; Prisoner Liu helpfully suggests that the cadre check the trunk of the camp commandant's car for stray seeds. With help from old Dr. Kou, another unjustly imprisoned inmate, the heroes also uncover a ring among the guards that sells prisoner flesh to starving inmates who can pay for it. Dr. Kou teaches Liu and Yang how to catch flies to meet their daily quota during a campaign to exterminate pests. They save his life when a campmate wants to kill the doctor to acquire his precious harvest of Diptera (a subplot less improbable than it sounds[12]).

The main case in Chapter One is the mass murder in 1953 of 13 people—prostitutes and their protection—in an old quarter of Beijing, Dazhalan Lane. The unfortunate Dr. Kou, called in by the PSB to consult on the night of the crime, was foreign-educated and thus the perfect scapegoat; the pinning of the crime on him and his assignment to *laogai* is what brings the plot into the prison camp.

The historical-event markers of this 1953–1972 plot are not the usual ones of the PRC's own authors' and exiles' exposés of prison conditions, a subgenre mostly written by former inmates, typically emphasizing starvation during the

Great Leap Forward.[13] Instead the big events here are the 1953 demobilization following the Korean War and the 1971 demise of Mao's expected successor Marshal Lin Biao and his son Lin Liguo, deputy director of the Air Force and alleged head of a conspiracy in life to kill Mao and seize power. The common thread in Imbert's novel is the PLA Air Force, for the murderer of the prostitutes is a physically and mentally damaged war hero, a pilot (fictional) who fought in Korea. His culpability in 1953 is discovered, and he is himself assassinated after being recruited to spy on Lin Liguo.[14]

Duckbill Wu sees the old doctor exonerated and gets Liu and Yang not only released but also admitted to a police academy. The travails of everyday life among the Beijing common folk become the focus. The good cadre weds, is promoted to people's judge, has a daughter he names Little Fish, and meets a flic nicknamed The Weasel, familiar names from the Judge Li series; Imbert has given his fans a prequel in disguise. As depicted in the late 1970s, Judge Li still has to spend time each week in the countryside helping with farmwork, like Judge Wu before him. Michel Imbert has conveyed impressions of residual Maoism in the basic-level police and legal institutions of China of the early post-Mao period.

The Return of Religious Mass Movements

Several mysteries depict new, generally fictional Chinese religious sects that revive specters of religious turmoil in Chinese history. It is another social interest mostly unique to the overseas crime authors, who clearly view collective Chinese religious revivalism with trepidation. The prototypes of the later-day sects in their imaginations need not be only the new Chinese Christian sects (of which many have arisen in post-Mao times[15]), or even the Falun Gong (Falun Dafa), whose image is fictionalized quite favorably by Rotenberg in his fourth and fifth mysteries and by Flint. They wrote after the 1999 PRC banning of the sect but before it gained bad press in the late 2010s as a wealthy global empire covertly supporting right-wing politics internationally. Adam Brookes's *Night Heron* (2014) also mentions CCP persecution of a generic South China religious cult. Overseas concerns about Chinese clampdowns on religious freedom are overshadowed in the mysteries by fear of the new sects as potential promoters of a new cycle of social violence. In the background might be figurations of groups like the Unification Church or Aum Shinrikyo, if not the Red Guards of the 1960s, or the Jonestown cult from America. Eliot Pattison's depictions of traditional Tibetan Buddhism as a nearly underground religion are by contrast entirely sympathetic, though Eric Stone's *Shanghaied* opens with Tibetan lamas

130   Chapter 5

eating steak dinners in Hong Kong prior to engaging detectives to provide due diligence before they invest their millions in the Mainland.

The first mysteries featuring religious cults were written around the time of the anxiety-producing approach of the millennium: West's *The Third Messiah* (2000; plot in 1999) and Alban Yung's *Pas de mantra pour Pékin* (2000; plot in 1999). Yung's fictional cult is scariest in principle, though least believable as a true threat to humankind, despite recherché detail about the cult's syncretistic native belief system. It is a secret society that combines Tibetan Buddhism, Red Hat Daoism, shamanism, millenarianism, and human sacrifice, with Falun Gong overtones. In the novel, the cult threatens mass murder and total destruction through explosive charges at the Guanghan Sanxingdui Museum (a real museum, north of Chengdu). The museum and its staff have to be liberated in a government commando raid aided by comic-heroic French Sinophiles who have esoteric Chinese martial-arts skills. The whole plot is so over-the-top, complete with satirical learned analyses of the cult by French religious studies professors, that this novel, like Yung's others, is more fun than mysterious.

The cults imagined by West and by Lisa See, previously described in Chapter 2, suggest broader national movements like the Falun Gong. The sects in those novels attach the appeals of modern Han nationalism to visions of restorationism: revival of neotraditional communal values and empowerment of a cult leader in fulfillment of a dangerously seductive chiliastic vision of a second coming. Lisa See's cult in *Dragon Bones* preaches destruction of the false idol of its age—the Three Gorges Dam—as the Taiping rebels of 1851–1864 preached destruction of pagan idols and temples. The neo-Christian sect in West's novel, the New Church of the Heavenly Kingdom, claims direct descent from the Taiping movement; its disciples believe that an all-seeing Hong Xiuquan, Jesus's younger brother in Heaven, has continued witnessing China's betrayals under gunboat imperialism, the false prophet Mao Zedong, and the Tiananmen tragedy, too. It is time for a new Christian millennium—and the original Heavenly Kingdom of 1851–1864 did almost topple the great Qing dynasty. Today, Inspector Wang Anzhuang thinks, religion might replace communism, which is what the CCP fears, besides Cultural Revolution–style chaos. "For a moment," a "terrible thought" occurs to him: "this place [the religious compound] was a kind of image of his own land, which had been so full of passion and noble intention but that had ended up on the brink of self-annihilation" (248).

Particularly alarming in its quest for national power through mobilization of hate instead of love or piety is the fictional cultic conspiracy imagined in Duncan Jepson's *Emperors Once More* (2014). In that novel, China has bailed out Europe from a great financial crash in 2014, one far worse than that of 2008. Presently, in

Retrospection: History and Nostalgia   131

2017 (three years in the future when the book was released), the pathetic Europeans want to default on their loans. China will dictate harsh repayment terms to Europe of its own choosing at an international meeting in Hong Kong—sweet historical revenge for the Boxer Indemnities and all the other foreign-imposed penalties since the Opium War! But there is a secret conspiracy beyond that, with its own aims.

Emperors Once More is another novel with a prologue, depicting a lone, undesignated actor whose identity will remain a mystery until the end. Interspersed through the rest of the narrative are more short chapters with anonymous, not-quite-identifiable characters, depicting the mysterious man in the preface (a villain) and his accomplices. The preface is moreover accompanied by the initial piece of an incomplete iconographic puzzle whose other pieces will be added one by one, chapter by chapter. The full image is of an octagon formed by an arrangement of the eight trigrams, familiar from Chinese popular religious societies of ancient and modern times. Each of the eight sides marks a location in Hong Kong, if its geography is conceived as an octagon, and each side corresponds to a particular crime or unsettling incident of the plot; each piece thus adds to a pattern of proper location in proper sequence. At the center is the anonymous man of the preface, whose ancestors are from Shandong, the starting point of the Boxer Rising of 1899–1900. Lisa See in *Dragon Bones* (2003) had constructed her own graphic puzzle to accompany and mark the progress of the plot in that China mystery. Her graphic images gradually fill in an expansion of concentric feudal enfeoffment zones radiating out from a central "capital domain." *Dragon Bones* likewise begins with an enigmatically premonitory prologue. Prologues had become a formula in mystery novels by the 1990s.[16]

The cult in *Emperors Once More* is an underground, tech-savvy neo-Boxer movement led by men who hope to use the internet and a revival of Boxer-era passions to reignite hatred of Europe and its historical imperialism. Part of the plan is to recruit Alex Soong, Hong Kong's immensely popular celebrity detective, and make him a major charismatic leader of a reborn Boxer revolutionary movement. He proves immune to such blandishments, even when they come from his partner, the Eurasian De Suza, who is at the end revealed to be the anonymous man in the preface, a traitor to the police force and the government. Preparing the way for the new rising are the conspirators' symbolic reenactments of the original Boxer Rising, beginning with an assassination of two Methodist ministers in Hong Kong, recalling the premonitory 1897 murder of two Catholic priests in Juye county, Shandong. To be sleuthed out are both the forensics of the contemporary 2017 crime (a sniper did it, from the old headquarters of the Independent Commission against Corruption founded in 1974, partly in response to

132   Chapter 5

extraordinary corruption by a white British colonial officer) and the century-old historical associations of other current crimes. The connections are sufficiently arcane that a professor of religious studies is called in to consult. The plotters hope that historic resentments reawakened by new acts of violence against Westerners and Christians will inspire patriots across China to join in a new mass movement.

More history resonates. The conspiracy's headquarters at the center of the octagon is a place in Kowloon where the fuse of the 1967 uprising was lit. The conjuring up of a new Boxer movement as a reincarnation of Chinese xenophobia might be seen as Orientalist if the novel had been written by a Caucasian. The conspirators see their East-West conflict in racial terms. Their historical view, and that even of Soong's forebears, is that "the white man took everything" (163), while the Chinese were compelled to accept his four poisons, "first opium, then religion [Christianity], political ideology [Marxism], and now debt" (140). Jepson, the author, is biracial, of British and Chinese descent. He felt the sting of racism both in the north of England, where he grew up, and from the Asian side in Singapore, where he resided before moving to Hong Kong. He created Alex Soong, his hero, to "explore" a Mainland Chinese type, "incorruptible and . . . a loyal friend. He is a part of a new generation of well-travelled, globally experienced Chinese, almost seeing themselves beyond nationality, and he comes up against a mastermind [De Suza's superior] who is Chinese of an older generation."[17]

The mystery as plotted does not show how a xenophobic internet movement, empowered by historical memory, could catch fire. It is instead mostly the story of Alex's relationship with his once trusted partner, who suffers from family trauma and a hidden racial identity crisis. When the plot is foiled at an economic summit thanks to Alex's integrity and prowess, an exciting mystery thriller concludes, following side trips into the psychology and problematic families of both detectives. Xi Jinping's summoning up of Great Han nationalism and neotraditionalism was not yet fully visible when Jepson (or West, Yung, or See) wrote.

Using Judge Dee to Comment on Contemporary China

Qiu Xiaolong entered his third decade as novelist looking for new directions. *Hold Your Breath, China* repeats passages from *Don't Cry, Tai Lake,* and Qiu's eleventh novel, *Becoming Inspector Chen,* recycles material from other previous writings.[18] It still proved engrossing to Inspector Chen fans, with its tales of his past life, and to critics and public intellectuals, who appreciated the work's new critical historical and social implications, including direct comment on China's

Retrospection: History and Nostalgia   133

increasing authoritarianism under Xi Jinping, China's new "emperor."[19] Chen Cao revisits his past in successive nightmares, following his 2018 political difficulty after the air pollution case. Dream imagery creatively transmogrifies tropes and beasts from Chinese classics, folklore, and recent political discourse. Qiu Xiaolong wanted the work to have an experimental, modernist feel. The novel leaves the chief inspector in suspended animation and a state of angst as he prepares to be demoted.

That is the inspector's situation in Qiu Xiaolong's thirteenth novel, which he originally intended to be printed together with what I count as his twelfth; Qiu's publishers, initially in France and Italy, split the original work into two. The resulting novels have historical and interliterary allusions suggesting, as already noted in this book's Chapter 3, that Qiu may all along have been writing for both popular and insider readers.

At issue are three mysteries: two by Qiu Xiaolong, one by Robert van Gulik; two historical, one contemporary. They are (1) Robert van Gulik's last Judge Dee historical mystery, *Poets and Murder* (1968; published posthumously);[20] (2) a new Judge Dee mystery "by Chen Cao" inspired by *Poets and Murder,* which may be called Qiu's twelfth novel and his first historical mystery, *The Shadow of the Empire* (French ed., 2020); and (3) Qiu's thirteenth, *Inspector Chen and the Private Kitchen Murder* (2021, first published as *Un dîner chez Min*), which unfolds ca. 2019. In all three mystery plots, a beautiful female socialite and hostess to the rich and famous (lover to some of them) is accused of having murdered her young woman servant. The servant might have betrayed the socialite, motivating the murder, but the evidence is dubious. The accused in the historical novels is a real figure from history: Yu Xuanji, a Tang dynasty courtesan and accomplished poet. She was executed for murder ca. 868, at the age of 28. (Not referenced in either novel is Yu's evidently open bisexuality.) In *Inspector Chen and the Private Kitchen Murder,* the accused is a fictional modern Shanghai woman named Min who throws private-table dinner parties for the rich and famous, then finds herself *shuanggui*'d in the Moller Villa by Internal Security. Min had trod on dangerous political ground, for her cheongsam-clad glamour and exclusive gourmet meals evoked nostalgia for Shanghai's high life under the precommunist Republic.[21] Chen Cao's self-appointed mission is to get justice for Min, who may be innocent. He has however been removed from the police force, kicked upstairs as director of a new Shanghai Judicial System Reform Office. The city government spies on him and further sidelines him by keeping him on sick leave.

The Private Kitchen Murder is enlivened by alternative suspects for the murder of Min's servant, including four of Min's dinner guests; by two more murders; and two attempted murders, first of Min, then of Chen Cao's young assistant

134   Chapter 5

Jin, an attractive woman who is his new surrogate sleuth and to whom he makes love at the end of the novel. The overarching mystery: What information does Min possess so important that she must be sequestered by Internal Security away from the police? Her louche and politically incorrect social reputation might not be her biggest offense. Meanwhile the social ills Qiu Xiaolong dramatizes are within the PRC legal system, embodied in Chen Cao's dismay at the irregular detention of Min and his separate inquiry into a second, unrelated corruption case. The latter leads Chen to argue that illegally obtained evidence is inadmissible, just when Western legal standards are being denounced in the press, in the novel as in life. Chen also worries that the judge in the corruption case has a conflict of interest, which contradicts the CCP view that its decisions *are* justice. Yet another prominent theme is Chen Cao's dual attractions to law and literature. In this novel they are not in conflict, however, for Chen conducts research to write a new Judge Dee mystery as *cover* for interviewing parties of interest in the Min case. Chen begins writing his Tang dynasty–themed novel at the end of the Private Kitchen case; that would be *The Shadow of the Empire*. Examining cases in parallel is part of China's traditional forensic legacy, passed on via Sinological research by none other than van Gulik.[22] *The Shadow of the Empire* foreshadows the contemporary plot about Chen Cao's quest to save Min, the Shanghai damsel in distress, because the ancient judge, in the new Judge Dee mystery "being written by Chen," collects Yu Xuanji's poems ostensibly to anthologize her creations, but really as cover while Dee gathers evidence to overturn Yu's murder accusation! This is both *mise en abyme* and a suggestion that Chinese justice in two eras is similarly subject to hidden dangers and inexplicable outcomes. Chen Cao's own disillusionment with the legal system is greater than ever in this novel. A drone flies up to his hotel window, perhaps to spy on him. He thinks it may be time to retire from public service. Chen already speaks to his coinvestigators in code to protect all concerned—from the authorities.

Van Gulik's 1968 novel introduced the useful anachronism of Judge Dee (Di Renjie, CE 630–700) encountering "Yoo-lan," the fictional courtesan accused of murder whom he identifies in a postscript (173) as Yu Xuanji (born ca. 840). The Dutch author reprised his usual formula, staging three present cases of murder or inexplicable death while portraying three high-ranking poet-literati gathered together who make excellent suspects. Most characters are fictitious except for Dee and Yu Xuanji, and she and her prior legal difficulty are marginal at first. Instead of recycling van Gulik's original victims and suspects, Chen's/Qiu's 2020 Judge Dee novel inserts other poets, judges, and friends of Yu Xuanji, some as informants, others as persons of interest. Most are invented, apart from Hanshan, another famous Tang dynasty poet, whose dates and biography are obscure. Qiu

Retrospection: History and Nostalgia   135

follows van Gulik in letting Judge Dee debunk popular suspicion that Yu is a fox spirit—a theme with Sinitic roots, though the foxes are black and have shrines to them as in Japan, where the Dutchman served as ambassador while he wrote *Poets and Murder*. In Chen's/Qiu's novel, Judge Dee is caught in a power struggle between the reigning Empress Wu Zetian's son Li and her nephew Wu. This is true to history for Di Renjie and Wu Zetian, though it necessarily underlines the plot's fictionality regarding Yu Xuanji, who in life was not yet born. However, a suggestion in Chen's/Qiu's plot that Yu Xuanji's final confession means to provide cover for a secret lover and patron to help him survive a hidden power struggle at the capital suggests, by analogy, why Min might have been secretly detained in 2019. Her Beijing patron might have a nemesis who wants her to give evidence under torture.

Inspector Chen and the Private Kitchen Murder drops its own hints that a power struggle in Beijing is the reason for Min's extraordinary detention. But the politics leads to loose ends: What does Min know, who are the powerholders at war in Beijing, and who represents them locally? Both Director Chen Cao in the contemporary novel and Judge Dee in the historical novel "by Chen" are directed toward their respective damsel in distress by a legally unauthorized third party whose motives appear shady. Then Dee and Chen, respectively, are threatened by still more mysterious operatives opposed to any investigation. Who the modern sides are is much vaguer than in Qiu's novels a decade earlier, when it was Beijing Gang vs. Shanghai Gang. However, setting plots in history (or in SF, fantasy, and other alternate reality locations) is a method for commenting on current reality favored by resident authors in the PRC today.

The Authors in Their Era

Authors of the contemporary China mysteries in this book are concentrated within the baby boom (born 1946–1964), particularly its older end (born 1946–1955). Adding pre-boom authors David Bonavia (1940–1988), Bill Montalbano (1940–1998), and Leo Lee (b. 1942) to those of the early boom, I count 23 of the 41 authors, including all the pioneers and relatively prolific authors other than Imbert, who was born later in the boom (1961). That includes Roger Uren, Dinah Lee Küng, Alban Yung, David Rotenberg, Eliot Pattison, Peter May, Nicole Mones, Eric Stone, Carl Hiaasen, Qiu Xiaolong, Christopher West, Lisa See, and Zhang Xinxin; also the multibook latecomer to the genre, Ian Hamilton; plus James Church and Henning Mankell (1948–2015), who wrote mysteries before locating one in China. Another nine authors were born later during the boom (1956–1964), bringing the total to 32 and including, besides Imbert, series

136   Chapter 5

authors Nury Vittachi, Lisa Brackmann, Jan-Philipp Sendker, and Catherine Sampson. Gen-Xers (born 1965–1980) include Diane Wei Liang, Chan Ho-Kei, Brian Klingborg, and perhaps four others, unless there is a Millennial among them, in the generation of Daniel Nieh and An Yu.

Priority in publishing naturally accompanies seniority in birth, but the older authors kept writing. See, Rotenberg, and May were still publishing China mysteries in 2003, and Qiu, Imbert, and Hamilton might all be continuing now. (Pattison evidently completed his Tibet mystery series in 2019, with his tenth.) By 2022, only a dozen or so of the more than 100 China mysteries on offer were written by authors from post-boom generations.

The early authors grew to young adulthood or beyond and started a career—in many cases a China-related career (others had a cultural or ancestral connection to China, if they were not born there)—while China was still Maoist. Britain, France, and Canada established relations with the PRC earlier than the US, but China itself was still relatively "closed" until 1979, and large parts of the country remained off-limits to foreigners afterwards. Most foreign authors must have been excited to be able finally to explore the forbidden land; Qiu Xiaolong and Zhang Xinxin knew the exhilaration of being allowed to travel out of it (escape it, in Diane Wei Liang's case). All the authors surely felt privileged to witness first-hand the post-Mao transformation of the country and the first Sino-Western honeymoon—and then a second. China contributed to their sense of self. (Hiaasen is the exception; his fellow-journalist collaborator, Montalbano, was his link to China.) In the 1980s, many survivors of Maoism living in China and abroad were already publishing memoirs, in Chinese and other languages. Western scholars and sojourners to China in the 1980s similarly came, in the twenty-first century, to see themselves as eyewitnesses to post-Mao history. They, too, wrote accounts of what they had seen, though they lacked the prewar experiences in China of older Sinologists who knew China prior to communism.[23] The China mystery authors were in some ways forerunners of the reminiscing overseas China scholars of the Xi Jinping era—documentarians of odd spectacles of the already abundantly superseded early post-Mao years, with emphasis on strange initial encounters of "East and West."

In a genre that welcomes hobbies, hobbyhorses, even recipes and health tips, the personal is often present without anything overtly autobiographical. But the latter can be found in the mysteries, too. A recurring figure in David Rotenberg's mysteries is Geoffrey Hyland, a theater director and drama coach like the author. Hyland goes to China to direct the PRC's first production of a Canadian play, George Ryga's *The Ecstasy of Rita Joe,* as did the author in life. The series' debut novel inserts "Hyland's" theory of acting right into the text as a detailed

Retrospection: History and Nostalgia   137

manuscript, and the character is overheard deploring Stanislavski's influence on Chinese acting. Rotenberg's China mystery plots recreate scenarios from Shakespeare: *Twelfth Night, Measure for Measure,* and *Othello,* respectively, in the first three novels. The fourth is titled *The Hamlet Murders.*[24]

The original projection of one's own modern sensibilities into the figure of a Chinese detective, and vice versa, is that of the old master, Robert van Gulik. He once told a colleague: "I *am* Dee."[25] One cannot read Nicole Mones's *The Last Chinese Chef* or any of the Qiu Xiaolong mysteries without intuiting the authors' interests in haute cuisine, professional in Mones's case. Peter May's interest in forensic medicine is on display in his mysteries, as is L. H. Draken's in CRISPR technology and genetic engineering in her works. The heroes and recurring characters of Dinah Lee Küng, Jan-Philipp Sendker, and many other former journalists recall the professional work of their creators. From Alban Yung we acquire satiric portraits of the French diplomatic corps and Sinological profession; from Henning Mankell, evocative settings in Sweden and Mozambique. James Church depicts his North Koreans.

Fragments of personal life stories are particularly evident in the less publicized authors' narratives. Lee Barckmann calls his *Farewell the Dragon* "semi-autobiographical."[26] The hero, like the author in his China days, is a tall, handsome, 35-year-old redhead Oregonian born and raised on the Jersey shore, who in 1987 teaches English at the Beijing Foreign Languages Institute. The hero of Cheryl West Petty evokes images of the author as a young woman. With roots in northern California, her hero is a bonsai and horticultural expert employed by Peking University to edit its online media publications (in life, Petty worked nearby, at Tsinghua), and also a beautiful supersleuth fit for the silver screen—ready and able to pull her CIA husband's chestnuts out of the fire and to assist or thwart Chinese and North Korean operatives as needed. L. H. Draken's main hero in *The Year of the Rabid Dragon* is Nathan Troy, an American male, but the other major positive protagonist is Dr. Laroque, a female French physician who works for the World Health Organization in Geneva, where Draken once resided and where the plot ends. *Rabbit in the Moon* (2008), from the married medical doctors Deborah and Joel Shlian, was conceived as a retrospective tribute to Chinese students for whom the Shlians were a host family in 1989. The Shlians first visited China in 1985.

It is however in the sense of a mystery doubling as *Bildungsroman,* wherein a beset hero is forced to grow wise in a hurry, that we can see the mysteries as displaced sympathetic biographies or autobiographies by proxy, and even as metaphors for the maturation of the *newer* China that replaced Chairman Mao's "New China." China is where non-Chinese heroes of Mones, Brackmann,

138   Chapter 5

Sendker, Walker, Kjeldsen, and Nieh "find" themselves, discovering ways of coping they never realized they had. Perhaps Lisa See reimagined herself as Liu Hulan. Qiu Xiaolong likes to tantalize his fans about how much of him dwells in Chen Cao. However, most of the amateur sleuths' emotional vulnerabilities, physical handicaps, and war wounds are fictional, not autobiographical.

Nostalgia

Nostalgia comes easily to the China mysteries. Many particulars of background and daily life derive from the authors' personal reminiscences, not just research, and often from memories of a departed youth that China helped shape. Most works were written years after the initial separation from the country, a separation not always desired. Rather different are the many kinds of nostalgia attributed to the Chinese people, about real and imagined eras and places.

Post-communist Russian and East European nostalgias have been theorized by Svetlana Boym and colleagues.[27] Boym left the USSR in 1980 and was surprised that she could return to Russia ten years later. Rather similarly, Qiu Xiaolong, Zhang Xinxin, and Diane Wei Liang felt constrained to remain outside of or leave the PRC in 1989, were pleased to be allowed a return visit within a decade, and marveled to see how fast their homeland had changed. Unlike Russia, China had "progressed," materially and in citizen morale. And unlike Gary Shteyngart of Russia, or Xiaolu Guo, Ha Jin, and Geling Yan (who writes in Chinese and in English), Qiu Xiaolong and Diane Wei Liang have focused their fictional imaginations entirely on the old country.[28]

Notable Russian and East European mass nostalgias have embodied longings for the Stalin era or goulash communism of Nagy, for tsarist or Hungarian imperial times, even the Brezhnev decades of the USSR. Post-Soviet detective stories were popular in 1990s Russia, feeding on reader longing for the certainties of Soviet society.[29]

That sort of nostalgia among Chinese citizens is a theme in several Qiu Xiaolong mysteries. The characters—and occasionally the chief inspector himself—feel wistful about the "old" socialist China, remembered as egalitarian, in *A Case of Two Cities* (2006). In *The Mao Case* (2008), a full-blown, pathological longing for Mao is the theme. *When Red Is Black* (2004) instead features longing for the glamour of 1930s Shanghai; *Red Mandarin Dress* (2007) also notes "the new culture of nostalgia" for prewar times (206), though the inspector thinks it is based in "myth" (43). By 2019, when *Inspector Chen and the Private Kitchen Murder* unfolds, authorities in the fiction perceive nostalgia for the precommunist era to be a threatening political deviation. Qiu Xiaolong's mixed-genre writing

Retrospection: History and Nostalgia   139

sometimes memorializes the "old" Shanghai, as in his book of poetry with photographs by Howard French, *Disappearing Shanghai* (2012).

Boym is known for her distinction between "restorative nostalgia" and "reflective nostalgia." "Restorative nostalgia stresses *nostos* (home) and attempts a transhistorical reconstruction of the lost home" (xviii). That includes the more programmatically constructed—and implanted—Russian (and, by my extrapolation, Chinese) longings for past national greatness under communism, or an imperial era before that, or both, conflated. Those are the nostalgias favored by Putin and Xi Jinping and by many Russians and Chinese the exiles left behind in the old countries. Such nostalgias are public interpretations of the lost home and purport to represent collective knowledge and memory. Boym's foil to the restorative nostalgias, "reflective" nostalgias, are contemplative and individually constructed. They would include the nostalgias felt by our China mystery authors (not their characters), and by Boym's fellow emigrants—nostalgias that are variable, complex, and closely held, unencumbered by anyone's will to power. Whether the two types of nostalgia are tendencies that might overlap, as Boym contends, or separate and even antithetical, is a bone of theoretical contention.[30] "Home" is what one would expect to be the yearning of the emigrants.

Today, "nostalgia" in English (and in Chinese, *huaijiu*) denotes longing for the past or things of the past, but Boym instructs us that the word was coined by a Swiss doctor in 1688 as a medical term referring to pining for a place, one's old home: "homesickness," conceived as a malady and curable (3–4). The location factor intensifies nostalgic longing among exiles and also the foreign long-term former residents of China. The object of longing can be for China the land, and a happy past spent there; for an imagined Mao era; and for a rustic, or contrarily, freewheeling urban era before Mao. In modern centuries, the ideation of nostalgia, Boym emphasizes, accompanies the idea of progress, "like Jekyll and Hyde: alter egos" (xvi). "Nostalgia is rebellion against the modern idea of time, the time of history and progress" (xv).

Progress is indeed the uniform background scenery in these mysteries, and it is not entirely wished away when it means the diversification and streamlining of daily life in shopping, traveling, importuning city officials, and just finding a space to sleep or pursue leisure. The focus on material life, travel, and its many material "clues," goes with the genre. There is little attention to parenting, working, schooling, or extra-professional friendships, though in modern discourses they, too, can be depicted as "traditional," "premodern," even "backward."

Resistance to change is certainly visible; nostalgias have acquired negative connotations in global discourses as "mechanisms of seduction and manipulation"

140   Chapter 5

(Boym, xviii). Those nostalgias are thought of as a longing for a time or place that never existed, even a "romance with one's own fantasy" (xiii). Boym, however, writes to deny that nostalgia must always be "to longing as kitsch is to art" (as put by Charles Maier[31]) or "taboo" (xiv, xv). It need not be an evasion of "personal responsibility," as Michael Kammen characterizes it: "Nostalgia . . . is essentially history without guilt. Heritage is something that suffuses us with pride rather than shame."[32] The responsible nostalgia Boym prizes departs from historical verisimilitude in ways that have their own critical edge. But as this book noted in Chapter 4, academic historians of Western crime fiction tend to argue that the crime genre, with its emphasis on solutions, already upholds a conservative, status-quo worldview.[33]

The nostalgias unconsciously felt or described among the authors and characters of the China mysteries are different from the same novels' sobering and impersonal historical vignettes of China during the Great Leap Forward and Cultural Revolution eras. That distinction maintains a line between nostalgia, which is personal when it is of the reflective sort, and "history," which has previously been constructed by others in books, like Boym's "restorative nostalgia." The history of ancient peasant revolts and rebellions is as insistently rewritten by the CCP as that of recent events, but our China mysteries seldom set out to revise any official "history." That would distract from the mystery plots.[34]

The past times longed for in China are as ambiguously defined and mutually conflicting as those of the Russians. If the Mao era was "the time of certainty and order,"[35] that might really be only "the seventeen years" from 1949 until the Cultural Revolution, or just the years of New Democracy, prior to the transition to socialism in the mid-1950s and famines after the Great Leap Forward. Maoist memes and iconography from those times are recognizable to older Western readers and can evoke nostalgia even among them. Shanghai before the revolution, with its cosmopolitanism and wild night life, is often celebrated in Western media, including global Chinese-origin films. Then there is imperial-era Beijing—its hutongs and courtyard homes, the imagined communal life within, the ditties of street peddlers outside, and palaces, temples, and old city gates beyond—but these, too, are globally known in this age of tourism, though many were rebuilt in post-Mao times. The Russians are seldom nostalgic for their short era of *perestroika,* 1986–1991. It is in the China mysteries that one sees fondness for China's *perestroika,* ca. 1978–1987, a time of still undelimited progress in every realm, with a "golden triennium" toward the end, 1984–1986, whose tolerance of freethinking and avant-garde arts unleashed the creativity of Inspector Chen and the poet who would imagine him. It was also a storied time for Diane Wei Liang, Nicole Mones, Lee Barckmann, and others who lived in China during

Retrospection: History and Nostalgia   141

those years. These authors can feel nostalgic for both a distant place and a receding time.

On-the-spot nostalgia is shared among characters, author, and readers when the novels (more than half of the 40 with major action in Beijing) depict the bulldozing of old hutong housing. That, too, can be seen from another side. Imbert writes of the bulldozing in nearly all his novels, but he and others offset the sense of loss by emphasizing that the old buildings lacked modern facilities and were rotting away. Factories were built next door to housing in the 1960s, right in the center of town (*Rouge Karma,* 116). The courtyard houses were malodorous and dusty, by 2015 just a come-on for "Western tourism, which was open to this incomprehensible nostalgia" (*Pékin de neige et de sang,* 135). But rebuilding often leads to something worse, government-built "monstrosities" (Hamilton, *The Goddess of Yantai,* 223). The perpetually disabused Luke Slade observes: "Above the dust of falling walls was a picture of what would replace [the old "courtyard houses"]: towers not more than a few years old, already scuffed and worn. It seemed almost deliberate, a ruin aesthetic—the new Beijing so poorly built that it counterfeited the age of hutongs being destroyed" (Walker, *Last Days in Shanghai,* 78). Restoration is an alternative to knocking-down, but in the new era, the result is ersatz "heritage" kitsch, as in the old Dazhalan neighborhood where Dr. Kou took the blame for the prostitutes murdered in 1953. In the twenty-first century, Dazhalan "mostly got *chai'*d [demolished] for the Olympics, the main street rebuilt into a Disneyfied version of itself, a fancy pedestrian mall that's half empty" (Brackmann, *Dragon Day,* 117). The hero Chinese cop in Shenzhen of Sendker's *Whispering Shadows* thinks of all the knockdowns as "a desperate attempt to flee from history, and the new high-rise buildings, roads, highways, airports, and factories were not so much progress as giant memorials to the desire to forget" (193).

The reader, generally white and middle-class, experiences nostalgia also from textual references to international commercial brands that have expired, pop songs from home (oldies), even discontinued Chinese things the reader may have encountered as a tourist, such as hard sleeper train accommodations and foreign exchange certificates.[36] Much of that nostalgia comes not from longing for what was lost in our age of mechanical reproduction, but from the satisfaction of remembering: "national or even global marketing is the inciting cause."[37] Deliberate appeal to nostalgic memories rather than the "exoticism" of new knowledge, visions, and interpretations helps differentiate popular from literary fiction, though irony can enter popular novels, too. When urban Chinese cops snicker at yahoos so behind the times they have kept their old alarm clocks adorned with Maoist kitsch, Western readers who have been to China may realize that these

142   Chapter 5

objects now enjoy a second life as collectors' items (Imbert, *Rouge Karma* [2005], 138). Authors who have lived many years abroad will on the other hand have "missed out" on their own country's recent pop culture trends, and therefore be alienated from nostalgia for them. Qiu Xiaolong's deficits in that regard emerged when his works were translated into Chinese for readers back home, and perhaps some of his readers detected in his works nostalgia for Chinese things that was "too dated." Nostalgia within a culture evolves.

These nostalgias are urban. Another Chinese nostalgia seeks an unspoiled rural China, imbued with simple, preindustrial and extra-bureaucratic values, and this nostalgia has ancient native roots. Nostalgia amid the rush of progress mostly reacts to the building of conventional urban Westernized "modernity." The China mysteries reflect that. Rural nostalgia is to be satisfied in China's Southwest and Tibet—where Shan Tao Yun and An Yu's hero have epiphanies, not unlike those of the Western authors when years ago they first came to China's newly opened cities. In official China today, the countryside is to be pitied and transformed—like Tibet.

Do the Mysteries Illuminate Recent Change?

Is there an internal chronicle within this dynamic "current era," whose start is unclear (is it after Mao died in 1976, or only after 1992?) and whose end cannot be known? Or is it all a blur, a rush toward progress without end? Time is seldom marked in the novels by policy or leadership changes. Several mysteries mention the now terminated one-child policy, but it began already in 1979. "Strike Hard" law enforcement campaigns occur in the plots, but many are generic, not referring to campaigns in particular years (e.g., 1983). The main temporal markers are the 1997 Hong Kong handover, 2008 Olympics, and incidents, mostly unhappy, in Sino-American and Sino-French relations. The events of 1989 are a subject of interest in only a few works, and therefore also the changing thought, temper, and social role of China's intelligentsia.

The narratives highlight change in the economy, infrastructure, and fashion, with occasional references to Chinese, other Asian, and Western cultural icons. (Cui Jian, Ai Weiwei, and Gong Li have spot mentions in the novels of Brackmann, Imbert, and Hamilton.) Progress is not always "Mr. Hyde" in these novels, and it will overpower nostalgia when the focus is development, the unleashing of a new middle class, new shops, entertainments, electronic devices, and the means to enjoy them for the citizenry at large. These are often emblems of Westernization, like the avant-garde architecture that came to Beijing before the Olympics. Peter May in 2016, looking back at his China thrillers 12 years on, felt they bore

Retrospection: History and Nostalgia   143

witness to "one of the most astonishing cultural transformations in recent history."[38] L. H. Draken read May's mysteries and was amazed at how they described a "phenomenally different time period" from what she experienced.[39] But the emphasis is on tangible culture. May remembers the setting of his first six novels as Beijing, 1999 to 2004,[40] and Draken lived in Beijing from 2011 to 2016. May writes,

> As I look back now, I can see [my] books as bearing witness to that change. From six empty ring roads [in 1991] to nine ring roads jammed end to end with private and commercial vehicles. From rivers of bicycles to the merest trickle of cyclists. From the Mongolian[-era] *siheyuan* courtyards which had been the traditional home of Beijingers for centuries, to high-rise modern apartment blocks. . . .
>
> The "bread cars"—the ubiquitous yellow vans used as taxis and referred to frequently in *The Firemaker*—had been banned by the time I returned in 1999 in an attempt to reduce pollution.
>
> The 50th anniversary of the People's Republic that year saw the abolition of the old green military-style uniform, to a new smart black uniform similar to those found in police forces elsewhere around the world.
>
> In the run-up to the 2008 Beijing Olympics, great swathes of the city were demolished by armies of hammer-wielding workmen. . . .
>
> Mao suits disappeared, to be replaced by the latest Western fashions. Everyone got mobile phones. Showrooms sprang up everywhere selling Mercedes and BMW. The insidious invasion of foreign culture brought McDonald's to Beijing street corners and, God forbid, even a Starbucks in the Forbidden City. English was becoming the common currency. (xvii–xviii)

May's comments are overstated, though there was a movement to promote English just before the Olympics. It is still fun to see Section Chief Li Yan's shock when he learns for the first time (as did I) that the new bourgeoisie spend 360 yuan a day to ski on man-made snow at a Beijing Snow World out near the Ming Tombs (*The Runner* [2003], 108–110). The historical point not mentioned is that May's year of empty ring roads, 1991, was during the "pause" in economic reform and global connectedness for three years after June 4, 1989. And despite having visited China in 1983 and 1991, May chose only to write about China since 1998 or 1999.

The primacy of unidirectional progress is stated by Chief Inspector Chen to his American opposite number Catherine Rohn in 1995 (which here allows a rare, specified baseline for the beginning of the new era: 1980): "Fifteen years

144   Chapter 5

ago, those brands were never heard of here. Chinese people were content to wear one style of clothes: Mao jackets, blue or black. Things are so different now. They want to catch up with the newest world fashions. From an historical perspective, you have to say that it's progress" (*A Loyal Character Dancer,* 223). Progress does come with regrets: Chen Cao feels that "capitalistic consumerism has grown out of control" (222). To commune with the past, he takes refuge in poetry.[41]

A Chinese citizen in Sendker's *The Language of Solitude* looks down from his high-rise hotel room and sees: "Lights, billboards, illuminated skyscrapers, elevated highways, cars, stretching to the horizon. The face of a new China, the fabric of the Chinese dream. The skyline had filled him with pride only a few weeks ago. His sister had been right: it was nothing but a façade" (301). This is the modern apprehension of emptiness in the spiritual realm that accompanies material progress. It is commonly depicted by the mystery authors. The newness of materialism lies not in the desire itself but in its open display. Roger Uren wrote, in retrospect, that one aim of *The China Lovers* (1985) was to bear witness to "the renaissance of a long-suppressed Chinese passion for the material and spiritual values of the outside world."[42] That is a rare positive view, and an "early" one. The "new materialism" of post-Mao China is mentioned frequently and more critically in the later novels by Sampson, Brackmann, Hamilton, and An Yu, directly or in their portraits of the new rich and aspiring young. It is a major theme in the pioneering China mysteries of Christopher West described in Chapter 2. James Church's Inspector O, who is to be sure a North Korean, decries money obsession this way to his Chinese nephew in *A Drop of Chinese Blood*: "Why are you so obsessed with money? The grand crypto-capitalism that has infected this society seems to have only one thing on its mind—money. Getting, saving, keeping, spending, owing, or paying money. More money. Not enough money. Money just around the corner" (109). This acquisitiveness may come not just from consumerism but from insecurity; the inspector sounds as much like Balzac as Mao.

The native-born authors are concerned. Wang Mei's selfish younger sister, Lu, is Diane Wei Liang's unappealing embodiment of the new worship of wealth and disdain for society's "losers," such as the detective's quite competent and educated male secretary and assistant from the much-maligned nearby province of Henan. The word "materialistic" recurs almost 50 times in Qiu Xiaolong's first ten mystery novels, practically as a Homeric-style epithet, deploring, explaining, or excusing new social trends. "In an increasingly materialistic society, who would take notice of a bookworm [Chen Cao] capable of nothing except penning a few sentimental lines?" (*Death of a Red Heroine,* 348). This new materialism is mentioned as background regarding the Chinese people's new turn toward religion as a counterweight; the heightened pressures they feel just to survive; their

Retrospection: History and Nostalgia   145

penchant for bargaining (which is, most historians would say, very old and not just Chinese); the new embarrassment of appearing to be poor; and Chen Cao's professional predicament even when he succeeds in his cases: "In an increasingly materialistic society, a cop was nobody" (*When Red Is Black,* 219). It is bound up with the times.[43]

The Inspector Chen novels voice special concern for the vulnerability of young women to the lure of unchecked materialism. They fall into bad marriages and even prostitution as never before, thinks the inspector. Wealth and power as enablers of a generation gap are just as important in Imbert's mysteries. One of Lt. Ma's challenges in *Pékin de neige et de sang* (2018) is training his subordinate, Sub-Lt. Zhou. He belongs to the one-child, Little Emperor generation that has never known a China without double-digit economic growth. It would be pointless of Ma to try to get him to understand a crime case in light of "Tiananmen, 1989." The erasure of memory applies also to the further past, in *La diplomatie du panda* (2019). The young interpreter whom Judge Li hires when he visits Jiangxi cannot even be convinced that there were communal mess halls during the Great Leap Forward, much less a famine as aftermath (181–218). It was not taught in school.

Another generational shift in cultural-moral values noted in Qiu's novels, often taken for granted by the other authors, is the rapid post-Mao change in sexual mores. The Red Heroine of his debut novel pays a price for it, but there is little condemnation of extramarital sex in principle, even from Chief Inspector Chen or Detective Yu, who is older and more old-school. Yu feels he is behind the times while listening to a female artist who had an affair with the major criminal in *Death of a Red Heroine* (276).

> "Come on, Comrade Detective Yu. We're in a new decade, a new time. Who lives any longer like in the Confucian books? If a marriage is a happy one, no outsider could ever destroy it," she said, scratching her ankle. "Besides, I never expected him to marry me."
>
> Maybe he was an old-fashioned man. Yu certainly felt ancient sitting beside the artist, to whom an affair could be just like the change of her clothes. But he also felt it tempting to imagine the body under her loose coverall.

Qiu and other mystery authors further note the revival of conventional Buddhism and Daoism in post-Mao times, not just the new sects. And yet the old faith of the Maoist age, Marxism-Leninism–Mao Zedong Thought, is rarely mentioned in the novels,[44] or therefore its rapid disappearance. Mention of Marx

146   Chapter 5

is particularly in abeyance. That, however, is true to the reality of post-Mao China, except in the schools. The China mysteries take place in a progressing, urban, post-ideological age. It is part of the glue that binds (or bound) together China and the West during their second honeymoon.

Aftermath

By the later 2010s, the second honeymoon was souring, just when Xi Jinping was insisting that storytellers everywhere "tell the good China story," about the PRC's development and progress. Overseas authors, even with crime and scandal as their themes, had been telling that very story. Famous highbrow Chinese authors resident in the PRC had written more shockingly, more allegorically, sometimes more gruesomely about social decay and dysfunction at home.[45] Outside his own country, Xi Jinping's policy shifts were endangering the very narratives he craved, just when race-based nationalisms and international polarization were on the rise globally and antipathy toward China, even Chinese people, was running rampant again in the West. But tales of China in the throes of development were no longer new anyway.

Michel Imbert's Judge Li and Ian Hamilton's heroes need not be affected by changes in the international climate if they continue or return to adventures set in earlier decades. Other series heroes have ventured outside China, including current and potential venues for the PRC's Belt and Road Initiative: Myanmar, in Brian Klingborg's 2022 mystery, and Mexico, in Daniel Nieh's 2022 thriller. The Initiative is an official Chinese program to project its power internationally through investment abroad. Criminals and operatives of diverse nationalities follow the money, and so do the good guys, in mystery fiction.

In his 2021 whodunit set in about 2019, Qiu Xiaolong briefly but explicitly notes dramatic policy reversals in the PRC. "In China's fast-changing political landscape, a number of entrepreneurs had gotten into trouble of late, as the Party government made an abrupt shift, trying to boost the state-run enterprises at their expense. In an apparent attempt to turn the clock back to Mao's time, 'official scholars' began clamoring about the 'state capitalism,' 'the Red emperor' or 'the historical justification for the Cultural Revolution,' like cicadas in the summer" (*Inspector Chen and the Private Kitchen Murder,* 118). Meanwhile Shan Tao Yun, already in Pattison's seventh novel, *Mandarin Gate* (2012), observes forced exchanges of resident populations between Tibet and eastern China. The work's opening line, "The end of time was starting in Tibet," suggests a historical and even theological mystery. The motif recurs in the next novel, in a plot about Tibetan self-immolations as political protest. Yet the crimes needing solving are duly solved, well satisfying genre expectations, even in the tenth volume. Shan and his son moreover enjoy happy endings for themselves. That is probably the final book in the series, the end of Shan Tao Yun's odyssey in our imaginations.

If the China mystery as described in this book is approaching its end or a fundamental transformation, that might well exemplify Franco Moretti's theory of literary genres (or subgenres) as formations with a life cycle of about a generation (25–35 years), after which new genres replace them, taking other paths like the branches of a tree. Moretti moreover posits political change as the prime external cause in genre differentiation and replacement.[46] That seems relevant here. My monograph is based far more on close readings of texts than quantitative analysis; it has a quasi-quantitative authority simply because it aims to characterize practically all works within a genre small enough to make that feasible. A methodological problem that keeps both Moretti's and my analyses from being "scientific" is that definitions of generic boundaries can be subjective. I exclude mysteries with ghosts, fantasy, and emphasis on espionage and sabotage. Moretti, in his account of "British novelistic genres, 1740–1900," gives the Kailyard school, invasion literature, and imperial romances phylogenetically equal rank with mysteries and historical novels, which are in principle much broader in scope, though Moretti's spy novel of ca. 1770–1800 is not our spy novel of today. His idea of (sub-)genre differentiation and replacement remains persuasive. It occurs before our eyes in popular fiction, in the West and also in the PRC, evidently accelerated by internet publication.[47]

Is globalization in secular decline, in realms both real and fictional? Andrew Pepper and David Schmid have advanced the theme of "globalization and the state" in crime fiction to counter emphasis on globalization alone.[48] The globalization of their focus is the neoliberal kind. Authoritarianism, ethnic nationalism, even protectionism and isolationism can also be global advocacies with transnational backing, we know today and from history a century ago. Attention to the state is surely necessary in analyzing China mysteries. Chapter 3 of this monograph has argued, like Pepper and Schmid, that plots about individual crimes thwarted by heroes tend to turn crime and bigger social problems into relatively incidental and local issues. China mysteries conceived overseas have many themes yet to explore, even exclusive of international complications: internet commerce, income inequality, new urban-rural disparities and interactions, changes in values besides consumerism (nationalism, for instance), the building of a monocultural surveillance and indoctrination society with reeducation camps, as in Xinjiang, the birth of a cashless society, and unprecedented approaches to preventing pandemics. Probing of such topics need not be done in

148   Chapter 5

science fiction. However, a sense of activity on the ground in China might become increasingly difficult for nonresident authors to acquire.

For the authors featured in this book, "the location's the thing," the source of their inspiration and competitive edge. Yet "the mystery's the thing" if they want readers for their second book. When one has ideas to convey about a land and a people and wants to reach a global mass audience, are crime themes and mystery plotting then a stimulus, a straitjacket, or a distraction? That is bound to vary with the talent, experiences, and opportunities of authors ready to accept the challenge of creating a new China mystery.

Appendix
The China Mysteries in Three Lists

This appendix lists thirteen authors' China-sited novels published in a police procedural series, followed by thirteen other authors' China-related series volumes starring a civilian hero (a recurring hero, except for Mones's), then another fifteen authors' relevant stand-alone novels. Annotations characterizing the authors' experience are selective and emphasize China connections.

Procedurals with a Series Police Detective

CHRISTOPHER WEST (ENGLISH), 4 MYSTERIES (HIS "CHINA QUARTET")

Backpacker in China, 1985, the basis of his travel book, *Journey to the Middle Kingdom*, 1991.

Hero: Inspector Wang Anzhuang of the Beijing Central Investigations Department.
1. *Death of a Blue Lantern*, 1994
2. *Death on Black Dragon River*, 1996
3. *Death of a Red Mandarin*, 1997
4. *The Third Messiah*, 2000

ALBAN YUNG (PSEUDONYMS ALBERT WENG, RÉMI GEDOIE) (FRENCH, WRITING IN FRENCH), 5 MYSTERIES

International banker in China and official French foreign trade adviser with contacts at the French embassy in Beijing; mother from Corsica, father from Wenzhou, China.

Hero on the Chinese side, with colorful sidekicks: Weng, evidently renamed Peng after the first two novels, variously described as Chief of Police in Beijing and a figure in Interpol. On the French side, diverse recurring security operatives, active and retired, for example, Grodaeg (Grodègue, in the fifth novel), Delamarne, Faudrey.

149

150   Appendix

1. *Message COFACE à Pékin* (COFACE Message in Beijing), 1997
2. *Pas de mantra pour Pékin* (No Mantra for Beijing), 2000
3. *Touche pas aux pékins* (Don't Mess with the Locals), 2002
4. *Pékin ce n'est pas de la tarte* (Beijing Is No Piece of Cake), 2006
5. *SCTIP Poker à Pékin* (SCTIP Poker in Beijing), 2012

LISA SEE 邝丽莎 (AMERICAN), 3 MYSTERIES SET IN CONTEMPORARY CHINA
Journalist, multicultural novel coauthor, historian of her Chinese American forebears. Subsequent to her mystery writing, author of historical novels set in China.

Hero: Inspector Liu Hulan in the Ministry of Public Security, Beijing, a "Red Princess."

1. *Flower Net,* 1997
2. *The Interior,* 1999
3. *Dragon Bones,* 2003

DAVID ROTENBERG (CANADIAN), 5 MYSTERIES, FOLLOWED BY ANOTHER CHINA NOVEL
Professor of theater arts; first person to direct a Canadian play in China, 1994.

Heroes: Zhong Fong, head of Special Investigations unit, Shanghai Public Security Bureau. Geoffrey Hyland, Zhong's acquaintance and love rival, later murdered, a Canadian drama teacher and writer.

1. *The Shanghai Murders,* 1998
2. *The Lake Ching Murders,* 2001
3. *The Hua Shan Hospital Murders,* 2003
4. *The Hamlet Murders,* 2004
5. *The Golden Mountain Murders,* 2005

Historical novel with an appearance by Zhong Fong as a four-year-old
Shanghai, 2008

PETER MAY (SCOTTISH, RESIDING IN FRANCE), 6 MYSTERY NOVELS AND A NOVELLA SET IN CHINA; ALSO THE AUTHOR OF OTHER MYSTERY THRILLERS
Journalist, television writer, and novelist, with visits to China in 1983 and 1991; hosted by Chinese police officials in subsequent trips, including 1997, 1999, and 2004.

Heroes: Detective Li Yan, Beijing Public Security Bureau; by the second novel promoted to Deputy Section Chief in the Criminal Investigation Department. Dr. Margaret Campbell, Li's American colleague, forensic pathologist.

The China Mysteries in Three Lists   151

1. *The Firemaker,* 1999
2. *The Fourth Sacrifice,* 2000
3. *The Killing Room,* 2001
4. *Snakehead,* 2002
5. *The Runner,* 2003
6. *Chinese Whispers,* 2004
7. *The Ghost Marriage,* 2010 (novella, bound with *Chinese Whispers*)

ELIOT PATTISON (AMERICAN), 10 MYSTERIES SET IN TIBET AND XINJIANG; ALSO THE AUTHOR OF A MYSTERY SERIES SET IN COLONIAL AMERICA

Attorney in international law, traveler in China and Tibet.

Hero: Shan Tao Yun, of Han nationality, formerly Inspector General in the "Ministry of the Economy," Beijing; sentenced to *laogai* (forced labor) in Tibet in the first novel; subsequently released without papers; appointed to local government positions in the last four novels, ultimately as a constable.

1. *The Skull Mantra,* 1999
2. *Water Touching Stone,* 2001
3. *Bone Mountain,* 2002
4. *Beautiful Ghosts,* 2004
5. *Prayer of the Dragon,* 2007
6. *The Lord of Death,* 2009
7. *Mandarin Gate,* 2012
8. *Soul of the Fire,* 2014
9. *Skeleton God,* 2017
10. *Bones of the Earth,* 2019

QIU XIAOLONG 裘小龙 (AMERICAN, WRITING IN ENGLISH; SOME WORKS WERE PUBLISHED IN FRENCH TRANSLATION PRIOR TO PUBLICATION OF THE ENGLISH ORIGINAL), 13 MYSTERIES IN ENGLISH SO FAR, PLUS STORY COLLECTIONS FEATURING CHIEF INSPECTOR CHEN AND OTHER BOOKS OF RELATED POETRY, SHANGHAI VIGNETTES, AND INSPECTOR CHENIANA

Born and raised in Shanghai; poet, interpreter, literary translator, and scholar of T. S. Eliot, prior to his move to the US in 1988. Returned to China annually in the twenty-first century.

Hero: Chief Inspector Chen Cao (Mandarin: Chen Chao 陈超), of the Shanghai PSB.

1. *Death of a Red Heroine,* 2000
2. *A Loyal Character Dancer,* 2002
3. *When Red Is Black,* 2004

152   Appendix

4. *A Case of Two Cities,* 2006
5. *Red Mandarin Dress,* 2007
6. *The Mao Case,* 2008 (pub. first in French, as *La Danseuse de Mao;* English, 2009)
7. *Don't Cry, Tai Lake,* 2010 (pub. first in French, as *Les Courants fourbes du lac Tai;* English, 2012)
8. *Enigma of China,* 2012 (pub. first in French, as *Cyber China;* English, 2013)
9. *Shanghai Redemption,* 2015 (pub. first in French, as *Dragon bleu, tigre blanc;* English, 2015)
10. *Hold Your Breath, China,* 2018 (pub. first in French, as *Chine, retiens ton souffle;* English, 2020)
11. *Becoming Inspector Chen,* 2020 (Contains some chapters pub. first in French, in *Il était une fois l'inspecteur Chen,* 2016, and revisions of some chapters first published in English in *Inspector Chen and Me,* 2018)
12. *The Shadow of the Empire,* 2020 (pub. first in French, as *Une enquête du vénérable juge Ti;* also Italian, *Processo a Shanghai;* English, 2022)
13. *Inspector Chen and the Private Kitchen Murder,* 2021 (pub. first in French, as *Un dîner chez Min,* 2021)
14. *Love and Murder in the Time of Covid* (forthcoming)

Story collections
Il était une fois l'inspecteur Chen (Once Upon a Time, Inspector Chen), 2016
Inspector Chen and Me: A Collection of Inspector Chen Stories (overlaps *Il était une fois l'inspecteur Chen*), 2018
Stories depicting the neighborhood and people of the novels
Years of Red Dust, 2008 (pub. first in French, as *Cité de la poussière rouge;* English, 2010)
Original poetry
Disappearing Shanghai, 2012 (with photographs by Howard W. French)
Poems of Inspector Chen, 2016

MICHEL IMBERT (SOMETIME PSEUD. MI JIANXIU) (FRENCH, WRITING IN FRENCH), 10 MYSTERIES AND ONE NON-*POLAR*

Traveler in China since 1986. Artist and arts professor in Lyon, France.

Heroes: Li Jianjia, Judge in the People's Court, Chongwen District, Beijing, and his friend and colleague, Peng Yetaï, Deputy Chief, later Inspector, in a nearby Public Security Bureau.

1. *Jaune camion* (Yellow Truck), 2004
2. *Rouge Karma* (Red Karma), 2005

3. *Bleu Pékin* (Beijing Blue), 2007
4. *Lotus et bouches cousues* (Keep It on the Down-Liu), 2009
5. *La diplomatie du panda* (Panda Diplomacy), 2019

Outside the Judge Li series
1. *La Mort en comprimés* (Death in Capsule), 2008
2. *Les disparus du laogaï* (The Disappeared of the *Laogai*), 2010
3. *En revenant de Tiananmen* (Back from Tiananmen), 2013
4. *Fang Xiao dans la tourmente* (Fang Xiao in Turmoil), 2016

With a new hero, Lt. Ma Gong
Pékin de neige et de sang (Beijing in Snow and Blood), 2018

Historical novel
Marche rouge montagnes blanches (Red March, White Mountains), 2015

DIANE WEI LIANG 梁暐 (HOLDING BRITISH AND AMERICAN CITIZENSHIP),
3 MYSTERY NOVELS

Born and raised in the PRC; participated in the 1989 democracy movement; university teacher in the US and UK. Wrote a popular 2003 memoir of her life in China.

Hero: Wang Mei ("Mei Wang" on the book covers; the text calls her "Mei"), a private detective operating under the legally tolerated designation of "information consultant"; a Peking University graduate now retired from the Ministry of Public Security in Beijing with contacts and relatives in the Ministry of State Security.
1. *The Eye of Jade,* 2008
2. *Paper Butterfly,* 2008
3. *The House of Golden Spirit,* 2011 (written in English but available only in translation, notably Spanish, as *La Casa del Espíritu Dorado*)

JAMES CHURCH (PSEUD.; AMERICAN), 6 INSPECTOR O NOVELS; NO. 5 IS
SET IN CHINA

"A former Western intelligence officer with decades of experience in Asia," including North Korea.

Heroes: Inspector O, a North Korean police official, and in this volume his nephew, Chinese citizen Maj. Bing Zong-yuan, head of the Yanji Sector Special Bureau of the PRC's Ministry of State Security.
A Drop of Chinese Blood, 2012

154   Appendix

SHAMINI FLINT (SINGAPOREAN; BORN IN KUALA LUMPUR), 7 NOVELS
FEATURING INSPECTOR SINGH; NO. 6 IS SET IN CHINA

International corporate lawyer; author also of children's literature.

Hero: Inspector Singh of Singapore.

Inspector Singh Investigates: A Calamitous Chinese Killing, 2013

DUNCAN JEPSON (BRITISH; RESIDENT IN HONG KONG SINCE 2000), FIRST
MYSTERY IN AN EXPECTED SERIES

Hong Kong–based solicitor; filmmaker; global NGO director and college teacher;
author of a historical novel (*All the Flowers in Shanghai,* 2011). Born in England,
first went to China in 1981. Mother is Singaporean, of Xiamen ancestry.

Hero: Senior Inspector Alex Soong of the Hong Kong Police.

Emperors Once More, 2014

BRIAN KLINGBORG (AMERICAN), 2 CHINA MYSTERIES

Long-term publishing and other employment in Asia; Harvard East Asian MA
program graduate. Also authored the thriller *Kill Devil Falls,* 2017, and writings
on Chinese martial arts.

Hero: Inspector Lu Fei, stationed in China's Northeast.

1. *Thief of Souls,* 2021 (pub. in the UK as *City of Ice*)
2. *Wild Prey,* 2022

Serial Productions with a "Beset Citizen" Hero

Heroes caught up in crime scenarios in these works are not under anyone's pro-
tection, least of all the CCP. Nieh's second novel is a spy thriller set in the US and
Mexico, not a China mystery, but it has PRC intrigues and continues the story of
Victor Li.

DINAH LEE KÜNG (AMERICAN, NOW SWISS), 3 MYSTERIES; ALSO
AUTHORED OTHER NOVELS

Journalist in China and Hong Kong; former Hong Kong bureau chief.

**Hero: American journalist Claire Raymond, Bureau Chief for a US busi-
ness weekly.**

1. *The Wardens of Punyu,* 2011 [early drafts, 1992]
2. *Left in the Care of,* 1997; republished as *The End of May Road,* 2011
3. *The Shadows of Shigatse,* 2011 [written in 2004]

The China Mysteries in Three Lists 155

NICOLE MONES (AMERICAN), 3 MYSTERIES SET IN CONTEMPORARY CHINA

Ran a textile business in China for 18 years, beginning in 1977; later, a food writer.

Heroes: Alice Mannegan, translator turned amateur archeologist in China; Lia Frank, art historian and dealer specializing in Chinese pots; Maggie McElroy, food writer for a US magazine.

1. *Lost in Translation,* 1998
2. *A Cup of Light,* 2002
3. *The Last Chinese Chef,* 2007
Historical novel with crime themes
Night in Shanghai, 2014

NURY VITTACHI (HONG KONG WRITER, WRITING IN ENGLISH, BORN IN CEYLON); THE FOURTH OF HIS 5 FENG SHUI DETECTIVE NOVELS IS SET IN THE PRC

Journalist and writer.

Hero: Singapore *fengshui* consultant and detective C. F. Wong, born in the PRC.

The Shanghai Union of Industrial Mystics, 2006

CATHERINE SAMPSON (ENGLISH), 2 CHINA-THEMED NOVELS, WHICH CONSTITUTE NOS. 3 AND 4 IN HER SERIES OF FOUR ROBIN BALLANTYNE NOVELS

Chinese studies in college; journalist for the BBC, *The Times* of London in Beijing, etc.

Heroes: British journalist Robin Ballantyne and private investigator Song Ren, an ex-cop.

1. *The Pool of Unease,* 2007
2. *The Slaughter Pavilion,* 2008
Short stories with Song Ren as hero
3. "Hit and Run," 2009
4. "Takeaway," 2013

JAN-PHILIPP SENDKER (GERMAN, WRITING IN GERMAN), 3 CHINA MYSTERIES AND OTHER NOVELS, INCLUDING MYSTERIES WITH BURMESE AMERICAN CHARACTERS

Correspondent for *Stern,* reporting from the US and Hong Kong. Has traveled in China since 1995. Published a nonfiction book about China in 2000.

156   Appendix

Christine Lo, translator

Heroes: German-born former journalist living in Hong Kong, Paul Leibo-vitz; Paul's 1980s friend and sometime coinvestigator living in Shenzhen, Detective Superintendent Zhang Lin, originally from Sichuan; Paul's girlfriend and lover, Christine Wu.

1. *Das Flüstern der Schatten,* 2007 (Whispering Shadows, 2016)
2. *Drachenspiele,* 2009 (Dragon Games, 2016) (The Language of Solitude, 2017)
3. *Am Anderen Ende der Nacht,* 2016 (The Far Side of the Night, 2018)

LEE BARCKMANN (AMERICAN), 1 CHINA MYSTERY, NO. 1 OF TWO NATE SCHUETTE MYSTERIES; ALSO THE AUTHOR OF A "SWIFTPAD" TRILOGY OF ALT-HISTORY THRILLERS

Taught English in China for nearly three years in the late 1980s.

Hero: Nate Schuette, American teaching English in China.

Farewell the Dragon, 2007; rev. ed., 2017–2020

ERIC STONE (AMERICAN), NO. 4 OF HIS FOUR RAY SHARP THRILLERS IS SET IN CHINA

Journalist in the US, Hong Kong, and Southeast Asia.

Hero: Ray Sharp, private investigator in Hong Kong, former journalist in Jakarta for *Asian Industry* magazine.

Shanghaied, 2009

LISA BRACKMANN (AMERICAN), 3 ELLIE MCENROE MYSTERY THRILLERS; HAS ALSO AUTHORED OTHER THRILLERS

China travel beginning in 1979; screenplay writer and novelist, rock musician, singer, and songwriter; blogger on current affairs, including events in China, since 2005.

Hero: Ellie McEnroe, Iraq war veteran, came to China with a husband working in shadowy security outfits.

1. *Rock, Paper, Tiger,* 2010
2. *Hour of the Rat,* 2013
3. *Dragon Day,* 2015

The China Mysteries in Three Lists   157

IAN HAMILTON (WELSH-BORN, SCOTTISH-EDUCATED CANADIAN), 4 NOVELS SET IN THE PRC WITHIN A SERIES OF 15 THRILLERS (TO DATE) FEATURING AVA LEE AND HER UNCLE CHOW TUNG; OTHERS ARE SET IN HONG KONG, MACAU, SOUTHEAST ASIA, LAS VEGAS

Former journalist, international business executive, Canadian civil servant, and 1970s diplomat overseeing Canadian immigration.

Hero: Ava Lee, Chinese Canadian forensic accountant with triad connections.

1. *The Wild Beasts of Wuhan,* 2012 (#3 in the Ava Lee series)
2. *The King of Shanghai,* 2014 (#7 ")
3. *The Princeling of Nanjing,* 2015 (#8 ")
4. *The Goddess of Yantai,* 2018 (#11 ")

ADAM BROOKES (CANADIAN-BORN, BRITISH-EDUCATED, RESIDENT IN THE US), 1 NOVEL OPENING A PHILIP MANGAN SERIES; SUBSEQUENT WORKS ARE MORE PURELY SPY NOVELS

Journalist based in Indonesia, China, then the US.

Hero: British journalist Philip Mangan.
Night Heron, 2014

CHERYL WEST PETTY (PSEUD. SHA LI; AMERICAN), 3 MYSTERIES

Worked for PRC universities, including Tsinghua, editing publicity texts and advising on web communications.

Hero: Mai Martin, blogger and editor for Chinese internet publications at a university in Beijing.

1. *Beijing Abduction,* 2014
2. *Wounds of Attachment,* 2014
3. *Escape from Here,* 2016

L. [LAUREN] H. DRAKEN (AMERICAN RESIDENT IN GERMANY, WRITING IN ENGLISH), 1 NOVEL AND 1 SHORT STORY SO FAR

Worked five years in China, first as a researcher at an electron-positron collider in southwest Beijing and then as an engineer at a Volkswagen plant in Beijing.

Hero: Nathan Troy, journalist and blogger; teaches English on the side.

1. *The Year of the Rabid Dragon,* 2018
2. *The Months of the Toxic Rat,* 2019 (short prequel to the title above)

158   Appendix

Daniel Nieh (American), 2 mysteries so far

Chinese American; Mandarin translator and professional model with past residence in China.
> **Hero: Victor Li, college student in the California State University system.**
> 1. *Beijing Payback,* 2019
> 2. *Take No Names,* 2022 (action is outside of China)

Stand-Alone Mysteries

These mysteries tend to be in the beset adventurer category, except for the book by Bonavia/Uren. Most are thrillers; Lee's might be called a spy thriller. Kjeldsen has also written *East* (2019), a China-themed near-future novel set in a dystopian US.

Carl Hiaasen and Bill Montalbano (1940–1998) (American)

Journalists and colleagues; Montalbano was posted to Beijing, 1979–1981.
> **Hero: Tom Stratton, art history professor and former US special ops officer.**
> *A Death in China,* 1984

David Bonavia (1940–1988; English) and John Byron (pseud. of Roger Uren) (Australian)

Bonavia: journalist in Hong Kong and China. Uren: Australian intelligence officer and diplomat in various countries, including China.
> **Hero: Li Chunlong, head of Criminal Affairs Division, Beijing PSB.**
> *The China Lovers,* 1985

Leo Ou-fan Lee 李歐梵 (Born in China, educated in Taiwan and the US, later resident in Hong Kong, writing in standard Chinese)

Professor, creative writer, cultural commentator, critic, and literary historian.
> **Hero: Pierre Fang, investigator for a multinational company.**
> *Dongfang lieshou* 東方獵手 (The Hunter of the East), 2001

Henning Mankell (1948–2015; Swedish, writing in Swedish)

Mystery novelist, traveler in China, enthusiast of the Chinese revolution.
> **Laurie Thompson, translator**
> **Hero: Birgitta Roslin, Helsingborg district judge.**
> *Kinesen* (Chinese), 2008 (*The Man from Beijing,* 2010)

The China Mysteries in Three Lists   159

DEBORAH AND JOEL SHLIAN (AMERICAN)

Medical doctors, married; first traveled to China in 1985 and thereafter hosted Chinese students studying at UCLA, where the Shlians taught; Deborah has subsequently written other thrillers.

Hero: Ni-Fu Cheng, Chinese physician.
Rabbit in the Moon, 2008

PAUL MASON (ENGLISH)

Journalist, writer, broadcast media personality, editor, and consultant.

Hero: David Brough, reporter.
Rare Earth, 2012

KIRK KJELDSEN (AMERICAN, RESIDENT IN GERMANY, THE US, SHANGHAI)

Filmmaker and college instructor, formerly resident in China.

Hero: Brendan Lavin, baker and ex-con from Queens, New York City.
Tomorrow City, 2013

160   Appendix

CASEY WALKER (AMERICAN)

Writer, traveler in China.
Hero: Luke Slade, aide to a California Congressman.
Last Days in Shanghai, 2014

CHAN HO-KEI 陳浩基 (BORN AND RAISED IN HONG KONG; RESIDENT IN TAIWAN, WRITING IN STANDARD CHINESE)

Writer of mysteries, science fiction, and combinations of the two.
Jeremy Tiang, translator
Heroes: Supt. Kwan Chun-dok and "Sonny" Lok, Hong Kong cops.
Yisan · liuqi 一三·六七 (2013 · 1967), 2014 (English trans., "The Borrowed," 2016)
Heroes: Au Nga-Yee, Hong Kong librarian, and "N," mystery hacker.
Wangneiren 網內人 (Woman in the Web), 2017 (English trans., "Second Sister," 2020)

JOHN GAPPER (ENGLISH)

Journalist and book author; editor and business commentator at the *Financial Times,* with China travel and expertise.
Heroes: Song Mei, Discipline Inspection Commission trainee in Guangzhou, and her American identical twin sister, Elizabeth Lockhart (Song Ping).
The Ghost Shift, 2015

ZHANG XINXIN 张辛欣 (AMERICAN, WRITING IN STANDARD CHINESE)

Born and raised in China; Beijing drama director in the 1980s and writer of avant-garde fiction. Since moving to the US in 1988, has written fiction, graphic novels, and blogs in Chinese.
Hero: Luoma Suisu (When-in-Rome Do-as-the-Romans), newly minted PhD in Chinese philosophy, American, hired by a Hollywood firm to investigate PRC theft of Intellectual Property.
Haolaiwu tongjifan 好莱坞通缉犯, 2015, 2021 (English trans., "Hollywood Wanted," forthcoming)

AN YU 安於 (CHINESE, WRITING IN ENGLISH; RESIDENT IN CHINA, THE US, AND OTHER COUNTRIES)

Writer, born and raised in China. New York University MFA.
Hero: Wu Jia Jia, artist.
Braised Pork, 2020

Notes

Chapter 1: Introduction

1. Yiman Wang, "Made in China," and Aijun Zhu, *Feminism and Global Chineseness*, discuss ambiguities of the term "Chinese."

2. Japan has however published detective stories from Mainland China, Taiwan, and Hong Kong in Japanese translation, such as Inamura Bungo's three-volume 2015–2016 set, *Gendai Kabun suiri shiretsu.*

3. Mysteries by Robert van Gulik, Elsa Hart, P. A. De Voe, Amanda Roberts, Zhu Xiao Di, and Frédéric Lenormand are set in imperial China. For the early twentieth century, try Paul French's true crime tales. Damrosch, in Nilsson et al., eds., *Crime Fiction as World Literature,* 257–270, analyzes Jamyang Norbu's pastiche of Conan Doyle and Kipling, *The Mandala of Sherlock Holmes,* which has Holmes spending his missing years, 1891–1894, in Tibet.

4. Henry Chang's and Ed Lin's Chinatown mysteries might have influenced PRC-sited mysteries. Lin has followed up with crime novels set in Taiwan. Francie Lin's crime novel *The Foreigner* (2008) features a Taiwanese American who goes from San Francisco to Taipei. Leslie Glass mysteries feature NYPD female detective April Woo. Vivien Chien sets her Noodle Shop Mysteries, culinary cozies such as *Death by Dumpling,* in the US. Earlier there were Chinatown crime novels like Robert Daley's *Year of the Dragon* (1981), the basis for Michael Cimino's film by that name (1985). S. J. Rozan's "Lydia Chin/Bill Smith Mysteries" are set in New York City, with some Chinese themes. A 1981–1992 BBC TV series set in London was called *The Chinese Detective.* The Honolulu police detective Charlie Chan visited prerevolutionary China in the movies—one movie—but not in any novel. A "female Charlie Chan" (a Chinese American from Hawaii) is Lily Wu, created by Juanita Sheridan. Chandra analyzes whodunits in Malay languages, some with ethnically Chinese detectives, who sleuth outside China in pre-1949 times.

5. David Michie's Matt Lester "spiritual thrillers" are set in Tibet. Liz Williams takes her Detective Inspector Chen into the underworld. My bibliography includes series-opener books by some authors in these related subgenres.

6. As in Damrosch, *What Is World Literature?*; D'haen et al., eds., *The Routledge Companion to World Literature;* and Nilsson et al., eds., *Crime Fiction as World Literature.*

7. English-language publishers demand higher profits than Continental European ones. Qiu's later books have appeared in French translation prior to their publication in the original English.

8. Hillenbrand, *Negative Exposures,* analyzes "public secrecy" in PRC photographs.

9. See Hellgren, *Swedish Marxist Noir.* Quotation from Jameson, *Raymond Chandler,* 80.

10. Peter Gordon, "[Review of] 'Blockchain Chicken Farm: And Other Stories of Tech in China's Countryside' by Xiaowei Wang," *Asian Review of Books,* Oct. 14, 2020, https://

162   Notes to Pages 3–5

asianreviewofbooks.com/content/blockchain-chicken-farm-and-other-stories-of-tech-in -chinas-countryside-by-xiaowei-wang/.

11. Alain Nicolas, "Qiu Xiaolong: 'Pour écrire sur la société, le flic est ce qu'il y a de mieux," *l'Humanité*, April 10, 2014, https://www.humanite.fr/qiu-xiaolong-pour-ecrire-sur -la-societe-le-flic-est-ce-quil-y-de-mieux. Qiu originally did not expect to write his first novel in mystery form. Stalling, "Bilingual Poetics," 96.

12. Anon., "An Interview with Diane Wei Liang," *BookBrowse*, n.d. (2009), https://www .bookbrowse.com/author_interviews/full/index.cfm/author_number/1526/diane-wei -liang#interview.

13. Muriel Plantier, "Le Gardois Michel Imbert est l'auteur de romans policiers chinois," *Midi Libre*, Nov. 16, 18, 2017, https://www.midilibre.fr/2017/11/16/le-gardois-michel-imbert -est-l-auteur-de-romans-policiers-chinois,1589609.php.

14. Chris West, "Autorenkommentar," https://www.amazon.de/-/en/Christopher-West /dp/0425172627.

15. Hilary Williamson interviewing Eliot Pattison, *BookLoons*, July 2004, http://www .bookloons.com/cgi-bin/Columns.asp?type=Interview&name=Eliot%20Pattison.

16. Peter May, *The Firemaker*, 2018 edition, xviii; D. R. Meredith, "The Firemaker (Murder in China)," *New York Journal of Books*, March 21, 2018, https://www.nyjournalofbooks.com /book-review/firemaker.

17. Layla Dabby, "China Itself Part of Mystery in Lake Ching Murders," *The Gazette* [Montreal], July 13, 2002, http://www.davidrotenberg.com/novels/reviews/LakeChing _Rev_2002.pdf.

18. Michael Handelzalts, "A Canadian in China," *Haaretz*, Oct. 28, 2008, https://www .haaretz.com/1.5052026.

19. Anjum, "The Challenge Was to Find the Pace and Voice: Duncan Jepson."

20. Gelder, *Popular Fiction*, 71–74. See Jack W. Chen et al., eds., *Literary Information in China: A History*, and Detwyler, "The Aesthetics of Information in Modern Chinese Literary Culture, 1919–1949"; Jiwei Xiao, *Telling Details: Chinese Fiction, World Literature*.

21. Not just for information about China. Hamilton's *The Wild Beasts of Wuhan* instructs us about a museum of the slave trade and an ancient synagogue in Curaçao (5–7). There's also a listing of famous forgers (77). Rignall, *Realist Fiction and the Strolling Spectator* (7, etc.) argues that the amateur detective character (with Holmes as the archetype) is successor to the flaneur figure. Pondering whether crime fiction might be "a new form of travel writing" is Anderson et al., eds., *The Foreign in International Crime Fiction*, 1–2.

22. Eidetic notables: Imbert, *La Mort en comprimés*, 12. Vegetarians: Vittachi, *The Shanghai Union of Industrial Mystics*, 137.

23. Mones, "Favorite Recipes from China," https://www.nicolemones.com/food-lovers /recipes/favorite-recipes-from-china/.

24. Yan Wei, *Detecting Chinese Modernities: Rupture and Continuity in Modern Chinese Detective Fiction (1896–1949)*, provides examples.

25. The neighborhood is "Red Dust Lane" or Hongchenfang, near the intersection of Fujian Rd. and Jinling Rd. "Red dust" has an ancient history as a term in Chinese literature and religion, referring variously to the prosperity and hubbub of urban life; daily life generally; and, less approvingly, the vulgar, distracting, and misleading nature of it all, as in the pursuit of material goods. Multiple ironies emerge as Qiu's focus shifts from the materially spartan Mao years to consumerist post-Mao times.

Notes to Pages 5–10   163

26. *Years of Red Dust* begins in 1949. Its stories originally appeared serially in *Le Monde,* translated from English to French, then were published in a 2008 French book. The plots concern post-Mao China after p. 71, in the English edition. A 1980 story is then told in the voice of Chen Cao (82). In Qiu's later linked story books, the subject is Chen Cao himself, mostly in post-Mao times: *Il était une fois l'inspecteur Chen* (2016); *Inspector Chen and Me* (2018); and *Becoming Inspector Chen* (2020), in which Chen Cao flashes back to his earlier life in dreams within the frame of a 2018–2019-era novel. My Appendix lists the 2020 book as Qiu's eleventh full-length Chen Cao novel. That is the author's view of it.

27. Ian Johnson, "The Flowers Blooming in the Dark," *The New York Review of Books* 67.5 (March 26, 2020): 46.

28. Mark Hughes, "Novel Ideas for 1997," *South China Morning Post,* April 6, 1995, https://www.scmp.com/article/113189/novel-ideas-1997.

29. Anon., "Ses polars sont censurés en Chine," *Le Parisien,* April 19, 2014, http://www.leparisien.fr/espace-premium/culture-loisirs/ses-polars-sont-censures-en-chine-19-04-2014-3778955.php. Magagnin, "Qiu Xiaolong's *Death of a Red Heroine* in Chinese Translation: A Macro-Polysystemic Analysis," discusses the Chinese translation of Qiu's debut novel. See also Qiu, "Bilingual Writing vs. Translating."

30. Luo Hui, "Shanghai, Shanghai," 55–57. My web browsing supports Luo's summary. A Yi, "Jingti Qiu Xiaolong shi de jingji wenren" (Be on Guard against Cultural Brokers like Qiu Xiaolong), *Xinjingbao,* Nov. 4, 2005, faults Qiu's novels (which he read in Chinese translation) as popular works mixing poetry, travelogue, and folk romance, in less than airtight plots to suit foreign readers. This rings true in some ways, but is oblivious to Qiu's mission and his readers' tastes. A Yi found unpoetic a verse he took to be a poem written or translated by Qiu, but it is from a poem by Louis MacNeice, which was poetic when Qiu reproduced the original in English and named the poet. If Luo Hui is right that Qiu sometimes quotes poetry and "Chinese culture" as a matter of irony and self-parody, that, too, was lost in translation, https://web.archive.org/web/20141014182855/http://culture.163.com/05/1104/10/21N5PF5O00280015.html.

31. Even for An Yu, Beijing "is much like a recurring dream to me." An Yu, "An Yu: Stuck in New York Because of Coronavirus, Thinking of Beijing," *Literary Hub,* April 22, 2020, https://lithub.com/an-yu-stuck-in-new-york-because-of-coronavirus-thinking-of-beijing/.

32. See Bakken, ed., *Crime and the Chinese Dream.*

33. Kelly in *Mystery Fiction and Modern Life* argues that mystery readers suspend disbelief because modern life itself is now implausible.

34. Ralph Arnote's Hong Kong handover thriller, *Hong Kong, China,* appeared in 1996. Reviews of the book were not favorable, and the author does not appear to have had a prior connection to China. He previously wrote a thriller about a Hong Kong drug lord operating in Hollywood, pursued by Arnote's series hero Willy Hanson, in *Fatal Secrets* (1994).

35. Lee, *Dongfang lieshou,* Postface, 311–315, and personal correspondence, April 22, 2020. Chan Ho-Kei's *Second Sister,* but not *The Borrowed,* I believe, has been printed in the PRC under a special dispensation by a Beijing press that specializes in publishing works from Taiwan, Jiuzhou chubanshe.

36. Paul French, "The Crime Fiction of Taipei," *CrimeReads,* Jan. 7, 2019, https://crimereads.com/the-crime-fiction-of-taipei/. Bertrand Mialaret, "Ed Lin with His Detective Novels Helps Us Understand the Latest Elections in Taiwan," https://mychinesebooks.com/ed-lin-detective-novels-helps-understand-latest-elections-taiwan-2/.

164   Notes to Pages 10–15

37. In 2017, five of China's top 30 best sellers, including the no. 1, were mysteries and thrillers by Higashino; Porter Anderson, "China's Fiction and Nonfiction Bestsellers of 2017," *Publishing Perspectives,* Jan. 31, 2018, https://publishingperspectives.com/2018/01/china-bestsellers-2017-openbook-cites-14–55-percent-growth/. On problems for China's home-grown crime fiction, and about Yokoyama, see Paul French, "Is China about to Witness a Crime Wave?," *CrimeReads,* June 12, 2019, https://crimereads.com/is-china-about-to-witness-a-crime-wave/.

38. Emily Bobrow, "Weekend Confidential: Liu Cixin," *Wall Street Journal,* Aug. 22–23, 2020, C6; Steven Lee Myers, "How to Catch a Killer in China: Another Chinese Crime Novel Goes Global," *New York Times,* June 4, 2018, https://www.nytimes.com/2018/06/04/books/zhou-haohui-death-notice-chinese-crime-thrillers.html.

39. Tom Mitchell, "Lunch with the *Financial Times:* He Jiahong," *Financial Times,* Feb. 20, 2015, https://www.ft.com/content/2e447276-b6fd-11e4-95dc-00144feab7de; Bertrand Mialaret, "He Jiahong, the Rule of Law through the Detective Novel," May 30, 2008, http://mychinesebooks.com/jiahong-rule-law-detective/. Marie-Claude Cantournet-Jacquet cotranslated He Jiahong's mysteries after writing a master's thesis on the author and his works.

40. The original is discussed in Kinkley, "The Cultural Choices of Zhang Xinxin," 147–151.

41. Dong Muzi and Peng Jingtao, "Cai Jun: Wo kaishi xiezuo de shihou, guonei hai meiyou xuanyi xiaoshuo zhege gainian" (Cai Jun: When I Started Writing, There Was No Domestic Concept of Suspense Fiction Yet), *Xinjingbao,* Oct. 14, 2020, https://www.163.com/dy/article/FOTKHQVJ0512D3VJ.html, accessed April 4, 2021.

42. Jemimah Steinfeld, "New Dog, Old Tricks," *Index on Censorship,* Sept. 18, 2015, doi/pdf/10.1177/0306422015605694a. On exposure novels, see Lu Hsun, *A Brief History of Chinese Fiction,* 372–388.

43. A major author of "Asian mystery fiction" online and in print is Barry Hughart (1930–2019), born in Peoria, Illinois, and later resident in Arizona, https://en.wikipedia.org/wiki/Barry_Hughart. Others with Wikipedia entries include Sean Russell (Canada, b. 1952), Guy Gavriel Kay (Canada, b. 1954), Gillian Rubinstein (UK, b. 1954), and Alison Goodman (Australia, b. 1966). The PRC's own popular and online fiction is not to be outdone in queer and cutting-edge trends. See Walsh, *The Subplot: What China Is Reading and Why It Matters,* and in Chinese, https://www.qidian.com. *Anime* and TV adaptations of "cultivation" novels are available with English subtitles on Netflix and YouTube. Online sites featuring English translations of Chinese novels come and go.

Chapter 2: Birth and Anatomy of a Genre

1. By the early 1960s, some of Robert van Gulik's whodunits' book covers announced "A Judge Dee Mystery" or "A New Judge Dee Mystery." This device was not of course unprecedented in mystery publications.

2. Gelder, "The Fields of Popular Fiction," in Gelder, ed., *New Directions,* 13, suggests we "think of popular genres as sites that both generate and come to depend on levels of readerly specialization." One common specialization is reading all works by a particular author.

3. Munt, "Grief," 135. The same is true of the *writing* of popular fiction. Gelder, *Popular Fiction,* 22–23.

Notes to Pages 16–18   165

4. Allan et al., eds., *The Routledge Companion to Crime Fiction*, 16. See also Rushing, *Resisting Arrest*, and Nilsson et al., eds., *Crime Fiction as World Literature*. Erdmann, "Nationality International," 17–18, summarizes formulaic elements. Ironically phrased "rules" for detective stories by Fr. Ronald Knox and then by S. S. Van Dine appear in Haycraft, ed., *The Art of the Mystery Story*, 189–199. The classic history is by Julian Symons, *Bloody Murder*.

5. See Carroll, *A Philosophy of Mass Art*, and Swirski and Vanhanen, eds., *When Highbrow Meets Lowbrow*.

6. Plain, *Twentieth-Century Crime Fiction*, 1–16, and Kinkley, *Chinese Justice*, 1–10, explore implications of the crime fiction concept. Link, *The Uses of Literature*, provides the classic analysis of PRC literary control.

7. Chinese terms for crime fiction are *zuian xiaoshuo*, or more recently *fanzui xiaoshuo*, probably after the Japanese *hanzai shōsetsu*. Prior to 1949, most crime fiction in China, foreign and domestic, was called "detective fiction" (*zhentan xiaoshuo*). It was in fact focused on detection, often by private investigators; after the reappearance of common crime themes in 1980s PRC publications, a more widely used term, already current in Taiwan, was "deductive fiction" (*tuili xiaoshuo*), after the long-standing Japanese term *suiri shōsetsu*. Nearly all PRC crime fiction is technically police procedural, called "legal system literature" (*fazhi wenxue*) in the 1980s, then "public security fiction" or "police fiction" (*gongān xiaoshuo*, not to be confused with *gongàn*, the designation for China's ancient "court case" fiction). Among competing genre terms today are *xuanyi xiaoshuo* and *jingsong xiaoshuo*, indicating suspense or thriller fiction.

8. Kinkley, *Chinese Justice*.

9. YA or "young adult" is a major genre today, and in the mystery field, pre-YA Nancy Drew and Hardy Boys series were once gateways to the adult genre. The crux need not be the reading level necessary for full understanding of a text, but simply to keep the reader reading. PRC translation studies publications use Flesch-Kincaid readability scores to compare English translations of Chinese highbrow literature.

10. Early analyses are Gans, *Popular Culture and High Culture* (1974) and Bourdieu, *The Field of Cultural Production* (which collects mostly 1980s articles translated from the French). See also Driscoll, *The New Literary Middlebrow*, and Sandberg, "Contemporary Crime Fiction."

11. Gulddal et al., eds., *Criminal Moves*, 1.

12. Gelder, *Popular Fiction*, 1, 11. Since 2012, the presence of popular or genre-fiction characteristics in novels by award-winning literary authors has led to a "genrefication" debate questioning whether there remains a difference between literary and popular fiction.

13. Murphy, *Key Concepts in Contemporary Popular Fiction*. See also Murphy and Matterson, eds., *Twenty-First Century Popular Fiction*. Walsh, *The Subplot*.

14. Driscoll, *The New Literary Middlebrow*, 81.

15. Rushing, *Resisting Arrest*. Swirski, *From Lowbrow to Nobrow* and *American Crime Fiction*. Also Swirski and Vanhanen, eds., *When Highbrow Meets Lowbrow*.

16. As in Northrup Frye, *Anatomy of Criticism*.

17. Interview at the 2020 EU-China Literary Festival, https://eu-china.literaryfestival .eu/a-yi-x-stina-jackson-noir-suspense-and-setting-the-scene/.

18. Driscoll, *The New Literary Middlebrow*, 37, addresses antagonisms between middlebrow culture and academe.

166 Notes to Pages 18–20

19. Yunte Huang, "Robert Hans van Gulik and the Reinvention of Chinese Detective Fiction," details Chinese cultural aspects van Gulik was able to incorporate in his Judge Dee books.

20. Todorov, "The Typology of Detective Fiction," 51.

21. Lucias J. P. Banks, *Beijing Is Dead: A Zombie Outbreak* (Scotts Valley, CA: CreateSpace, 2015).

22. Santaulària i Capdevila, "'This Is Getting a Little Too Chinese for Me,'" 67–68; Mukherjee, *Crime and Empire*; Reitz, *Detecting the Nation*; Christian, ed., *The Post-Colonial Detective*; Matzke and Mühleisen, eds., *Postcolonial Postmortems*.

23. Many observers trace the boom in *translated* contributions to Anglophone (and global) crime fiction to the debut of Stieg Larsson's *Millennium* trilogy in English in 2008. See Nilsson et al., eds., *Crime Fiction as World Literature*.

24. Pepper and Schmid, eds., *Globalization and the State*, "Introduction," 2, cites, among others, Clive James: "In most of the crime novels coming out now, it's a matter not of what happens but of where. Essentially, they are guidebooks." From *The New Yorker*, April 9, 2007. See also Anderson et al., eds., *The Foreign in International Crime Fiction*, 1–2.

25. This is the premise of Tally, ed., *The Routledge Handbook of Literature and Space*. See also King, "Place," 213, citing geographers Tuan, Howell, and Hausladen. George J. Demko writes on crime mysteries at http://www.dartmouth.edu/~gjdemko/toc.htm.

26. Christian, ed., *The Post-Colonial Detective*; Fischer-Hornung and Mueller, eds., *Sleuthing Ethnicity*; Matzke and Mühleisen, eds., *Postcolonial Postmortems*; Krajenbrink and Quinn, eds., *Investigating Identities*; Pearson and Singer, eds., *Detective Fiction in a Postcolonial and Transnational World*; Baker and Shaller, eds., *Detecting Detection*; Evans and White, eds., *Crime across Cultures*; Anderson et al., eds., *The Foreign*; Pepper and Schmid, eds., *Globalization and the State*; Nilsson et al., eds., *Crime Fiction as World Literature*; Gulddal et al., eds., *Criminal Moves*; Gulddal et al., eds., *The Cambridge Companion*; and Elias and Sienkiewicz-Charlish, eds., *Crime Scenes*. For an overview, see King, "Place," in Allan et al., eds., *The Routledge Companion to Crime Fiction*. Rzepka and Horsley, eds., *A Companion to Crime Fiction*, 296–307, emphasizes European authors.

27. See King, "Crime Fiction as World Literature," 9–10. King, "The Reader and World Crime Fiction," 195–198. My own *Chinese Justice* and Yan Wei's *Detecting Chinese Modernities* are not exceptions to the national literatures approach. On mobility, see Piipponen et al., eds., *Transnational Crime Fiction*.

28. Jim Nelson, "The New American Regionalism," blog, July 23, 2017, rev. Nov. 19, 2020, http://j-nelson.net/tag/writing-of-local-color/.

29. Erdmann, "Nationality International," 16; King, "Place," 214. A rare reference book with entries on Africa, China, Japan, and Latin America is Herbert, ed., *The Oxford Companion to Crime and Mystery Writing*, 9, 64–67, 241–243, and 255–256.

30. Michelle Deeter got Zijin Chen's permission to specify locations for the English version of *The Untouched Crime*, she says in Angus Stewart's "The Translated Chinese Fiction Podcast" 16 (Oct. 22, 2019), https://www.youtube.com/watch?v=BBgGYyTpCNA, accessed April 3, 2021.

31. Bakhtin, *The Dialogic Imagination*.

32. Leitch, "The Many Pasts of Detective Fiction." See also Todorov, "The Typology of Detective Fiction"; Champigny, *What Will Have Happened*; Sandberg, "Crime Fiction and the Past"; Browne and Winks, eds., *The Detective as Historian*; Herbert, ed., *The*

Oxford Companion, 207–210; Rzepka and Horsley, eds., *A Companion to Crime Fiction*, 222–232.

33. Damrosch, *What Is World Literature?*, 6–7, 212–213; King, "Crime Fiction as World Literature," 10–15. See D'haen et al., eds., *The Routledge Companion*; Nilsson et al., eds., *Crime Fiction*; and Allan et al., eds., *The Routledge Companion*. Regarding China, see Shu-mei Shih, "Global Literature"; Shih et al., eds., *Sinophone Studies*; Jing Tsu, *Sound and Script*; and Flair Shi, "Post-Mao Chinese Literature as World Literature." Nilsson et al., eds., *Crime Fiction as World Literature*, 2, finesses the question of whether crime fiction is "literature" by arguing that it is more global than the novel as such and much hybridized with canonical works. A recent contribution, Gulddal et al., eds., *The Cambridge Companion to Crime Fiction*, replaces "literature" with "fiction" and usefully speaks of the nineteenth-century "'first globalization' of crime fiction" (7), implying that more recent ones have come in a series.

34. King, "Crime Fiction as World Literature," 14, 16; King, "The Reader and World Crime Fiction," 200–207.

35. Exceptions are Kinkley, *Chinese Justice;* Yan Wei, *Detecting Chinese Modernities;* and Saito, "East Asian Crime Fiction," in Gulddal et al., eds., *The Cambridge Companion*, 117–140.

36. Idema, *Judge Bao and the Rule of Law*.

37. Silver, *Purloined Letters;* Kawana, *Murder Most Modern*. Japan, too, in the prewar period had modern detective fiction set in historical Japan, feudal Judge Dees so to speak, written by Okamoto Kidō and others.

38. Van Gulik's original Judge Dee novels unfold within a generalized imperial-era China, adorned with details from the author's Sinological research. His plots are rather "Western" (even cozy), but his Judge Dee hero resembles prototypes from Chinese tradition. Some of the crimes come from old Judge Bao stories and forensics books. Van Gulik's chapter titles in couplets, illustrations in the style of woodblock prints, and end-of-chapter suspense recall traditional Chinese fiction more generally. See Hao, "Transcending Cultural Boundaries," and Yunte Huang, "Robert Hans van Gulik." Van Gulik entered the world of Judge Dee through an anonymous Chinese novel, *Wu Zetian qi'an* or *Di gongan*, which he translated and adapted in a 1949 book he called *Celebrated Cases of Judge Dee*. Scholars now think it was written about 1890, not in the eighteenth century; Benedetti, "Killing Di Gong." By the later nineteenth century, so-called *gongan* narratives had evolved into martial-arts sagas. Contemporary martial-arts fiction and media productions are the modern heirs to China's Great Judge narratives. "Kung fu" works, too, are now a global genre. Mok, "Martial Arts Fiction."

39. Van Gulik from the start wanted his works translated into Chinese and Japanese for native readers, thinking this might give ideas to East Asian writers. He might never have heard of Okamoto Kidō. Ad Blankestijn, Nov. 21, 2015 blog, https://adblankestijn.blogspot .com/2015/11/judge-dee-novels.html. The samurai detective series is by the German-born US Japanologist Ingrid J. Parker.

40. Uxó, "The Representation of Chinese Characters," discusses Cuban historical crime fiction featuring Chinese Cubans. The noted Italian crime writer Carlo Lucarelli has written *Febbre gialla* (Yellow Fever, 1997), set in Bologna and translated into German as *Mafia alla Chinese: Ein Italienkrimi*, 2004. The 1997 novel and other works by Lucarelli inspired a 2006 TV series called *Vendetta cinese*, with heroes l'ispettore Coliandro and l'ispettore Suyi (a woman).

168   Notes to Pages 22–28

41. As by Huang Wenrui and Geling Yan. Their novels were initially published in Taiwan.

42. Anderson et al., eds., *The Foreign,* has chapters about individual crime authors' mistakes, misunderstandings, and diverse differences of viewpoint from natives' when authors write about crime in a place that is foreign to them.

43. Said, *Orientalism.*

44. Žižek, "Parallax," unpaginated.

45. Žižek, "Parallax," unpaginated.

46. See Yunte Huang, "Robert Hans van Gulik," 114, 120–122.

47. The "Worlds" issue could be factored out in a comparison of Iceland Noir novels by Arnaldur, Yrsa, Lilja, Ragnar, and Sólveig with those by foreign-origin resident authors such as Grant Nicol, Quentin Bates, and Michael Ridpath. The latter write in English and the former write in Icelandic, globalized through translations.

48. St. André, *Translating China as Cross-Identity Performance.*

49. The hero of Ha Jin's *The Crazed* has been called a detective by some critics, but the lack of overt signals of recognized crime or detective themes well illustrate the difference between what is perceived as genre fiction (by Qiu Xiaolong) and what is not (by Ha Jin).

50. See Rolls, Vuaille-Barcan, and West-Sooby, "Introduction: Translating National Allegories: The Case of Crime Fiction," which opens their themed 2016 issue of *The Translator.*

51. Jameson, "Third-World Literature," 69. The most forceful criticism of Jameson's stance came not from scholars of Chinese literature, but from Aijaz Ahmad, "Jameson's Rhetoric of Otherness and the 'National Allegory.'"

52. Rolls, "Whose Allegory Is It Anyway?" is a case study of French translators superimposing French allegories of France as hard-boiled-American on to revised translations of American crime fiction that originally served the French, in postwar translations, as national allegories of the US.

53. "Conference: Telling Truths—Crime Fiction and National Allegory." Jameson was the keynote speaker; his talk is unavailable, and he might not have concurred, https://partnersin crimesydney.wordpress.com/2012/11/11/conference-telling-truths-crime-fiction-and -national-allegory/.

54. "William Montalbano, 57, Prize-Winning Reporter," *New York Times,* March 22, 1998, 43, https://www.nytimes.com/1998/03/22/nyregion/william-montalbano-57-prize-winning -reporter.html.

55. By "John Byron": *Portrait of a Chinese Paradise: Erotica and Sexual Customs of the Late Qing Period* (London: Quartet, 1987); *The Claws of the Dragon: Kang Sheng* [Mao's spymaster] (Riverside, NJ: Simon & Schuster, 1992); *To Eastern Lands* [Uren's own poetry, prose, and photos] (Hong Kong: Proverse, 2013). I cannot verify that Yan Zhen, *The China Dream,* tr. John Byron (Beijing: Chinese Writers Press, 2014) came into print.

56. William D. Montalbano, "The Giant Awakens," *Los Angeles Times,* June 15, 1993, 2.

57. Derek Davies, "Obituary: David Bonavia," *The Correspondent,* Oct. 4, 1988, https:// issuu.com/fcchk/docs/1988–10/4.

58. John Byron website, https://johnbyron.net/books.html. Judy Bonavia Boillat, who typed up the manuscript, confirmed this in an Aug. 26, 2020, email to me. She adds that David Bonavia also contributed to characterization.

59. An update: "Former Intelligence Official Avoids Jail for Breaching National Secrecy Over 'Forgotten' Documents," *ABC News,* Sept. 7, 2020, https://www.abc.net.au/news/2020 –09–08/former-intelligence-officer-roger-uren-avoids-jail-time/12641896.

Notes to Pages 30–41   169

60. Jake Needham, "Jake Needham Asks: Read Any Good Asian Crime Fiction Lately?" *Shots: Crime & Thriller Ezine,* n.d. [post-2011] relates that best-selling author Stephen Leather "abandoned Asia as source material for his fiction" (that would be after 1993; Leather had penned a couple plots with Vietnam War themes, after two spy thrillers tangentially related to China), though "he hadn't really wanted to, but his publisher had insisted. They warned him to stop writing about Asia or it would kill his career," http://www.shotsmag.co.uk/feature_view .aspx?FEATURE_ID=180, accessed Nov. 13, 2020.

61. Küng considered Bonavia a mentor at the *Far Eastern Economic Review,* for which she was a London-based correspondent, 1978–1982. The Küng and Bonavia families became close when Küng was based in Hong Kong, 1983–1986, and remained so after David Bonavia's passing in 1988. From personal correspondence.

62. The book has a retrospective thrust, for China's globalization had been thrown into reverse after "June Fourth" (1989). West's postscript is almost an apology, reaffirming his view of China as a land still poised to move in any direction.

63. Chris West, web autobiographical notes, https://www.amazon.com/Christopher-West /e/B001HCYT0W/ref=ntt_dp_epwbk_1. https://www.chriswest.info/. Hausladen, *Places for Dead Bodies,* 138–140, discusses West's first China mystery.

64. West, "Autorenkommentar," https://www.amazon.de/-/en/Christopher-West/dp/ 0425172627.

65. Named as the Yiguandao, which was secret and ran businesses, but was not a criminal triad society; this plot detail might be called a mistake.

66. Chris West, biographical blurb for Amazon, undated, post-2012, https://www.amazon .de/-/en/Christopher-West/dp/0425172627.

67. Personal correspondence from Küng, Aug. 20, 2019, and her website, archived at https://web.archive.org/web/20190208074421/http://www.dinahleekung.com/events .htm.

68. Correspondence from Küng, April 21, 2020. Fr. Nalet brought the *China News Analysis* to Taiwan in 1994: https://www.ucanews.com/story-archive/?post_name=/1993/11/11/40yearold -china-analysis-fortnightly-moves-to-taiwan&post_id=44267; https://taiwantoday.tw/print.ph p?unit=20,29,35,45&post=24740; https://www.taiwan-panorama.com/en/Articles/Details?Guid =0a9eb041-3117-41fb-a266-f4f83bfd5ec8&CatId=11.

69. Correspondence from Küng, Aug. 20, 2019.

70. Even a book with the then-trendy title of *The Post-Colonial Detective* (Ed Christian, ed.) took time to land a publisher. Its essays, first assembled in 1992, saw print in 2001. My first essay on PRC crime fiction appeared in 1985, in Kinkley, ed., *After Mao.*

71. Jean-Claude Perrier, "Un Chinois en Chine," *Livres Hebdo,* Nov. 10, 2013, https:// www.livreshebdo.fr/article/un-chinois-en-chine.

72. Kinkley, *Corruption and Realism in Late Socialist China.*

73. Speculation about the case also fueled a documentary-style episode called "Chinese Murder Mystery" in the UK Channel 4 series *Dispatches,* aired Nov. 12, 2012, and one of three fictionally dramatized cases tied to the leak of the Panama Papers in *The Laundromat* (2019 film), distributed by Netflix, Steven Soderbergh, director, starring Meryl Streep, Gary Oldman, and Antonio Banderas.

74. Another 1997 film is the sole James Bond film so far with a Chinese connection, *Tomorrow Never Dies.* Agent 007 collaborates with a female Chinese spy in a notably China-honeymoonish plot.

170   Notes to Pages 41–49

75. https://www.lisasee.com/faq/. See says she had been a journalist for more than a dozen years, ending in 1996 (the year before publication of *Flower Net*). Chauncey Mabe, interviewing Lisa See, *South Florida Sun Sentinel*, "Author Q&A," June 19, 2011, https://www.sun-sentinel.com/entertainment/events/fl-xpm-2011-06-19-fl-books-lisa-see-20110619-story.html.

76. Lisa See, "The Funeral Banquet," 138.

77. Akshita Nanda, interviewing Lisa See, "Lisa See and the Roots of Her Success," *The Star* (Petaling Jaya, Malaysia), Nov. 8, 2011, https://www.thestar.com.my/lifestyle/books/2011/11/08/lisa-see-and-the-roots-of-her-success.

78. So said See when I asked her at her book talk in Beaverton, Oregon, April 12, 2017.

79. Kendall, who in 2009 founded the L.A.-based law firm of Kendall Brill & Kelly, was a partner at Shearman & Sterling LLP, New York, 1988–1997. That firm, hired by the Bank of China, pursued the international fraud case with the FBI. John J. Fialka, *War by Other Means* (New York: Norton, 1999), 145–148.

80. From See's website, https://www.lisasee.com/faq/.

81. Lisa See, answer to a question in Goodreads, ca. 2012, https://www.goodreads.com/questions/809037-how-much-do-you-know-about-chinese. Elisabeth Sherwin, "See 'The Interior' through the Eyes of Someone Who's Been There," blog, http://virtual-markets.net/~gizmo/1999/see2.html (Nov. 14, 1999).

82. Lisa See, *Flower Net,* cites two equivalent, genderless phrases commonly used in China: "He is a Red Prince, *Gaogan Zidi*" (37); and "These are the *taizi*—princelings" (112).

83. Gary Krist, "Pacific Overtures," *New York Times,* Oct. 26, 1997, http://movies2.nytimes.com/books/97/10/26/reviews/971026.26kristt.html.

84. See also Anderson et al., eds., *Serial Crime Fiction.*

85. Kinkley, interviewing Qiu Xiaolong, 56.

86. The Keller Entertainment Group has promoted a possible TV series featuring Chen Cao and Catherine Rohn; see the "cop buddies" section in Chapter 4 of this book. BBC Radio 4 has produced a series of "Inspector Chen Mysteries" radio plays, https://archive.org/details/bbcr4chen.

87. I met Qiu Xiaolong at this stage of his career, at Wang Meng's international conference on contemporary Chinese literature in Jinshan, Shanghai, Nov. 4–6, 1986.

88. The editor of Qiu's first book was averse to having poetry in the mystery. Stalling, "Bilingual Poetics," 96–97.

89. Eliot liked English cozies. Paul Grimstad, "What Makes Great Detective Fiction, According to T. S. Eliot," *The New Yorker,* Feb. 2, 2016, https://www.newyorker.com/books/page-turner/what-makes-great-detective-fiction-according-to-t-s-eliot.

90. "Inspector Chen Series is a Reflection of Evolving China, Says Author," *Hindustan Times* (New Delhi), June 17, 2015, https://web.archive.org/web/20170721005302/http://www.hindustantimes.com/books/inspector-chen-series-is-a-reflection-of-evolving-china-says-author/story-QlG7QUFGgx8pczazpJI1kK.html.

91. *Hindustan Times.*

92. Stalling, "Bilingual Poetics," 97. Qiu mentions W. B. Yeats's poem "The Mask."

93. Her third novel, available only in Spanish, is set in 2008, unlike the first two.

Notes to Pages 50–52   171

Chapter 3: China

1. Said, *Orientalism;* Damrosch and Spivak, "Comparative Literature/World Literature"; Sheng-mei Ma, "Zen Keytsch"; Young, "World Literature and Postcolonialism." Hao, "Transcending Cultural Boundaries," on pitfalls for Caucasians writing novels featuring non-Caucasians, 551–554. About China mysteries: Santaulària i Capdevila, "'This Is Getting a Little Too Chinese for Me.'"

2. More broadly, see Salomone, *The Rise of English: Global Politics and the Power of Language.*

3. Yingchi Chu, "The Politics of Reception"; Luo Hui, "Shanghai, Shanghai." On the double bind Chinese American writers face: Gish Jen, *Tiger Writing;* Jennifer Ho, *Understanding Gish Jen.* Walsh, *The Subplot,* 81–85, discusses Han Chinese writers in the PRC who write about and then are inevitably viewed as torchbearers for non-Han ethnic groups.

4. Yunte Huang, *Charlie Chan.*

5. Hiaasen and Montalbano, *A Death in China,* 272, has its Caucasian hero "dying with cruelty and calculated humiliation that no Western mind could fashion." It is not ameliorative that page 137 drops the phrase "no Chinese artist could ever express such a horror." May, *The Firemaker,* 1, mentions "dark oriental eyes," though page 133 says its hero cop Li Yan's training in Chicago "opened his eyes to a crime culture and the means of combating it that was unknown in China." Kjeldsen, *Tomorrow City,* Ch. 18, mentions "*lingchi* photographs he'd seen in an old book" (death by a thousand cuts). Draken's *The Year of the Rabid Dragon* is at times jaw-dropping, as is Jepson's imagination of a neo-Boxer cult in *Emperors Once More* (see Chapter 5 in this book).

6. Lisa See mentions poisoning by liquification of internal organs in *Flower Net,* but the poison is Spanish fly.

7. An exception: Draken, *The Year of the Rabid Dragon,* 301–310.

8. This topic is the poignant subject of highbrow author Jia Pingwa's *Jihua,* expertly translated by Nicky Harman as *Broken Wings.*

9. Lisa See: "What I want people to get from my books is that all people on the planet share common life experiences—falling in love, getting married, having children, dying—and share common emotions—love, hate, greed, jealousy. These are the universals; the differences are in the particulars of customs and culture," https://www.lisasee.com/faq/.

10. Many of these issues are discussed in Forsdick, "Travelling Concepts"; Segalen, *Essay on Exoticism;* and Bhabha, *The Location of Culture.*

11. Erdmann, a German scholar, takes exception in her "Nationality International" to Leon's portraits of Germans. Leon conjures up Venetian voices that comment ironically on other European and regional Italian types.

12. Toronto Public Library, Appel Salon, April 15, 2011, https://www.youtube.com/watch?v=NkXDbrYrSXs, 4:04–5:01.

13. There is an astounding assortment of regional Italian detectives for the reader of English, in novels variously translated from the Italian or originally written in English, http://italian-mysteries.com/crime-series/. Germans, too, write Italy mysteries, in German.

14. Inspector Chen would be shifting between Mandarin and Shanghainese in his work, but attention to that might slow the action and appear tedious to many readers. Some authors account for their heroes conversing with foreign actors by noting education abroad, etc. Others ignore such concerns.

172   Notes to Pages 52–61

15. Toronto Public Library, Appel Salon, April 5, 2016, https://www.youtube.com/watch?v=9HVs8a8x4N8, 48:00–49:00.

16. Qiu Xiaolong, "Bilingual Writing vs. Translating," 133–135.

17. Moretti, *Graphs, Maps, Trees,* 61–62.

18. Zhang Xinxin was born in Nanjing and rusticated in Heilongjiang, but her adult career in China is famously associated with Beijing.

19. On Shanghai in Qiu Xiaolong's works: Luo Hui, "Shanghai, Shanghai," 57–58, and Jiaying Cai, "Qiu Xiaolong and Linda Fairstein." Other detectives operating in or about Shanghai: David Rotenberg's Zhong Fong, head of special investigations for the Shanghai PSB; Eric Stone's private investigators Ray Sharp and Lei Yue; Ian Hamilton's forensic accountant Ava Lee in *The King of Shanghai* and two follow-on novels; Nury Vittachi's "Feng Shui Detective" in *The Shanghai Union of Industrial Mystics;* and Casey Walker's hero in *Last Days in Shanghai.*

20. Weijie Song, *Mapping Modern Beijing,* analyzes the city's literary topography.

21. Wholly fictional cities and areas, besides Pattison's Lhadrung, somewhere north of Arunachal Pradesh according to maps on the inside covers of early volumes, appear in Rotenberg, *The Lake Ching Murders;* Imbert, *La diplomatie du panda;* Sampson's *The Slaughter Pavilion* (Yidong city, though she describes Beijing's Anjialou neighborhood meticulously); and See's *Dragon Bones* (the Bashan site). Inner Mongolian towns in Mason's *Rare Earth* are fictional or composite.

22. Chan Ho-Kei, *Second Sister,* 286–288.

23. Wasserstrom, "Hour of the Rat."

24. The superhighway was in existence at the time of the plot. See leaves no loose threads, so the text gives a sort of apology for why Liu took the train, and via Datong, not Shijiazhuang—Liu couldn't get a ticket for the other route.

25. Uyghurs play a criminal role in Imbert, *Pékin de neige et de sang.* Brackmann's three novels feature a Uyghur artist whose disappearance *is* the mystery. He and his friends are suspected as friends of terrorism. Uyghurs stage a revolt as a small subplot at the end of Paul Mason's *Rare Earth.* Somewhat oddly, though in good conscience, Vittachi's otherwise comic and satirical novel *The Shanghai Union of Industrial Mystics* inserts a four-page manifesto and serious bill of accusations against Chinese government oppressors by a fictitious but real-sounding Uyghur committee in exile. The plight of Uyghurs is covered in a spy novel by Charles Cumming, *Typhoon* (2008).

26. See Kinkley, *Chinese Justice.* Whodunits by He Jiahong, the Beijing law professor, too, are based on real cases, but they are ones he researched, not his own cases.

27. *A Case of Two Cities* mentions a senior American Sinologist [in life, an Australian and later chair professor in Scotland], Bonnie Grant [Bonnie McDougall], known for translating a leading Misty Poet [Bei Dao], who Qiu however writes "had killed his wife and then committed suicide" [that would be Gu Cheng; Qiu Xiaolong, rest assured, knows the difference]. In *Red Mandarin Dress,* the inspector consults an old acquaintance, Shen Wenchang [Shen Congwen] (50), who after the revolution retired from his 1940s literary career to study ancient Chinese clothing. "Chen would not have remembered him [Shen] either but for a meeting with a British [American] sinologist [yours truly] who raved about Shen's earlier literary work" (52–53). One of Shen's poems, "Mutilated Earthworm" (65), looks like an inside joke for literary scholars referring to the signature poem of Shen's friend Wen Yiduo, "Sishui" ("Dead Water," or "Stagnant Water"). *Death of a Red Heroine,* Ch. 22, has an elderly woman author, Yang

Notes to Pages 62–67   173

Ke, who resembles Yang Mo, author of *Song of Youth* (in the novel, it is *Song of Revolution*). *Inspector Chen and the Private Kitchen Murder*, 3, mentions a French literary enthusiast called Bertrand—maybe Bertrand Mialaret. Qiu's Washington University mentor, Robert Hegel, is mentioned under his real name (86).

28. From, respectively: Pattison, *Water Touching Stone;* Mones, *Lost in Translation;* See, *Dragon Bones;* Pattison, *Prayer of the Dragon.* For *fengshui,* all of Vittachi's novels featuring C. F. Wong; medicine—various, beginning perhaps with See, *Flower Net.*

29. John F. Burns, "Peking Focuses on Execution of 3 Aides' Sons," *New York Times,* Feb. 25, 1986, A11. Qiu was not the only one to look at the case from the standpoint of making an example of extramarital sex. See Xinran Xue, *The Promise,* 114.

30. Chen Xiaomeng was Qiu's chief model for Wu Xiaoming. Anon., "Wue buzuo: Pandian Yanda zhong bei qiangbi de gaoganzidi" (Nothing Was Beyond Them: Inventorying Princelings Executed during the Strike Hard), Sept. 25, 2019. This article circulated on many media and webpages, under different titles. All have been scrubbed from the internet.

31. An inconsistency: Secretary Li says the Tiananmen event (1989) was "last summer" (338), yet Deng Xiaoping's 1992 southern tour to Shenzhen has already occurred (413). In either case, the time of the plot has been moved forward, although it is still in the past as judged by the time of writing. I asked about this, and Qiu said, "there's some poetic license about the time." Kinkley, interviewing Qiu Xiaolong, 55.

32. Laifong Leung, *Contemporary Chinese Fiction Writers,* 64–68.

33. A fictitious tell-all book mentioned in Qiu's novel (11) is *Cloud and Rain in Shanghai,* which suggests Edna Wu's memoiristic novel, *Clouds and Rain: A China-to-America Memoir.* Both Li's and Wu's books were published in 1994. Still another inspiration might be Nien Cheng's *Life and Death in Shanghai* (1986), which tells of that author's daughter, a would-be PRC movie actress.

34. Shangguan Yunzhu. See Zhang Jishun, "From Fallen Star to Red Star."

35. The *Golden Venture* incident must also have inspired Jeffery Deaver, *The Stone Monkey,* which was published in 2002, the same year as Qiu Xiaolong's novel.

36. Philip Shenon, "Suspect in Golden Venture Case Was Leading a Life of Luxury," *New York Times,* Nov. 19, 1995; Keefe, *The Snakehead.*

37. August, *Inside the Red Mansion.* Kinkley, *Corruption and Realism,* 124–143, discusses popular novelist Liu Ping's *roman à clef* about Lai Changxing and his depredations.

38. In this novel Zhou Keng originated in Shaoxing, Zhejiang, like Zhou Shuren (pseud. Lu Xun), China's preeminent modern writer. They could be related! Chen Cao goes there to sleuth (Chs. 18, 19).

39. Built in 1936 as the mansion of a shipping tycoon, the Moller Villa is today a luxury hotel.

40. The Guangxi case is somewhat altered, as usual. The novel moves the case from Guangxi to Yunnan. And the perp who was outed is moved to Shanghai. Not only did Han Feng not die, some netizens came to his defense, as a cadre whose greed was relatively restrained. Wikipedia has articles under "Li Gang incident" and also "Human flesh search engine."

41. Lu Hsun, *A Brief History of Chinese Fiction,* 317–336; Hsia, "The Scholar-novelist and Chinese Culture"; McMahon, "A Case for Confucian Sexuality."

42. A syndicate of villainous businessmen, mostly of Taiwan origins, is anxious to preserve Sino-US trade in Rotenberg, *The Shanghai Murders.*

174   Notes to Pages 68–77

43. See Chan, Selden, and Pun, *Dying for an iPhone.*

44. "Radioactive Scrap Metal Detected in Novorossiysk," Russia, *NTI,* Jan. 20, 2004, concerns contaminated scrap metal found in a port railyard, presumably bound for export, https://www.nti.org/analysis/articles/radioactive-scrap-metal-detected-novorossiysk -russia/.

45. Scott Pelley reporting, "Following the Trail of Toxic E-waste," *60 Minutes,* Nov. 6, 2008, updated Aug. 29, 2009, https://www.cbsnews.com/news/following-the-trail-of-toxic-e -waste/. Having seen the rough treatment of the crew of reporters, Brackmann decided not to visit in person. Wasserstrom, "Hour of the Rat."

46. Wasserstrom, "Hour of the Rat." The US fugitive would be Justin Franchi Solondz. See Dan Levin, "China Jails Environmentalist Wanted in U.S.," *New York Times,* Nov. 28, 2009, https://www.nytimes.com/2009/11/28/world/asia/28china.html.

47. Qiu Xiaolong visited some of the sites and he stayed in the former cadre vacation guesthouse in Wuxi where his police inspector lodges in the novel. Email from Qiu Xiaolong, Nov. 27, 2015.

48. Email from Qiu Xiaolong, Nov. 27, 2015.

49. In life, Wu Lihong, after repeated attempts by local officials to buy him off, succumbed and accepted a "pollution cleanup contract." Joseph Kahn, "In China, a Lake's Champion Imperils Himself," *New York Times,* Oct. 14, 2007, https://www.nytimes.com/2007/10/14/world /asia/14china.html.

50. Chai Jing, *Under the Dome,* with English subtitles. 144 min, https://www.youtube .com/watch?v=V5bHb3ljjbc, accessed April 20, 2021. Qiu Xiaolong responded quickly, producing a short-story-length Inspector Chen narrative, "China's Smoke-Smothered Sky," for the July 2015 special issue on global pollution of Duke University's *World Policy Journal.*

51. In the novel, China's fictional petroleum czar, named Kang, falls from power. Cf. Zhou Yongkang, head of the China National Petroleum Corp. (1996–1998). In life, Zhou had already fallen from power in 2013. See also Alex L. Wang, "Contamination: On Qiu Xiaolong's Inspector Chen Mysteries," *Los Angeles Review of Books,* Oct. 8, 2020, https://lareviewofbooks.org /article/contamination-on-qiu-xiaolongs-inspector-chen-mysteries/.

52. Zhang Xinxin, "Wenyi nian jishi" (What I Did in the Year of the Pandemic), unpublished ms.

53. Kinkley, *Chinese Justice,* 199. For stories in English, see Cheng Xiaoqing, *Sherlock in Shanghai.*

54. Especially in Pattison, *The Lord of Death,* Chs. 2 and 3.

55. Imbert, *Pékin de neige et de sang.*

56. West's first and third, See's first, Rotenberg's first and second, and Qiu's second, third, and fourth.

57. Brackmann, *Rock Paper Tiger,* Ch. 30, features a village protest against corrupt officials. Characters from See and Brackmann mention local protests against pollution. Sampson, *The Pool of Unease,* dramatizes Beijing citizen protests against inadequate police protection (122–123, 169).

58. Personal email from Qiu Xiaolong, Nov. 27, 2015.

59. In *The Eye of Jade,* red princess Wang Mei's mother is said to have worked for the MSS before the Cultural Revolution, but that would be a predecessor of the MSS.

60. Brackmann, *Hour of the Rat,* 18, says the operatives have badges saying *Guo Nei Anquan Bao [Bu];* the next page translates this as "Domestic Security Department."

Notes to Pages 78–89   175

61. "Normal" kidnappings occur in Imbert, *Fang Xiao dans la tourmente* (62), and Sendker, *The Far Side of the Night*.

62. Sampson, "China Trembles at the Power of the Blog," *The Independent*, Aug. 6, 2007, https://www.independent.co.uk/news/media/china-trembles-at-the-power-of-the-blog-5334456.html, and "Break the Tiananmen Taboo," *The Guardian*, June 30, 2008, https://www.theguardian.com/commentisfree/2008/jun/30/china.

63. For works written in Chinese about the protests and massacre, see Kong, *Tiananmen Fictions Outside the Square*.

64. Liang, in *Lake with No Name*, 244, recalls her post-massacre change in attitude toward novels about "life and death in the Cultural Revolution": "Personally I did not feel like reading fictionalized political tragedies anymore."

65. Robert Mugabe appears as a positive character in a cameo appearance as president of Zimbabwe.

66. James Rothwell, "Bo Guagua: The Student Playboy Whose Lavish Lifestyle Could Be His Downfall—As Father Bo Xilai Faces Prosecution," *The Independent*, Sept. 10, 2013, https://www.independent.co.uk/student/news/bo-guagua-student-playboy-whose-lavish-lifestyle-could-be-his-downfall-father-bo-xilai-faces-prosecution-8807074.html.

67. Kinkley, *Corruption and Realism in Late Socialist China*.

68. Pattison, *The Skull Mantra*, 219. Also his *Water Touching Stone*, 73–74.

Chapter 4: Actors

1. Erlich, "Russian Formalism," 632, states the position of fellow Russian Formalists: "in the fairy tale, not unlike the detective story, character, usually stereotyped, is no more than a tool."

2. A Yi was in fact influenced by *L'Étranger*. Helen Roxburgh, "*A Perfect Crime* by A Yi," *Time Out Shanghai*, May 20, 2016, https://www.timeoutshanghai.com/features/Books_-Book_features/36237/A-Perfect-Crime-by-A-Yi.html.

3. Not so for PRC novels. On Amazon websites regarding *A Devil's Mind* (which features dismemberment, forensic pathology, and profiling), the author Gangxueyin, a PRC resident, credits Thomas Harris's novels about Lecter "with having made a major impression on him," https://www.amazon.com/Devils-Mind-Gangxueyin/dp/1503937038.

4. In the PRC, Liang Liang has a series about "the stupid detective" and comical Japanese mysteries have been translated into Chinese. On the variety of global police heroes, see Andrew Nestingen, "Crime Fiction and the Police," in Allan et al., eds., *The Routledge Companion to Crime Fiction*, 301–309.

5. May, *The Fourth Sacrifice*, 413. In a new, 2016 "Introduction" to the reissue of his six-volume "China Thriller" series, vol. 1, *The Firemaker*, ix–xviii, May tells of several trips, 1997–2004, when he met with Beijing PSB officers. May mentions the criminologist Richard Ward of the University of Illinois Chicago, who trained 500 Chinese police officers during several years' residence in Shanghai. May previously visited China in 1983 and 1991. Li Yan and Uncle Yifu have biographies fairly close to their models in life.

6. Two agents who threaten to shut down Wang Mei's "information consultancy" business appear to be from the *Chengguan*, there called the municipal "Bureau of Regulation." Liang, *Paper Butterfly*, 174.

176 Notes to Pages 89–102

7. Kinkley, interviewing Qiu Xiaolong, 55.

8. Chen Fang wrote a famous banned novel, *Tian nu* (Heaven's Wrath), about this senior vice mayor, who served Beijing's leader, Chen Xitong. See Kinkley, *Corruption and Realism*, 47–77.

9. Kinkley, interviewing Qiu Xiaolong, 55.

10. As in Stone, *Shanghaied*, 137. Brackmann, *Hour of the Rat*, 124–134.

11. Zhong Fong's ancestors were night soil collectors, but they cornered the market and became "capitalists" in the "old society."

12. Qiu Xiaolong, *Il était une fois l'inspecteur Chen*, 59.

13. There is also a story about him, "Overseas Chinese Lu," in Qiu, *Inspector Chen and Me*, 43–91, and again in *Becoming Inspector Chen*.

14. The major work on Chinese lyricism is David Der-wei Wang, *The Lyrical in Epic Time*. Gish Jen, *Tiger Writing*, discusses "Chinese vs. Western" gestalts of individualism vs. collectivism.

15. A 2012 postscript in Draken, 601, says, "In a Confucian culture, an individual is only as valuable as his role in his family and society."

16. *Paper Butterfly*, 104; *The Eye of Jade*, 211.

17. Diane Wei Liang, Richard Moreland, Linda Argote, "Group Versus Individual Training and Group Performance: The Mediating Role of Transactive Memory," *Personality and Social Psychology Bulletin* 21.4 (April 1, 1995): 384–393. Liang taught at the Carlson School of Management, University of Minnesota.

18. Qiu Xiaolong, *Inspector Chen and the Private Kitchen Murder*, 7–12.

19. Shan unknowingly fathers a daughter in the sixth mystery. He meets her in the tenth; his relation to her is revealed to him only in that novel.

20. *The Lord of Death*, 203.

21. Annabel Gutterman, "An Yu's *Braised Pork* Is an Engrossing Portrait of Isolation," *Time*, April 8, 2020, https://time.com/5817495/an-yu-braised-pork/.

22. Hyland's biography has points of similarity with Rotenberg's, yet even the latter is hard to pin down and I see inconsistencies in interviews and so forth. I prefer to rely on the first novel by itself. From it we learn (109) that China has just stopped issuing Foreign Exchange Certificates; that happened in 1994. *The Shanghai Murders* (32) says Hyland performed the premiere of *The Ecstasy of Rita Joe* in China 11 years earlier than the novel's present time, which would come to 1983 or 1984.

23. In Imbert's *Rouge Karma*, The Weasel (a cop) likes to arrest homosexual and heterosexual lovers he finds making love in parks. A predatory gay man is a villain in Cai Jun's *A Child's Past Life*. Queer readers of the book will not be amused.

24. Ping Zhu and Hui Faye Xiao, eds., *Feminisms with Chinese Characteristics*.

25. Porter, *The Pursuit of Crime*, 125; Knight, *Form and Ideology in Crime Fiction*; Klein, *The Woman Detective*, 223–225; Kinkley, *Chinese Justice*, 12, 99. On feminism and women detectives in fiction, see Klein, *The Woman Detective*; Klein, ed., *Diversity and Detective Fiction*; Johnsen, *Contemporary Feminist Historical Crime Fiction*; Irons, *Feminism in Women's Detective Fiction*; Munt, *Murder by the Book?*; Beyer, ed., *Contemporary Crime Fiction*; Messent, *The Crime Fiction Handbook*, 85–95; and Rzepka and Horsley, eds., *A Companion to Crime Fiction*, 258–269. Horsley, *A Companion to Crime Fiction*, 242–289, summarizes critical reevaluations of interwar whodunits and provides a literary history up through late twentieth-century lesbian crime fiction and "women's noir." See also Gill Plain, "Gender

Notes to Pages 102–115   177

and Sexuality," in Allan et al., eds., *The Routledge Companion,* 102–110. Authors from Christie to the hard-boiled writers are being reinterpreted by some scholars now as socially subversive.

26. Seaman, *Bodies of Evidence;* Kawana, *Murder Most Modern.* Natsuo Kirino is a leading writer.

27. Wu Ye is cited as a woman author of fiction featuring female detectives, https://baike .baidu.com/item/%E5%8D%88%E6%99%94. Also Feng Hua, https://baike.baidu.com/item/% E5%86%AF%E5%8D%8E/4513954.

28. TV cop hits in China in the 1980s were *Hunter* (US) and *Derrick* (West Germany).

29. Elizabeth Ho, "'I Think It's Really about Us,'" *Neo-Victorian Studies* 4.2 (2011): 191–202, http://www.neovictorianstudies.com/past_issues/4-2%202011/NVS%204-2-10%20%20 L-Ho%20Review.pdf. Tammy Lai-Ming Ho, "A Review of Lisa See's *Snow Flower and the Secret Fan,*" *Asiatic* 10.1 (June 2016): 249–250, https://journals.iium.edu.my/asiatic/index.php /ajell/article/view/772. Neurina Fajriyatul Islamiyah and Much Koiri, "Female Subjectivity in Lisa See's *Snow Flower and the Secret Fan,*" *Advances in Social Science, Education and Humanities Research* 108 (2017), https://doi.org/10.2991/sochec-17.2018.27.

30. Magras, "The Ties that Bind," quoting from an interview of See that accompanied the film, posted on June 30, 2011, at https://www.youtube.com/watch?v=txMp1iTTLEM.

31. This is Magras's viewpoint, which I share.

32. Jana Siciliano and Dana Schwartz, "Interview [of Gail Tsukiyama]: September 8, 1999," *Book Reporter,* Sept. 8, 1999, https://www.bookreporter.com/authors/gail-tsukiyama /news/interview-090799.

33. Murphy, *Key Concepts in Contemporary Popular Fiction,* 107–111.

34. Driscoll, 29. The series novel (and the late nineteenth-century and early twentieth-century novel more generally) is linked to female readership in Langbauer, *Novels of Everyday Life.*

35. Wikipedia entry for Ian Hamilton, https://en.wikipedia.org/wiki/Ian_Hamilton _(writer), accessed July 31, 2022. Casey Stepaniuk dissents, in "An Ass-Kicking Sleuthing Heroine Who Needs A Queer Feminist Makeover," July 22, 2013 blog, https://caseythecanadian lesbrarian.com/2013/07/22/an-ass-kicking-sleuthing-heroine-who-needs-a-queer-feminist -makeover-a-review-of-ian-hamiltons-the-wild-beasts-of-wuhan/.

36. Multicultural sleuths in other crime fiction are discussed in Anderson et al., eds., *The Foreign,* 75–149.

37. The same name as the Hong Kong film director. This is strictly humorous.

38. The "Federation's" humorous satiric articles about China by "Professeur Grosçon" (Yung), previously at http://fipep.org/, are no longer available, even at archive.org.

39. Keller Entertainment Group, https://web.archive.org/web/20171013080408/http:// inspectorchen.com/files/Inspector-Chen-n-Me_pp-book_ENG.pdf, captured from Aug. 24, 2018. Anton Diether, Co-Executive Producer; Qiu Xiaolong, Associate Producer; Max Keller, Micheline Keller, and David Joseph Keller, Executive Producers. There may have been plans to do some filming in Shanghai.

40. On Feb. 4, 2021, Zhang posted on Weibo a 2017 Biekan Studio video about such a group, produced by Joshua Frank, for Yishi Yise Wenhua Chuanfan Youxian Gongsi. Zhang says the fansubs were shut down, https://weibo.com/u/1961813155?refer_flag=1005050010_&ssl _rnd=1619395609.2976&is_all=1.

41. Qiu Xiaolong stresses this in his many recent interviews. But I recall Chen Cao's insecurity in the earlier post-Mao period, when Chen was just a rookie.

178   Notes to Pages 117–129

Chapter 5: Retrospection

1. From Jepson, *Emperors Once More,* 142, and May, *The Fourth Sacrifice,* 16, 327, 329ff.

2. Leitch, "The Many Pasts of Detective Fiction," 157, 168–170.

3. These are Imbert's five Judge Li mysteries and the novels by Hiaasen/Montalbano, Bonavia/Uren, the Shlians, and Barckmann.

4. Brooks, "Freud's Masterplot," 285; Shklovsky, *Theory of Prose;* Todorov, "The Typology of Detective Fiction." See also Champigny, *What Will Have Happened,* 4–5; and Sandberg, "Crime Fiction and the Past."

5. C. Hugh Holman, "*Absalom, Absalom!:* The Historian as Detective," *The Sewanee Review* 79.4 (Autumn 1971): 542–553.

6. Winks, in Browne and Kreiser, eds., *The Detective as Historian,* ix–x, apologizes for his previous criticism of the novel, without providing a reference. His list is at http://www.classiccrimefiction.com/winks-recommended-detective-fiction.htm. See also: Nina King, with Robin Winks, *Crimes of the Scene: A Mystery Novel Guide for the International Traveler* (New York: St. Martin's, 1997). Catherine E. Hoyser names a few later novels inspired by Tey, including some written to refute Tey's view of Richard III. See Herbert, ed., *The Oxford Companion,* 209–210; also 207–209. Of further interest is Rush and Winks, eds., *Asia in Western Fiction.*

7. Examples are Wan Zhi, "Open Ground," and Ge Fei, "The Lost Boat." Later and longer works that rewrite official narratives of modern Chinese history are discussed in Kinkley, *Visions of Dystopia in China's New Historical Novels.*

8. Kong, *Tiananmen Fictions,* analyzes works in English by Ha Jin and Annie Wang and works by Gao Xingjian, Ma Jian, and others, translated from the Chinese.

9. They were Wong Yee Man and Wong Siu Fan, https://en.wikipedia.org/wiki/1967_Hong _Kong_riots.

10. In another Imbert mystery, *Lotus et bouches cousues,* Judge Li, in 1982 in a poor, rural district of northwestern Jiangsu, examines the ruins of steel smelters built in the Great Leap Forward. Some bricks are out of place and he finds some bones. The memory of the Leap is an embarrassment to characters in the novel. Ian Hamilton's Ava Lee mysteries also have incidental mentions of the Leap. Nicole Mones's *The Last Chinese Chef* recalls the subsequent famine.

11. At the end of the novel (321), Imbert provides a nonfiction page of historical commentary on the post-Leap famine. He notes that between 30 and 60 million perished.

12. An American Korean War POW imprisoned in China's Northeast told me how he and his campmates discovered the place where their captors were burying their catches of flies. The prisoners dug up and resubmitted previously turned-in flies to meet their daily quotas.

13. Translated from the Chinese: Zhang Xianliang, *Grass Soup* and *My Bodhi Tree.* Williams and Wu, *The Great Wall of Confinement;* Williams and Wu, eds., *Remolding and Resistance;* and Kinkley, *Chinese Justice,* 27, provide analyses.

14. In Imbert's novel, Lin Biao and his wife die by assassination in their limousine, not in a plane crash.

15. Besides the Church of Almighty God or Eastern Lightning, founded in 1991 and active in India by 2020, Wikipedia named eight other noteworthy sects when accessed on Feb. 27, 2021, https://en.wikipedia.org/wiki/Chinese_lists_of_cults#In-state.

Notes to Pages 131–138   179

16. Elmore Leonard, "Writers on Writing; Easy on the Adverbs, Exclamation Points and Especially Hooptedoodle," *New York Times,* July 16, 2001, E-1, https://www.nytimes.com/2001/07/16/arts/writers-writing-easy-adverbs-exclamation-points-especially-hooptedoodle.html. Deborah and Joel Shlian, *Rabbit in the Moon,* also has a short prologue, set in 1949.

17. Anjum, "The Challenge."

18. Prefaces to the first eight chapters, and Ch. 9, are original to *Becoming Inspector Chen.* The rest of the book repeats chapters from *Il était une fois l'inspecteur Chen* and *Inspector Chen and Me,* with revisions.

19. In the novel, Chen Cao realizes he might know a dissident Red Lane creator of a poem titled "Reading *Animal Farm*" (83) that seems to liken China to a pigsty (in 2018, a time of swine flu). He quotes a supreme leader who says "I'm the Emperor, the only one," and likens him to the pig Napoleon (representing Stalin in Orwell's classic). Again, Qiu is riffing on the news. In July 2018, police in Sanya, Hainan, detained a man for referring to Xi Jinping on WeChat as "pig-head Xi" (dimwit Xi). Qiu's novel clarifies that this was generally understood as a meme for Xi (83–84). See Aris Teon, "Chinese Netizen Imprisoned for 10 Days after Insulting Xi Jinping on WeChat," *The Greater China Journal* (repeating Voice of America), Sept. 1, 2018, https://china-journal.org/2018/09/01/chinese-netizen-imprisoned-for-10-days-after-insulting-xi-jinping-on-wechat/, accessed April 20, 2021.

20. Van Gulik finished it in the year of his death, during China's Cultural Revolution. The novel mentions a rebellion and adds, "a number of false accusations were filed—evil people trying to utilize the opportunity for ridding themselves of personal enemies, as often happens in such serious cases with wide ramifications" (119–120).

21. Society—now the internet—calls Min the "Republican Lady" (15–16), invoking ideas of Lin Huiyin (1904–1955). Back-translating *la Dame Républicaine* (35) from the French, I thought of "the Belle of the Republic" and Vivien Leigh's embodiment of the Dixie Belle Scarlett O'Hara and *her* Lost Cause.

22. Kinkley, *Chinese Justice,* 144–145.

23. Furth, *Opening to China;* Murray et al., eds., *China Tripping;* Kin-ming Liu, ed., *My First Trip to China.* Patricia Ebrey is compiling references on the older Sinologist memoirists, such as John K. Fairbank and Fritz Mote.

24. Baker, "Shakespearean Authority in the Classic Detective Story," discusses Shakespearean themes in other detective fiction.

25. Van de Wetering, *Robert van Gulik,* 77, cited in Sheng-mei Ma, "Zen Keytsch," 136.

26. Barckmann's LinkedIn site, https://www.linkedin.com/in/barckmann/. The book cover of the first printing has a photo of the author during his Beijing years.

27. Boym, *The Future of Nostalgia;* Kalinina, "Mediated Post-Soviet Nostalgia"; Horvath, "Faces of Nostalgia." Salmose, "Introduction," in *Contemporary Nostalgia,* 2, lists many recent works. Updating physiological approaches to memory in narrative is Austin, *Nostalgia in Transition.*

28. On Shteyngart, see Friedman, "Nostalgia, Nationhood." In *Inspector Chen and Me,* 74, Qiu Xiaolong speaks of having felt "more and more nostalgic" as he spent his first years in exile from Shanghai, in St. Louis. Ha Jin, *The Writer as Migrant,* 6–12, writes movingly about the dilemma of Solzhenitsyn in exile. "Out of Time: Realms of Chinese Nostalgia," is the theme of *Made in China* 7.1 (2022), http://doi.org/10.22459/MIC.07.01.2022.

29. Elena Baraban, "A Little Nostalgia: The Detective Novels of Alexandra Marinina," *International Fiction Review* 32.1 (2005), https://journals.lib.unb.ca/index.php/IFR/article

180   Notes to Pages 139–145

/view/7802. Written originally in Hungarian, in post-communist Hungary, though set in the 1930s–1950s, are the Budapest Noir novels of Vilmos Kondor, https://crimereads.com/the-mysteries-of-budapest/.

30. Muller, "Notes Toward a Theory of Nostalgia," sees the two kinds of nostalgia as relatively separate.

31. Charles S. Maier, "The End of Longing? Notes toward a History of Postwar German National Longing," in *The Postwar Transformation of Germany: Democracy, Prosperity, and Nationhood,* ed. John S. Brady, Beverly Crawford, and Sarah Elise Wiliarty (Ann Arbor: University of Michigan Press, 1999), 273.

32. Ellipsis as in Boym, *The Future of Nostalgia,* xiv, citing Michael Kammen, *Mystic Chords of Memory: The Transformation of Tradition in American Culture* (New York: Knopf, 1991), 688. See also Scanlon, "Introduction: Nostalgia."

33. Porter, *The Pursuit of Crime,* 125; Knight, *Form and Ideology in Crime Fiction;* Klein, *The Woman Detective,* 223–225; and Kinkley, *Chinese Justice,* 12, 99.

34. Qiu Xiaolong provides some exceptions. In *A Loyal Character Dancer,* 2, Chen Cao is skeptical that the Bund Park in Shanghai really had a sign saying literally "No Chinese or dogs allowed," and from there he muses about "the line between truth and fiction" as it is "always being constructed and deconstructed by those in power." Chen reflects again that the sign, which he learned about in a middle school textbook, may have been apocryphal in *The Mao Case,* 245–246. *Enigma of China,* 203, says, of a temple dedicated to Yu the Great: "In recent years, a number of cities built temples or palaces to attract tourists, making far-fetched claims of connections to legendary figures." Yung, in *Pékin ce n'est pas de la tarte,* 1:9, has some criticism of officially rewritten history, but notes that France has the same problem.

35. Diane Wei Liang, *Lake with No Name,* 4, recalling a crowd lined up to enter the Mao mausoleum during her 1996 return to Tiananmen Square, her first since 1989.

36. Rotenberg provides a profile history of the certificates in *The Shanghai Murders,* 108–109.

37. Scanlon, "Introduction: Nostalgia," 5.

38. May, *The Firemaker,* 2018 edition, xviii.

39. Jo Frances Penn (podcast transcript of talk with L. H. Draken), "Ancient City, Modern Life. Beijing with L H Draken," Oct. 31, 2019, https://www.booksandtravel.page/beijing-draken/.

40. May, *The Firemaker,* 2018 edition, xviii. Working with evidence internal to the novels, I originally deduced that the novels, particularly the early ones, unfold about a year earlier than the dates May provided in 2018, but it would be tedious to argue the point. May visited Beijing in 1997 and 1999, and published his sixth novel in 2004. He published his seventh, shorter mystery, *The Ghost Marriage,* in 2010, with a plot set in that year, by my reckoning.

41. Shan Tao Yun when under stress remembers Daoist fortune-telling his father taught him using chichi sticks, and the poems of Su Dongpo. *The Skull Mantra,* 401, 402; and *The Lord of Death,* 202–203.

42. John Byron website, https://johnbyron.net/books.html.

43. In Qiu's mysteries I see the phrase "materialistic society" 11 times; "materialistic age" (or "new" or "current materialistic age"), 9 times; "materialistic" followed by "transition," "time," "transformation of Shanghai," "world," "temptation," "neighborhood," "waves today," "consideration,"

Notes to Pages 145–147   181

"basis," indeed "century," about 11 times. Depictions of materialistic young women appear about 7 times. These are just passages that literally use the word, "materialistic."

44. A Mao quotation begins each chapter of Klingborg's *Thief of Souls* as an epigraph. The chapters can be read as either exemplifying or negating the cited Maoist principle.

45. David Der-wei Wang, *Why Fiction Matters in Contemporary China*, opens with a reference to Xi Jinping's admonition.

46. Moretti, *Graphs, Maps, Trees*, 17–26.

47. As described by Murphy, *Key Concepts*, and by Walsh, *The Subplot*, respectively.

48. Pepper and Schmid, eds., *Globalization and the State in Contemporary Crime Fiction*.

Bibliography

A Yi [pseud. of Ai Guozhu]. "The Curse." Julia Lovell, tr. *The Guardian*. April 13, 2012. https://www.theguardian.com/books/2012/apr/13/curse-a-yi-story-china.

———. *A Perfect Crime*. Anna Holmwood, tr. London: Oneworld, Point Blank, 2015. Originally pub. in Chinese, as *Mao he laoshu* (Cat and Mouse). Hangzhou: Zhejiang wenyi chubanshe, 2012.

———. *Two Lives: Tales of Life, Love & Crime*. Alex Woodend, tr. London: Flame Tree, 2020.

———. *Wake Me Up at Nine in the Morning*. Nicky Harman, tr. London: Oneworld, 2022. Originally pub. in Chinese, as *Zaoshang jiudian jiaoxing wo*. Nanjing: Yilin chubanshe, 2018.

Ahmad, Aijaz. "Jameson's Rhetoric of Otherness and the 'National Allegory.'" *Social Text* 17 (Autumn 1987): 3–25.

Allan, Janice, Jesper Gulddal, Stewart King, and Andrew Pepper, eds. *The Routledge Companion to Crime Fiction*. Milton Park, UK: Routledge, 2020.

Anderson, Jean, Carolina Miranda, and Barbara Pezzotti, eds. *The Foreign in International Crime Fiction: Transcultural Representations*. London: Continuum, 2012.

———. *Serial Crime Fiction: Dying for More*. Basingstoke, UK: Palgrave Macmillan, 2015.

Andrew, Lucy, and Catherine Phelps. *Crime Fiction in the City: Capital Crimes*. Cardiff: University of Wales Press, 2013.

Anjum, Zafar. "The Challenge Was to Find the Pace and Voice: Duncan Jepson." *Kitaab*, March 1, 2014. https://kitaab.org/2014/03/01/the-challenge-was-to-find-the-pace-and-voice-duncan-jepson/.

Arnote, Ralph. *Fatal Secrets*. New York: Tor, 1994.

———. *Hong Kong, China*. New York: Tor, 1996.

August, Oliver. *Inside the Red Mansion: On the Trail of China's Most Wanted Man*. Boston: Houghton Mifflin, 2007.

Austin, Linda M. *Nostalgia in Transition, 1780–1917*. Charlottesville: University of Virginia Press, 2007.

Baker, Dallas John, Donna Lee Brien, and Jen Webb, eds. *Publishing and Culture*. Newcastle upon Tyne, UK: Cambridge Scholars, 2019.

Baker, Peter, and Deborah Shaller, eds. *Detecting Detection: International Perspectives on the Uses of a Plot*. New York: Continuum, 2012.

Baker, Susan. "Shakespearean Authority in the Classic Detective Story." *Shakespeare Quarterly* 46.4 (Winter 1995): 424–448.

184 Bibliography

Bakhtin, M. [Mikhail] M. *The Dialogic Imagination: Four Essays*. Michael Holquist, ed. Holquist and Caryl Emerson, tr. Rev. ed. Austin: University of Texas Press, 1982 [1981].

Bakken, Børge, ed. *Crime and the Chinese Dream*. Hong Kong: Hong Kong University Press, 2018.

Barckmann, Lee. *Farewell the Dragon*. Bloomington, IN: AuthorHouse, 2007. Rev. ed., Barckwards, 2017–2020.

Baudrillard, Jean. *Simulacra and Simulation*. Sheila Faria Glaser, tr. Ann Arbor: University of Michigan Press, 1994 [French, 1981].

Benedetti, Lavinia. "Killing Di Gong: Rethinking Van Gulik's Translation of Late Qing Dynasty Novel *Wu Zetian Si Da Qi'an*." *Ming Qing Studies 2014*. Paolo Santangelo, ed. Rome: Aracne, 2014.

Beyer, Charlotte, ed. *Contemporary Crime Fiction: Crossing Boundaries, Merging Genres*. Newcastle upon Tyne, UK: Cambridge Scholars, 2021.

Bhabha, Homi K. *The Location of Culture*. 2nd ed. New York: Routledge, 2004 [1994].

Bonavia, David. *The Chinese*. London: Penguin, 1980, 1982. Posthumously published rev. ed., 1989.

Bonavia, David, and John Byron [pseud. of Roger Uren]. *The China Lovers*. Hong Kong: South China Morning Post, 1985.

Bonnett, Alastair. *The Geography of Nostalgia: Global and Local Perspectives on Modernity and Loss*. Milton Park, UK: Routledge, 2016.

Bourdieu, Pierre. *The Field of Cultural Production*. Randal Johnson, ed. and intro. New York: Columbia University Press, 1993.

Boym, Svetlana. *The Future of Nostalgia*. New York: Basic Books, 2001.

Brackmann, Lisa. *Dragon Day*. New York: Soho, 2015.

———. *Hour of the Rat*. New York: Soho, 2013.

———. *Rock, Paper, Tiger*. New York: Soho, 2010.

Brookes, Adam. *Night Heron*. New York: Redhook, 2014.

Brooks, Peter. "Freud's Masterplot." *Yale French Studies* 55/56 (1977): 280–300.

Browne, Ray B., and Lawrence A. Kreiser, Jr., eds. *The Detective as Historian: History and Art in Historical Crime Fiction*. Bowling Green, OH: Bowling Green State University Popular Press, 2000.

Byron, Jennifer, and Enrico Minardi, eds. *Out of Deadlock: Female Emancipation in Sara Paretsky's V. I. Warshawski Novels, and Her Influence on Contemporary Crime Fiction*. Newcastle upon Tyne, UK: Cambridge Scholars, 2015.

Cai, Jiaying. "Qiu Xiaolong and Linda Fairstein: Representations of Crime Sites in Shanghai and New York." In Evans and White, eds., 77–89.

Cai Jun. *The Child's Past Life*. Yuzhi Yang, tr. Seattle: Amazon Crossing, 2014. Originally pub. in Chinese, as *Sheng si he* (lit., "River between Life and Death"). Beijing: Beijing lianhe chuban gongsi, 2013.

Carroll, Noël. *A Philosophy of Mass Art*. Oxford: Oxford University Press, 1998.

Cawelti, John G. "Canonization, Modern Literature, and the Detective Story." In Jerome H. Delamater and Ruth Prigozy, eds., *Theory and Practice of Classic Detective Fiction*, 5–16. Westport, CT: Greenwood, 1997.

Bibliography   185

Champigny, Robert. *What Will Have Happened: A Philosophical and Technical Essay on Mystery Stories*. Bloomington: Indiana University Press, 1977.

Chan, Jenny, Mark Selden, and Pun Ngai. *Dying for an iPhone: Apple, Foxconn, and the Lives of China's Workers*. Chicago: Haymarket Books, 2020.

Chan Ho-Kei. *The Borrowed*. Jeremy Tiang, tr. New York: Grove Atlantic, Black Cat, 2017 [2016]. Originally pub. in Chinese, as *Yisan · liuqi* (2013 · 1967; lit., "13 · 67"). Taipei: Huangguan, 2014.

———. *Second Sister*. Jeremy Tiang, tr. New York: Grove Atlantic, Black Cat, 2020. Originally pub. in Chinese, as *Wangneiren* (Woman in the Web). Taipei: Huangguan, 2017.

Chandra, Elizabeth. "The Chinese Holmes: Translating Detective Fiction in Colonial Indonesia." *Keio Communication Review* 38 (2016): 39–63. https://www.mediacom .keio.ac.jp/wp/wp-content/uploads/2016/03/03_Elizabeth.pdf.

Chen, Jack W., Anatoly Detwyler, Christopher M. B. Nugent, Xiao Liu, and Bruce Rusk, eds. *Literary Information in China: A History*. New York: Columbia University Press, 2021.

Chen Qiufan. *Waste Tide*. Ken Liu, tr. New York: Tor, 2019. Originally pub. in Chinese, as *Huangchao*. Wuhan: Changjiang wenyi chubanshe, 2013.

Cheng, Nien [pseud. of Yao Nianyuan]. *Life and Death in Shanghai*. New York: Grove, 1986.

Cheng Xiaoqing. *Sherlock in Shanghai: Stories of Crime and Detection by Cheng Xiaoqing*. Timothy C. Wong, tr. Honolulu: University of Hawai'i Press, 2006.

Christian, Ed, ed. *The Post-Colonial Detective*. Basingstoke, Hampshire, UK: Palgrave, 2001.

Chu, Yingchi. "The Politics of Reception: 'Made in China' and Western Critique." *International Journal of Cultural Studies* 17.2 (2014): 159–173.

Church, James. *A Drop of Chinese Blood*. New York: Minotaur, 2012.

Clancy, Tom. *The Hunt for Red October*. Annapolis, MD: Naval Institute Press, 1984.

Clancy, Tom, with Mark Greaney. *Threat Vector*. New York: Berkley, 2013 [2012].

Close, Glen S. *Female Corpses in Crime Fiction: A Transatlantic Perspective*. Cham, Switzerland: Palgrave Macmillan, 2018.

Cumming, Charles. *Typhoon*. New York: St. Martin's Griffin, 2011 [2008].

Daley, Robert. *Year of the Dragon*. New York: Simon & Schuster, 1981.

Damrosch, David. "A Sinister Chuckle: Sherlock Holmes in Tibet." In Nilsson, Damrosch, and D'haen, eds., 257–270.

———. *What Is World Literature?* Princeton, NJ: Princeton University Press, 2018 [2003].

Damrosch, David, and Gayatri Chakravorti Spivak. "Comparative Literature/World Literature." *Comparative Literature Studies* 48.4 (2011): 455–485.

De Voe, P. [Pamela] A. *Deadly Relations: A Ming Dynasty Mystery*. St. Louis, MO: Drum Tower Press, 2018.

———. *Judge Lu's Case Files*. St. Louis, MO: Drum Tower Press, 2020.

———. *No Way to Die: A Ming Dynasty Mystery*. St. Louis, MO: Drum Tower Press, 2020.

Deaver, Jeffery. *The Stone Monkey*. New York: Simon & Schuster, 2002.

186 Bibliography

Detwyler, Anatoly. "The Aesthetics of Information in Modern Chinese Literary Culture, 1919–1949." PhD diss., Columbia University, 2015.

D'haen, Theo, David Damrosch, and Djelal Kadir, eds. *The Routledge Companion to World Literature*. London: Routledge, 2012.

Dobrescu, Caius. "Identity, Otherness, Crime: Detective Fiction and Interethnic Hazards." *Acta Universitatis Sapientiae, Philologica* 5.1 (2013): 43–58. https://doi.org/10.2478/ausp-2014-0004.

Draken, L. [Lauren] H. *The Months of the Toxic Rat*. München: Graubär, 2019.

———. *The Year of the Rabid Dragon*. München: Graubär, 2018.

Driscoll, Beth. *The New Literary Middlebrow: Tastemakers and Reading in the Twenty-First Century*. Basingstoke, UK: Palgrave Macmillan, 2014.

Eisler, Barry. *Graveyard of Memories*. Grand Haven, MI: Brilliance Audio, 2014.

Elias, Urszula, and Agnieszka Sienkiewicz-Charlish, eds. *Crime Scenes: Modern Crime Fiction in an International Context*. Frankfurt am Main: Peter Lang, 2014.

Erdmann, Eva. "Nationality International: Detective Fiction in the Late Twentieth Century." Fiona Fincannon, tr. In Krajenbrink and Quinn, eds., *Investigating Identities: Questions of Identity in Contemporary Crime Fiction*, 11–27.

Erlich, Victor. "Russian Formalism." *Journal of the History of Ideas* 34.4 (Oct.–Dec. 1973): 627–638.

Evans, Lucy, and Mandala White. *Crime across Cultures*. [Themed edition of] *Moving Worlds* 13.1 (2013). Leeds: University of Leeds.

Fischer-Hornung, Dorothea, and Monika Mueller, eds. *Sleuthing Ethnicity: The Detective in Multiethnic Crime Fiction*. Madison, NJ: Fairleigh Dickinson University Press, 2003.

Flint, Shamini. *Inspector Singh Investigates: A Calamitous Chinese Killing*. London: Piatkus, 2013.

Forsdick, Charles. "Travelling Concepts: Postcolonial Approaches to Exoticism." *Paragraph* 24.3 (Nov. 2001): 12–29.

French, Paul. *City of Devils*. New York: Picador, 2018.

———. *Midnight in Peking*. New York: Penguin, 2012 [2011].

Friedman, Natalie. "Nostalgia, Nationhood, and the New Immigrant Narrative: Gary Shteyngart's *The Russian Debutante's Handbook* and the Post-Soviet Experience." *Iowa Journal of Cultural Studies* 5 (Fall 2004): 77–87.

Frye, Northrop. *Anatomy of Criticism: Four Essays*. Princeton, NJ: Princeton University Press, 1957.

Furth, Charlotte. *Opening to China: A Memoir of Normalization, 1981–1982*. Amherst, NY: Cambria, 2017.

Gangxueyin [Gang Xueyin]. *A Devil's Mind*. George A. Fowler, tr. Seattle: Amazon Crossing, 2016. Originally pub. in Chinese, as *Fanzui xinli dang'an* (Case Files in Criminal Psychology). Beijing: Beijing xiandai chubanshe, 2013.

Gans, Herbert J. *Popular Culture and High Culture*. Rev. ed. New York: Basic Books, 2008 [1974].

Gapper, John. *The Ghost Shift*. New York: Ballantine, 2015.

Bibliography   187

Ge Fei [pseud. of Liu Yong]. "The Lost Boat." Caroline Mason, tr. In Henry Y. H. Zhao, ed., *The Lost Boat: Avant-garde Fiction from China*, 77–100. London: Wellsweep, 1993. Originally pub. in Chinese, as "Mizhou." *Shouhuo* 1987, no. 6.

Gelder, Ken. *Popular Fiction: The Logics and Practices of a Literary Field*. New York: Routledge, 2004.

Gelder, Ken, ed. *New Directions in Popular Fiction: Genre, Distribution, Reproduction*. Basingstoke, UK: Palgrave Macmillan, 2016.

Goldberg, Lee. *Killer Thriller*. Seattle: Thomas & Mercer, 2019.

Gulddal, Jesper, Stewart King, and Alistair Rolls, eds. *The Cambridge Companion to World Crime Fiction*. Cambridge, UK: Cambridge University Press, 2022.

———. *Criminal Moves: Modes of Mobility in Crime Fiction*. Liverpool: Liverpool University Press, 2019.

Hamilton, Ian. *The Goddess of Yantai*. Toronto: Anansi, 2018.

———. *The King of Shanghai*. Toronto: Anansi, 2014.

———. *The Princeling of Nanjing*. Toronto: Anansi, 2015.

———. *The Wild Beasts of Wuhan*. New York: Picador, 2012.

Hao, Sabrina Yuan. "Transcending Cultural Boundaries: Robert van Gulik's Judge Dee Detective Stories." *Canadian Review of Comparative Literature* 43.4 (Dec. 2016): 551–567. https://doi.org/10.1353/crc.2016.0041.

Hart, Elsa. *Jade Dragon Mountain*. New York: Minotaur, 2015.

Hausladen, Gary. *Places for Dead Bodies*. Austin: University of Texas Press, 2000.

Haycraft, Howard, ed. *The Art of the Mystery Story*. New York: Grosset & Dunlap, 1946.

He Jiahong. *Fengnü* (Madwoman), 1995; retitled *Xue zhi zui* (Blood Crime); retitled *Rensheng qingyuan: Shuang xuexing ren* (Psychological Depths of Humankind: The Man with Two Blood Types), 2007. In French, *Crime de sang* (Blood Crime). Marie-Claude Cantournet-Jacquet and Xiaomin Giafferri-Huang, tr. La Tour-d'Aigues: L'Aube, 2005. In English, *Hanging Devils: Hong Jun Investigates*. Duncan Hewitt, tr. New York: Penguin Viking, 2012.

———. *Longyanshi zhi mi* (The Mystery of the Dragon's Eye Stone), 1995. Retitled *Rensheng wuqu: Longyanshi zhi mi* (Misconceptions of Humankind: The Mystery of the Dragon's Eye Stone). In French, *L'énigme de la pierre Œil-de-Dragon* (The Mystery of the Dragon's Eye Stone). Marie-Claude Cantournet-Jacquet and Xiaomin Giafferri-Huang, tr. La Tour-d'Aigues: L'Aube, 2003.

———. *Rensheng xialu: Heibianfu, baibianfu* (The Narrow Path of Humankind: Black Bat, White Bat), n.d. [2007 or earlier].

———. *Shenmi de guhua* (The Mysterious Ancient Painting), 1997. Retitled *Rensheng guaiquan: Shenmi de guhua* (An Abnormality of Humankind: The Mysterious Ancient Painting). Retitled *Wuzui tanguan* (The Unpunished Corrupt Official). In French, *Le mystérieux tableau ancient* (The Mysterious Ancient Painting). Marie-Claude Cantournet-Jacquet and Xiaomin Giafferri-Huang, tr. La Tour-d'Aigues: L'Aube, 2002.

———. *Wuzui mousha* (The Unpunished Murder), 1998? In French, *Crime impuni aux monts Wuyi* (The Unpunished Crime in the Wuyi Mountains). Marie-Claude Cantournet-Jacquet, tr. La Tour-d'Aigues: L'Aube, 2013.

188 Bibliography

———. *X zhi zui* (X Crime). 2nd ed., rev. Beijing: Zhongguo Renmin Daxue chubanshe, 2012 [1996?].

———. *Xing zhi zui* (Sex Crime). Retitled *Rensheng heidong: Gushi muhou de zui'e* (Black Holes of Humankind: Crimes of the Stock Market). In French, *Crimes et délits à la Bourse de Pékin* (Crimes and Misdemeanors at the Beijing Stock Market). Marie-Claude Cantournet-Jacquet and Xiaomin Giafferri-Huang, tr. La Tour-d'Aigues: L'Aube, 2005. In English, *Black Holes*. Emily Jones, tr. New York: Penguin Viking, 2014.

Hellgren, Per. *Swedish Marxist Noir: The Dark Wave of Crime Writers and the Influence of Raymond Chandler*. Jefferson, NC: McFarland, 2018.

Herbert, Rosemary, ed. *The Oxford Companion to Crime and Mystery Writing*. Oxford: Oxford University Press, 1999.

Hiaasen, Carl, and Bill [William D.] Montalbano. *A Death in China*. New York: Vintage Crime, 1998 [1984].

Higashino, Keigo. *The Devotion of Suspect X: A Detective Galileo Novel*. Alexander O. Smith, tr. New York: Minotaur, 2012.

Hillenbrand, Margaret. *Negative Exposures: Knowing What Not to Know in Contemporary China*. Durham, NC: Duke University Press, 2020.

Ho, Jennifer Ann. *Understanding Gish Jen*. Columbia: University of South Carolina Press, 2015.

Horsley, Lee. *Twentieth-Century Crime Fiction*. Oxford: Oxford University Press, 2005.

Horvath, Gizela. "Faces of Nostalgia: Restorative and Reflective Nostalgia in the Fine Arts." Jednak Książki. Gdańskie Czasopismo Humanistyczne (April 2018). https://doi.org/10.26881/jk.2018.9.13.

Howell, Phillip. "Crime and the City Solution: Crime Fiction, Urban Knowledge, and Radical Geography." *Antipode* 30.4 (1998): 357–378.

Hsia, C. T. "The Scholar-novelist and Chinese Culture: A Reappraisal of *Ching-hua yuan*." In Andrew H. Plaks, ed., *Chinese Narrative: Critical and Theoretical Essays*, 266–305. Princeton, NJ: Princeton University Press, 1977.

Huang, Yunte. *Charlie Chan: The Untold Story of the Honorable Detective and His Rendezvous with American History*. New York: W. W. Norton, 2011.

———. "Robert Hans van Gulik and the Reinvention of Chinese Detective Fiction." In Zong-qi Cai and Stephen Roddy, eds., *The Western Reinvention of Chinese Literature, 1910–2010: From Ezra Pound to Maxine Hong Kingston*, 114–138. Leiden: Brill, 2022.

Huang Wenrui ("Wenrui Terry: H"). *Xiaoshi de Boluoke* ("Chasing Pollock," as translated on the cover). New Taipei: INK, 2020; Shanghai: Huadong Shifan Daxue chubanshe, 2020.

Hutcheon, Linda. "Irony, Nostalgia, and the Postmodern." In *Methods for the Study of Literature as Cultural Memory*. Raymond Vervliet and Annemarie Estor, eds., 189–207. Atlanta, GA: Rodopi, 2000.

Hutcheon, Linda, and Mario Valdés. "Irony, Nostalgia, and the Postmodern: A Dialogue." 2000. http://revistas.unam.mx/index.php/poligrafias/article/viewFile/31312/28976%20.

Bibliography 189

Huyssen, Andreas. *Present Pasts: Urban Palimpsests and the Politics of Memory*. Stanford, CA: Stanford University Press, 2003.

Idema, Wilt L. *Judge Bao and the Rule of Law: Eight Ballad-Stories from the Period 1250–1450*. Singapore: World Scientific, 2010.

Iles, Greg. *Cemetery Road*. New York: William Morrow, 2019.

Imbert, Michel [pseud. Mi Jianxiu]. *Bleu Pékin* (Beijing Blue). La Tour-d'Aigues: L'Aube, 2007.

—— [Mi Jianxiu]. *La diplomatie du panda* (Panda Diplomacy). La Tour-d'Aigues: L'Aube noire, 2019.

——. *Les disparus du laogaï* (The Disappeared of the *Laogai*). Paris: Rouergue, 2010.

—— [Mi Jianxiu]. *Fang Xiao dans la tourmente* (Fang Xiao in Turmoil). La Tour-d'Aigues: L'Aube noire, 2016.

—— [Mi Jianxiu]. *Jaune camion* (Yellow Truck). La Tour-d'Aigues: L'Aube noire, 2004.

—— [Mi Jianxiu]. *Lotus et bouches cousues* (Keep It on the Down-Liu). La Tour-d'Aigues: L'Aube, 2009.

——. *Marche rouge montagnes blanches* (Red March, White Mountains). Arles: Picquier, 2015.

—— [Mi Jianxiu]. *La Mort en comprimés* (Death in Capsule). La Tour-d'Aigues: L'Aube, 2008.

—— [Mi Jianxiu]. *Pékin de neige et de sang* (Beijing in Snow and Blood). Arles: Picquier, 2018.

——. *En revenant de Tiananmen* (Back from Tiananmen). Arles: Picquier, 2013.

—— [Mi Jianxiu]. *Rouge Karma* (Red Karma). La Tour-d'Aigues: L'Aube, 2005.

Inamura Bungo, tr. *Gendai Kabun suiri shiretsu* (Modern Chinese Language Detective Series). 3 vols. N.p.: Kindle edition, 2015, 2016.

Irons, Glenwood H. *Feminism in Women's Detective Fiction*. Toronto: University of Toronto Press, 1995.

Jameson, Fredric. *Raymond Chandler: The Detections of Totality*. New York: Verso, 2016.

——. "Third-World Literature in the Era of Multinational Capitalism." *Social Text* 15 (Autumn 1986): 65–88.

Jen, Gish. *Tiger Writing*. Cambridge, MA: Harvard University Press, 2013.

Jepson, Duncan. *Emperors Once More*. New York: Quercus, 2014.

Jia Pingwa. *Broken Wings*. Nicky Harman, tr. London: Alain Charles Asia, 2019. Originally pub. in Chinese, as *Jihua* (Nonesuch Flower), 2016.

Jin, Ha. *The Crazed*. New York: Vintage, 2002.

——. *The Writer as Migrant*. Chicago: University of Chicago Press, 2008.

Johnsen, Rosemary Erickson. *Contemporary Feminist Historical Crime Fiction*. London: Palgrave Macmillan, 2006.

Julien, Eileen. "The Extroverted African Novel, Revisited: African Novels at Home, In the World." *Journal of African Cultural Studies* 30.3 (2018): 371–381.

Kalinina, Ekaterina. "Mediated Post-Soviet Nostalgia." PhD diss., Södertörn University, Huddinge, Sweden, 2014.

Kawana, Sari. *Murder Most Modern: Detective Fiction and Japanese Culture*. Minneapolis: University of Minnesota Press, 2008.

190 Bibliography

Keefe, Patrick Raden. *The Snakehead: An Epic Tale of the Chinatown Underworld and the American Dream*. New York: Anchor, 2010.

Kelly, R. Gordon. *Mystery Fiction and Modern Life*. Jackson: University Press of Mississippi, 1998.

King, Stewart. "Crime Fiction as World Literature." *Clues: A Journal of Detection* 32.2 (Sept. 2014): 8–19.

———. "Place" (Chapter 23). In Allan et al., eds., *The Routledge Companion to Crime Fiction*, 211–218.

———. "The Reader and World Crime Fiction: The (Private) Eye of the Beholder." In Gulddal et al., eds., *Criminal Moves*, 195–210.

Kinkley, Jeffrey C. *Chinese Justice, the Fiction: Law and Literature in Modern China*. Stanford, CA: Stanford University Press, 2000.

———. *Corruption and Realism in Late Socialist China: The Return of the Political Novel*. Stanford, CA: Stanford University Press, 2007.

———. "The Cultural Choices of Zhang Xinxin, a Young Writer of the 1980s." In Paul A. Cohen and Merle Goldman, eds., *Ideas Across Cultures: Essays on Chinese Thought in Honor of Benjamin I. Schwartz*, 137–162. Cambridge, MA: Council on East Asian Studies, Harvard University, 1990.

———, interviewing Qiu Xiaolong. "Qiu Xiaolong." *Mystery Scene* 72 (2001): 54–57.

———. *Visions of Dystopia in China's New Historical Novels*. New York: Columbia University Press, 2015.

Kinkley, Jeffrey C., ed. *After Mao: Chinese Literature and Society 1978–1981*. Cambridge, MA: Council on East Asian Studies, Harvard University, 1985.

Kjeldsen, Kirk. *East*. N. p.: Grenzland, 2019.

———. *Tomorrow City*. Hong Kong: Signal 8, Typhoon Media, 2013.

Klein, Kathleen Gregory. *The Woman Detective: Gender and Genre*. 2nd ed. Urbana: University of Illinois Press, 1996 [1988].

Klein, Kathleen Gregory, ed. *Diversity and Detective Fiction*. Bowling Green, OH: Bowling Green State University Popular Press, 1999.

Klingborg, Brian. *Thief of Souls*. New York: Minotaur, 2021. UK title, *City of Ice*. London: Headline, 2021.

———. *Wild Prey*. New York: Minotaur, 2022.

Knight, Stephen. *Form and Ideology in Crime Fiction*. Bloomington: Indiana University Press, 1980.

Kong, Belinda. *Tiananmen Fictions Outside the Square: The Chinese Literary Diaspora and the Politics of Global Culture*. Philadelphia: Temple University Press, 2012.

Koontz, Dean. *The Eyes of Darkness*. London: Headline, 2016 [New York: Simon & Schuster, 1981].

Krajenbrink, Marieke, and Kate M. Quinn, eds. *Investigating Identities: Questions of Identity in Contemporary Crime Fiction*. Amsterdam: Rodopi, 2009.

Küng, Dinah Lee. *The End of May Road*. Rev. ed. New York: Eyes and Ears, 2011. Originally pub. as *Left in the Care of: A Novel of Suspense*. New York: Carroll & Graf, 1997.

———. *The Shadows of Shigatse*. New York: Eyes and Ears, 2011.

———. *A Visit from Voltaire*. London: Halban, 2003.

Bibliography   191

———. *The Wardens of Punyu*. New York: Eyes and Ears, 2011.

Kynge, James. *China Shakes the World: A Titan's Rise and Troubled Future—and the Challenge for America*. Boston: Houghton Mifflin Harcourt, 2006.

Langbauer, Laurie. *Novels of Everyday Life: The Series in English Fiction, 1850–1930*. Ithaca, NY: Cornell University Press, 1999.

Leather, Stephen. *The Chinaman*, paired with *The Hungry Ghost*. London: Hodder & Stoughton, 1992.

Lee, Leo Ou-fan. *Dongfang lieshou* (The Hunter of the East). Taipei: Maitian, 2001.

Lei, Mi (Chinese name Lei Mi). *Profiler*. Gabriel Ascher, tr. Beijing: Beijing Digital Technology Co., 2013. Originally pub. in Chinese, as *Xinlizui: Huaxiang* (Psycho Crimes: Profiles). Chongqing: Chongqing chubanshe, 2012.

Leitch, Thomas. "The Many Pasts of Detective Fiction." *Crime Fiction Studies* 1.2 (Sept. 2020): 157–172.

Lenormand, Frédéric. *Mort dans un champ de lotus: Une nouvelle enquête du juge Ti* (Death in a Lotus Field: A New Investigation by Judge Dee). N.p.: CreateSpace, 2018.

Leon, Donna. *Death at La Fenice*. New York: Harper, 2004 [1992; the first Commissario Guido Brunetti Mystery].

Leung, Laifong. *Contemporary Chinese Fiction Writers: Biography, Bibliography, and Critical Assessment*. New York: Routledge, 2016.

Li, Cheng. "Was the Shanghai Gang Shanghaied? The Fall of Chen Liangyu and the Survival of Jiang Zemin's Faction." *China Leadership Monitor* 20, n.d. [2007?]. https://www.hoover.org/sites/default/files/uploads/documents/clm20cl.pdf. Accessed June 18, 2020.

Li Zhisui. *The Private Life of Chairman Mao: The Memoirs of Mao's Private Physician*. New York: Random House, 1994.

Liang, Diane Wei. *The Eye of Jade*. New York: Simon & Schuster, 2009 [2008].

———. *The House of Golden Spirit*. Unavailable in English. Pub. in Spanish as *La Casa del Espíritu Dorado*. Lola Diez, tr. Madrid: Siruela, 2011.

———. *Lake with No Name*. New York: Simon & Schuster, 2009 [2008, 2003]. The new edition has a Nov. 2008 "Introduction."

———. *Paper Butterfly*. New York: Simon & Schuster, 2010 [2008].

Liang Liang. *Ba ziji tuili cheng xiongshou de ming zhentan* (The Famous Detective Who Took Himself to Be the Murderer). Wuhan: Changjiang wenyi chubanshe, 2015.

Lin, Francie. *The Foreigner*. New York: Picador, 2008.

Link, Perry. *The Uses of Literature: Life in the Socialist Chinese Literary System*. Princeton, NJ: Princeton University Press, 2000.

Liu, Kin-ming, ed. *My First Trip to China: Scholars, Journalists and Diplomats Reflect on Their First Encounters with China*. Hong Kong: Hong Kong University Press, 2012.

Liu Cixin. *The Three-Body Problem*. Ken Liu, tr. New York: Tor, 2014.

Liu Zhenyun. *The Cook, the Crook, and the Real Estate Tycoon*. Howard Goldblatt and Sylvia Li-chun Lin, tr. New York: Arcade, 2015. Originally pub. in Chinese, as *Wo jiao Liu Yuejin* (My Name Is Liu Yuejin). Wuhan: Changjiang wenyi chubanshe, 2007.

192 Bibliography

———. *I Did Not Kill My Husband: A Novel*. Howard Goldblatt and Sylvia Li-chun Lin, tr. New York: Arcade, 2016. Originally pub. in Chinese, as *Wo bu shi Pan Jinlian* (I Am Not Pan Jinlian). Wuhan: Changjiang wenyi chubanshe, 2012.

———. *Strange Bedfellows*. Howard Goldblatt and Sylvia Li-chun Lin, tr. New York: Cambria, 2021. Originally pub. in Chinese, as *Chigua shidai de ernümen* (The Watermelon-Eating Generation). Wuhan: Changjiang wenyi chubanshe, 2017.

Lu Hsun [Lu Xun, pseud. of Zhou Shuren]. *A Brief History of Chinese Fiction*. Yang Hsien-yi and Gladys Yang, tr. Peking: Foreign Languages Press, 1964 [1959; Chinese, 1923–1924, single volume 1925].

Ludlum, Robert. *The Bourne Supremacy*. New York: Random House, 1986.

Luo Hui. "Shanghai, Shanghai: Placing Qiu Xiaolong's Crime Fiction in the Landscape of Globalized Literature." In Anderson et al., eds., *The Foreign in International Crime Fiction*, 47–59.

Ma, Sheng-mei. "Zen Keytsch: Mystery Handymen with Dragon Tattoos." In Baker and Shaller, eds., 115–138.

Ma Xiaoquan. *Confession d'un tueur à gages* (Confession of a Hitman). Marie-Claude Cantournet-Jacquet, tr. Paris: Points, 2013.

Magagnin, Paolo. "Qiu Xiaolong's *Death of a Red Heroine* in Chinese Translation: A Macro-Polysystemic Analysis." *Annali di Ca' Foscari, Serie orientale* 51 (June 2015): 95–108. https://edizionicafoscari.unive.it/it/edizioni/riviste/annali-di-ca-foscari-serie-orientale/2015/1/qiu-xiaolongs-death-of-a-red-heroine-in-chinese-tr/.

Magras, Michael. "The Ties that Bind: Lisa See's China Dolls." *Los Angeles Review of Books*, June 16, 2014. https://lareviewofbooks.org/article/ties-bind-lisa-sees-china-dolls/.

Mai Jia. *Decoded*. Olivia Milburn and Christopher Payne, tr. New York: Farrar, Straus and Giroux, 2014. Originally pub. in Chinese, as *Jie mi*. Beijing: Zhongguo qingnian chubanshe, 2012.

Mankell, Henning. *The Man from Beijing*. Laurie Thompson, tr. New York: Vintage Crime/Black Lizard, 2011. Originally pub. in Swedish, as *Kinesen* (Chinese). Stockholm: Leopard, 2008.

Marshall, William. *Yellowthread Street*. London: Futura, 1988 [1975].

Mason, Paul. *Rare Earth*. Harpenden, Hertfordshire, UK: No Exit, 2012.

Matzke, Christine, and Susanne Mühleisen, eds. *Postcolonial Postmortems: Crime Fiction from a Transcultural Perspective*. Leiden: Brill, 2006.

May, Peter. *Chinese Whispers*. London: Riverrun, 2017 [2004].

———. *The Firemaker*. London: Quercus, 2016 [1999].

———. *The Fourth Sacrifice*. London: Riverrun, 2016 [2000].

———. *The Ghost Marriage*. London: Riverrun, 2017 [2010] (bound with *Chinese Whispers*).

———. *The Killing Room*. London: Riverrun, 2016 [2001].

———. *The Runner*. London: Riverrun, 2017 [2003].

———. *Snakehead*. London: Riverrun, 2017 [2002].

McMahon, R. Keith. "A Case for Confucian Sexuality: The Eighteenth-Century Novel *Yesou Puyan*." *Late Imperial China* 9.2 (Dec. 1988): 32–55. https://kuscholarworks.ku.edu/bitstream/handle/1808/16335/McMahon_3.pdf.

Bibliography 193

Messent, Peter. *The Crime Fiction Handbook.* Chichester, UK: Wiley-Blackwell, 2013.

Michie, David. *The Magician of Lhasa: A Matt Lester Spiritual Thriller.* Perth: Conch, 2020 [2010].

Mizejewski, Linda. *Hardboiled & High Heeled: The Woman Detective in Popular Culture.* New York: Routledge, 2004.

Mo Yan. *The Republic of Wine.* Howard Goldblatt, tr. New York: Arcade, 2000. Originally pub. in Chinese, as *Jiu guo.* Taipei: Hongfan, 1992.

Mok, Olivia Wai Han. "Martial Arts Fiction: Translational Migrations East and West." PhD diss., University of Warwick, UK, 1998.

Mones, Nicole. *A Cup of Light.* New York: Delacorte, 2002.

———. *The Last Chinese Chef.* Boston: Houghton Mifflin, 2007.

———. *Lost in Translation.* New York: Delacorte, 1998.

———. *Night in Shanghai.* Boston: Houghton Mifflin, 2014.

Moretti, Franco. *Graphs, Maps, Trees: Abstract Models for a Literary History.* London: Verso, 2005.

Mukherjee, Upamanyu Pablo. *Crime and Empire: The Colony in Nineteenth-Century Fictions of Crime.* Oxford: Oxford University Press, 2003.

Muller, Adam. "Notes Toward a Theory of Nostalgia: Childhood and the Evocation of the Past in Two European 'Heritage' Films." *New Literary History* 37.4 (Autumn 2006): 739–760.

Munt, Sally R. "Grief, Doubt and Nostalgia in Detective Fiction or . . . 'Death and the Detective Novel': A Return." *College Literature* 25.3 (Fall 1998): 133–144.

———. *Murder by the Book?: Feminism and the Crime Novel.* London: Routledge, 1994.

Murong [Murong Xuecun; pseud. of Hao Qun]. *Dancing Through Red Dust.* Harvey Thomlinson, tr. London: Make-Do, 2015. Originally pub. in Chinese, as "Yuanliang wo hongchen diandao." Zhuhai: Zhuhai chubanshe, 2008.

Murphy, Bernice M. *Key Concepts in Contemporary Popular Fiction.* Edinburgh: Edinburgh University Press, 2017.

Murphy, Bernice M., and Stephen Matterson, eds. *Twenty-First Century Popular Fiction.* Edinburgh: Edinburgh University Press, 2018.

Murray, Jeremy A., Perry Link, and Paul G. Pickowicz, eds. *China Tripping: Encountering the Everyday in the People's Republic.* Lanham, MD: Rowman & Littlefield, 2019.

Needham, Jake. *The Big Mango.* Bangkok: Asia Books, 1999.

Nieh, Daniel. *Beijing Payback.* New York: Ecco, 2019.

———. *Take No Names.* New York: Ecco, 2022.

Nilsson, Louise, David Damrosch, and Theo D'haen, eds. *Crime Fiction as World Literature.* New York: Bloomsbury Academic, 2017.

Norbu, Jamyang. *The Mandala of Sherlock Holmes.* New York: Bloomsbury USA, 2003 [1999].

O'Hearn, Claudine Chiawei, ed. *Half and Half: Writers on Growing Up Biracial and Bicultural.* New York: Pantheon, 1998.

Pattison, Eliot. *Beautiful Ghosts.* New York: Minotaur, 2004.

———. *Bone Mountain.* New York: Minotaur, 2004 [2002].

———. *Bones of the Earth.* New York: Minotaur, 2019.

194   Bibliography

———. *The Lord of Death*. New York: Soho, 2009.

———. *Mandarin Gate*. New York: Minotaur, 2012.

———. *Prayer of the Dragon*. New York: Soho, 2007.

———. *Skeleton God*. New York: Minotaur, 2017.

———. *The Skull Mantra*. New York: Minotaur, 1999.

———. *Soul of the Fire*. New York: Minotaur, 2014.

———. *Water Touching Stone*. New York: Minotaur, 2001.

Pearson, Nels, and Marc Singer, eds. *Detective Fiction in a Postcolonial and Transnational World*. Burlington, VT: Ashgate, 2009.

Pepper, Andrew, and David Schmid, eds. *Globalization and the State in Contemporary Crime Fiction: A World of Crime*. London: Palgrave Macmillan, 2016.

Petty, Cheryl West [pseud. Sha Li]. *Beijing Abduction*. Scotts Valley, CA: CreateSpace, 2014.

———. *Escape from Here*. Scotts Valley, CA: CreateSpace, 2016.

———. *Wounds of Attachment*. Scotts Valley, CA: CreateSpace, 2014.

Piipponen, Maarit, Helen Mäntymäki, and Marinella Rodi-Risberg, eds. *Transnational Crime Fiction*. London: Palgrave Macmillan, 2020.

Plain, Gill. *Twentieth-Century Crime Fiction: Gender, Sexuality and the Body*. Edinburgh: Edinburgh University Press, 2010 [2001].

Porter, Eric. *The Pursuit of Crime: Art and Ideology in Detective Fiction*. New Haven, CT: Yale University Press, 1981.

Qin Ming. *Murder in Dragon City*. Alex Woodend, tr. Seattle: Amazon Crossing, 2016. Originally pub. in Chinese, as *Dishiyi gen shouzhi* (The Eleventh Finger). Changsha: Hunan wenyi chubanshe, 2014.

Qiongding zhi xia (Under the Dome). Documentary film. Chai Jing, dir. Released on Tencent. Feb. 28, 2015.

Qiu Xiaolong. *Becoming Inspector Chen*. London: Severn, 2020.

———. "Bilingual Writing vs. Translating," *Asia Pacific Translation and Intercultural Studies* 6 (200): 129–136. https://www.tandfonline.com/doi/pdf/10.1080/23306343.2019.1674568.

———. *A Case of Two Cities*. New York: Soho, 2006.

———. "China's Smoke-Smothered Sky." *World Policy Journal* (Summer 2015). http://worldpolicy.org/2015/07/16/wpj-conversation-with-qiu-xiaolong/. Accessed June 21, 2020. Contains embedded video of Qiu Xiaolong interviewed by Westerly Gorayeb and Nellie Peyton [11 min., 24 sec.].

———. *Death of a Red Heroine*. New York: Soho, 2000. Tr. in Chinese as *Hongying zhi si*. Yu Lei, tr. Shanghai: Shanghai wenyi chubanshe, 2003.

———. *Don't Cry, Tai Lake*. New York: Minotaur, 2012. Pub. first in French, as *Les Courants fourbes du lac Tai*. Fanchita Gonzalez-Battle, tr. Paris: Liana Levi, 2010.

———. *Enigma of China*. New York: Minotaur, 2013. Pub. first in French, as *Cyber China*. Adélaïde Pralon, tr. Paris: Liana Levi, 2012.

———. *Hold Your Breath, China*. London: Severn, 2020. Pub. first in French, as *Chine, retiens ton souffle*. Adélaïde Pralon, tr. Paris: Liana Levi, 2018.

Bibliography   195

———. *Il était une fois l'inspecteur Chen* (Once Upon a Time, Inspector Chen). Adélaïde Pralon, tr. Paris: Liana Levi, 2016.

———. *Inspector Chen and Me: A Collection of Inspector Chen Stories.* Middletown, DE: Amazon, 2018.

———. *Inspector Chen and the Private Kitchen Murder.* London: Severn, 2021. Pub. first in French, as *Un dîner chez Min.* Adélaïde Pralon, tr. Paris: Liana Levi, 2021.

———. *Love and Murder in the Time of Covid.* Forthcoming.

———. *A Loyal Character Dancer.* New York: Soho, 2002. Tr. in Chinese as *Waitan huayuan* (Bund Park). Kuang Yongmei, tr. Shanghai: Shanghai wenyi chubanshe, 2005.

———. *The Mao Case.* New York: Minotaur, 2009. Pub. first in French, as *La Danseuse de Mao.* Fanchita Gonzalez-Battle, tr. Paris: Liana Levi, 2008.

———. *Poems of Inspector Chen.* Scotts Valley, CA: CreateSpace, 2016.

———. *Red Mandarin Dress.* New York: Minotaur, 2007. Tr. in Chinese as *Hong qipao.* Lu Chuangchuang, tr. Beijing: Xinxing chubanshe, 2012.

———. "A Selection of Poems by Inspector Chen." Alan R. Velie, ed. and intro. *Chinese Literature Today* 6.1 (2017): 78–88.

———. *The Shadow of the Empire.* London: Severn, 2022. Pub. first in French, as *Une enquête du vénérable juge Ti.* Adélaïde Pralon, tr. Paris: Liana Levi, 2020.

———. *Shanghai Redemption.* New York: Minotaur, 2015. Pub. first in French, as *Dragon bleu, tigre blanc.* Adélaïde Pralon, tr. Paris: Liana Levi, 2015.

———. *When Red Is Black.* New York: Soho, 2004. Tr. in Chinese as *Shikumen lige* (Farewell in the Row Houses). Ye Xujun, tr. Shanghai: Shanghai wenyi chubanshe, 2005.

———. *Years of Red Dust: Stories of Shanghai.* New York: St. Martin's, 2010. Pub. first in French, as *Cité de la poussière rouge.* Fanchita Gonzalez-Battle, tr. Paris: Liana Levi, 2008. Tr. in Chinese as *Hongchen suiyue.* Hu Chengwei, tr. Hong Kong: Xianggang Daxue chubanshe, 2008.

Qiu Xiaolong, ed. and tr. *Treasury of Chinese Love Poems.* New York: Hippocrene, 2003. Bilingual ed.

Qiu Xiaolong (author of poems) and Howard W. French (photographer). *Disappearing Shanghai: Photographs and Poems of an Intimate Way of Life.* Paramus, NJ: Homa & Sekey, 2012.

Red Corner (film). Directed by Jon Avnet. Los Angeles: MGM/United Artists, 1997.

Reitz, Caroline. *Detecting the Nation: Fictions of Detection and the Imperial Venture.* Columbus: Ohio State University Press, 2004.

Rignall, John. *Realist Fiction and the Strolling Spectator.* London: Routledge, 1992.

Roberts, Amanda. *The Emperor's Seal.* N. p. [Shenzhen, PRC?]: Red Empress, 2018.

Rolls, Alistair. "Whose Allegory Is It Anyway? Or What Happens When Crime Fiction Is Translated?" *Forum for Modern Language Studies* 52.4 (Oct. 2016): 434–448.

Rolls, Alistair, Marie-Laure Vuaille-Barcan, and John West-Sooby. "Introduction: Translating National Allegories: The Case of Crime Fiction." *The Translator* 22.2 (2016): 135–143. https://www.tandfonline.com/doi/full/10.1080/13556509.2016.1205707.

Rotenberg, David. *The Golden Mountain Murders.* Toronto: McArthur & Co., 2005.

———. *The Hamlet Murders.* Toronto: McArthur & Co., 2005 [2004].

———. *The Hua Shan Hospital Murders.* Toronto: McArthur & Co., 2003.

196   Bibliography

———. *The Lake Ching Murders.* Toronto: McArthur & Co., 2002 [2001].

———. *Shanghai.* Toronto: Penguin Canada, 2009.

———. *The Shanghai Murders.* New York: St. Martin's, 1998.

Rush, James R., and Robin W. Winks, eds. *Asia in Western Fiction.* Manchester, UK: University of Manchester Press, 1990.

Rushing, Robert A. *Resisting Arrest: Detective Fiction and Popular Culture.* New York: Other, 2007.

Rzepka, Charles J., and Lee Horsley, eds. *A Companion to Crime Fiction.* Chichester, UK: Wiley-Blackwell, 2010.

Said, Edward W. *Orientalism.* New York: Vintage, 1979.

Saito, Satoru. *Detective Fiction and the Rise of the Japanese Novel, 1880–1930.* Cambridge, MA: Harvard University Asia Center, 2012.

Salmose, Nicholas. "Introduction." *Contemporary Nostalgia.* Basel: MDPI, 2019.

Salomone, Rosemary. *The Rise of English: Global Politics and the Power of Language.* New York: Oxford University Press, 2022.

Sampson, Catherine. "Hit and Run." In Alexandra Pearson et al., *Beijing: Portrait of a City.* Hong Kong: Odyssey, 2009.

———. *The Pool of Unease.* London: Macmillan, 2007.

———. *The Slaughter Pavilion.* London: Macmillan, 2008.

———. "Takeaway." Kindle ebook, 2013.

Sandberg, Eric. "Contemporary Crime Fiction, Cultural Prestige, and the Literary Field." *Crime Fiction Studies* 1.1 (Feb. 2020): 5–22. https://www.euppublishing.com/doi/10.3366/cfs.2020.0004.

———. "Crime Fiction and the Past." *Crime Fiction Studies* 1.2 (Sept. 2020): 153–156.

Santaulària i Capdevila, Isabel. "'This Is Getting a Little Too Chinese for Me': The Representation of China in Crime Fiction Written in English." *Coolabah* 20 (2016): 67–82. https://repositori.udl.cat/bitstream/handle/10459.1/59766/025168.pdf?sequence=1&isAllowed=y.

Scaggs, John. *Crime Fiction.* London: Routledge, 2005.

Scanlon, Sean. "Introduction: Nostalgia." *Iowa Journal of Cultural Studies* 5 (Fall 2004): 3–9.

Scheen, Lena. *Shanghai Literary Imaginings: A City in Transformation.* Amsterdam: University of Amsterdam Press, 2015.

Seaman, Amanda C. *Bodies of Evidence: Women, Society, and Detective Fiction in 1990s Japan.* Honolulu: University of Hawai'i Press, 2004.

See, Lisa. *Dragon Bones.* New York: Random House Trade Paperback, 2007 [2003].

———. *Flower Net.* New York: Random House Trade Paperback, 2008 [1997].

———. "The Funeral Banquet." In O'Hearn, ed., 125–138.

———. *The Interior.* New York: Random House Trade Paperback, 2008 [1999].

———. *The Island of Sea Women.* New York: Scribner, 2019.

———. *On Gold Mountain.* New York: Vintage, 2012 [1995].

———. *Snow Flower and the Secret Fan.* New York: Random House, 2005.

Segalen, Victor. *Essay on Exoticism: An Aesthetics of Diversity.* Yaël Rachel Schlick, tr. Durham, NC: Duke University Press, 2002 [French, 1995; pub. posthumously].

Bibliography   197

Sendker, Jan-Philipp. *Dragon Games*. Christine Lo, tr. Edinburgh: Polygon, 2016. Also pub. as *The Language of Solitude*. New York: Simon & Schuster Atria, 2017. Originally pub. in German, as *Drachenspiele*. München: Karl Blessing, 2009.

———. *The Far Side of the Night*. Christine Lo, tr. Edinburgh: Polygon, 2019. Originally pub. in German, as *Am Anderen Ende der Nacht*. München: Karl Blessing, 2016.

———. *Whispering Shadows*. Christine Lo, tr. New York: Simon & Schuster Atria, 2016. Originally pub. in German, as *Das Flüstern der Schatten*. München: Karl Blessing, 2007.

Sheridan, Juanita. *The Chinese Chop*. Garden City, NY: Doubleday, 1949.

Shi, Flair Donglai. "Post-Mao Chinese Literature as World Literature: Struggling with the Systematic and the Allegorical." *Comparative Literature and World Literature* 1.1 (2016):20–34.http://www.cwliterature.org/uploadfile/2016/0422/20160422112507141.pdf#page=25.

Shih, Shu-mei. "Global Literature and the Technologies of Recognition." *PMLA* 119.1 (2004): 16–30.

Shih, Shu-mei, Chien-hsin Tsai, and Brian Bernards, eds. *Sinophone Studies: A Critical Reader*. New York: Columbia University Press, 2013.

Shklovsky, Viktor. *Theory of Prose*. Benjamin Sher, tr. Normal, IL: Dalkey Archive Press, 1990 [Russian original, 1925, 2nd ed., 1929].

Shlian, Deborah, and Joel Shlian. *Rabbit in the Moon*. Ipswich, MA: Oceanview, 2008.

Shortridge, J. R. "The Concept of the Place-Defining Novel in American Popular Culture." *Professional Geographer* 43.3 (1991): 280–291.

Silver, Mark. *Purloined Letters: Cultural Borrowing and Japanese Crime Literature, 1868–1937*. Honolulu: University of Hawai'i Press, 2008.

Song, Weijie. *Mapping Modern Beijing: Space, Emotion, Literary Topography*. New York: Oxford University Press, 2018.

Song Ying. *Apricot's Revenge: A Crime Novel*. Howard Goldblatt and Sylvia Li-chun Lin, tr. New York: Minotaur, 2016. Originally pub. in Chinese, as *Xing shao hong*. Guangzhou: Huacheng chubanshe, 2008.

St. André, James. *Translating China as Cross-Identity Performance*. Honolulu: University of Hawai'i Press, 2018.

Stalling, Jonathan. "Bilingual Poetics in the Global Age: An Interview with Qiu Xiaolong." *Chinese Literature Today* 6.1 (2017): 89–97.

Stone, Eric. *Shanghaied*. Madison, WI: Bleak House, 2009.

Sun Yisheng. "The Shades Who Periscope Through Flowers to the Sky." Nicky Harman, tr. *Words without Borders* (Dec. 2012). https://www.wordswithoutborders.org/article/the-shades-who-periscope-through-flowers-to-the-sky.

Swirski, Peter. *American Crime Fiction: A Cultural History of Nobrow Fiction as Art*. New York: Palgrave Macmillan, 2016.

———. *From Lowbrow to Nobrow*. Montréal: McGill-Queens University Press, 2005.

Swirski, Peter, and Tero Eljas Vanhanen, eds. *When Highbrow Meets Lowbrow: Popular Culture and the Rise of Nobrow*. New York: Palgrave Macmillan, 2018 [2017].

Symons, Julian. *Bloody Murder: From the Detective Story to the Crime Novel: A History*. 3rd rev. ed. New York: Mysterious Press, 1993 [1992, 1985, 1972].

198   Bibliography

Tally, Robert T., Jr., ed. *The Routledge Handbook of Literature and Space*. Milton Park, UK: Routledge, 2017.

Tey, Josephine. *The Daughter of Time*. New York: Macmillan, 1951.

Todorov, Tzvetan. "The Typology of Detective Fiction." In his *The Poetics of Prose*. Richard Howard, tr., 42–52. Ithaca, NY: Cornell University Press, 1977 [French book, 1971; this essay, 1966].

Trotter, David. "Theory and Detective Fiction." *Critical Quarterly* 33.2 (June 1991): 66–77.

Tsu, Jing. *Sound and Script in Chinese Diaspora*. Cambridge, MA: Harvard University Press, 2011.

Tuan, Yi-fu. "The Landscapes of Sherlock Holmes." *Journal of Geography* 84.2 (1977): 56–60.

Uxó, Carlos. "The Representation of Chinese Characters in Leonardo Padura's *La Cola de la Serpiente* (2000): Sinophobia or Sinophilia?" In Anderson et al., eds., *The Foreign in International Crime Fiction*, 200–211.

Van der Wetering, Janwillem. *Robert van Gulik: His Life, His Work*. New York: Soho, 1998 [1987].

Van Gulik, Robert. *Poets and Murder: A Judge Dee Mystery*. Chicago: University of Chicago Press, 1996 [1968].

Van Gulik, Robert, tr. *Celebrated Cases of Judge Dee (Dee Goong An)*. New York: Dover, 1976 [1949].

Van Lustbader, Eric. *The Bourne Retribution*. New York: Grand Central, 2013.

Velie, Alan R. "Introduction," to "A Selection of Poems by Inspector Chen." *Chinese Literature Today* 6.1 (2017): 79–80.

Vittachi, Nury. *The Feng Shui Detective*. New York: Minotaur, 2002.

———. *The Shanghai Union of Industrial Mystics*. New York: Felony & Mayhem Press, 2012 [2006].

Walker, Casey. *Last Days in Shanghai*. Berkeley, CA: Counterpoint, 2014.

Walsh, Megan. *The Subplot: What China Is Reading and Why It Matters*. New York: Columbia Global Reports, 2022.

Wan Zhi [pseud. of Chen Maiping]. "Open Ground." Bonnie S. McDougall, tr. *Bulletin of Concerned Asian Scholars* 16.3 (July–Sept. 1984): 6–7. Originally pub. in Chinese, as "Kaikuodi." *Jintian* 5 (1979). Reprint at https://www.jintian.net/today/?action-viewnews-itemid-3003.

Wang, David Der-wei. *The Lyrical in Epic Time*. New York: Columbia University Press, 2015.

———. *Why Fiction Matters in Contemporary China*. Waltham, MA: Brandeis University Press, 2020.

Wang, Xiaowei. *Blockchain Chicken Farm: And Other Stories of Tech in China's Countryside*. New York: Farrar, Straus and Giroux, 2020.

Wang, Yiman. "Made in China, Sold in the United States, and Vice Versa—Transnational 'Chinese' Cinema between Media Capitals." *Journal of Chinese Cinemas* 3.2 (2009): 163–176. https://www.tandfonline.com/doi/abs/10.1386/jcc.3.2.163_1.

Bibliography   199

Wang Shuo. *Playing for Thrills: A Mystery*. Howard Goldblatt, tr. New York: William Morrow, 1997. Originally pub. in Chinese, as *Wande jiushi xintiao*. Beijing: Zuojia chubanshe, 1989.

Wasserstrom, Jeffrey. "Hour of the Rat: A Q & A with Noir Author Lisa Brackmann." *Los Angeles Review of Books*, June 19, 2013.

Wei, Yan. *Detecting Chinese Modernities: Rupture and Continuity in Modern Chinese Detective Fiction (1896–1949)*. Leiden: Brill, 2020.

West, Christopher. *Death of a Blue Lantern*. New York: Berkley Prime Crime, 1998 [1994].

———. *Death of a Red Mandarin*. New York: Berkley Prime Crime, 1999 [1997].

———. *Death on Black Dragon River*. London: Allison & Busby, 1999 [1996].

———. *Journey to the Middle Kingdom*. London: Simon & Schuster, 1991.

———. *The Third Messiah*. New York: Minotaur, 2000.

Williams, Philip F., and Yenna Wu. *The Great Wall of Confinement: The Chinese Prison Camp through Contemporary Fiction and Reportage*. Berkeley: University of California Press, 2004.

Williams, Philip F., and Yenna Wu, eds. *Remolding and Resistance among Writers of the Chinese Prison Camp: Disciplined and Published*. London and New York: Routledge, 2006.

Winks, Robin W., ed. *The Historian as Detective: Essays on Evidence*. New York: Harper & Row, 1969.

Wu, Edna. *Clouds and Rain: A China-to-America Memoir*. Louisville, KY: Evanston Publishing, 1994.

Wu Jingzi [Wu Ching-tzu]. *The Scholars*. Yang Hsien-yi and Gladys Yang, tr. New York: Columbia University Press, 1992 [1972, 1957]. Originally pub. in Chinese, as *Rulin waishi*, 1750.

Xiao, Jiwei. *Telling Details: Chinese Fiction, World Literature*. New York: Routledge, 2022.

Xue, Xinran. *The Promise: Love and Loss in Modern China*. William Spence, tr. London: I. B. Taurus, 2020 [2018].

Yan, Geling. *The Secret Talker*. Jeremy Tiang, tr. New York: HarperVia, 2021. Originally pub. in Chinese, as *Miyuzhe*. Taipei: Sanmin shuju, 2004.

Ying, Yan. "Qiu Xiaolong. *Death of a Red Heroine; A Loyal Character Dancer; When Red Is Black*" [reviews]. *Modern Language Studies* 35.1 (Spring 2005): 75–83.

Yokoyama, Hideo. *Six Four*. Jonathan Lloyd-Davies, tr. New York: Farrar, Straus and Giroux, 2017.

Young, Robert J. C. "World Literature and Postcolonialism." In D'haen et al., eds., 213–222.

Yu, An. *Braised Pork*. New York: Grove, 2020.

Yung, Alban [pseud. Remi Gedoie]. *Message COFACE à Pékin* (COFACE Message in Beijing). Paris: Climats, 1997.

——— [pseud. Albert Weng]. *Pas de mantra pour Pékin* (No Mantra for Beijing). Arles: Picquier, 2000.

——— [Rémi Gedoie]. *Pékin ce n'est pas de la tarte* (Beijing Is No Piece of Cake). Online, 2006. PDF file available at *Question chine*. https://www.questionchine.net/?page =articlepdf&id_article=2042.

200   Bibliography

——— [Rémi Gedoie]. *SCTIP Poker à Pékin* (SCTIP Poker in Beijing). Bélaye, France: René Viénet, 2012.

——— [Albert Weng]. *Touche pas aux pékins* (Don't Mess with the Locals). Arles: Picquier, 2002.

Zhang Jishun. "From Fallen Star to Red Star: Shangguan Yunzhu." In Timothy Cheek, Klaus Mühlhahn, and Hans van de Ven, eds., *The Chinese Communist Party: A Century in Ten Lives*. Cambridge: Cambridge University Press, 2021.

Zhang Liang, comp. Andrew J. Nathan and Perry Link, eds. *The Tiananmen Papers*. New York: PublicAffairs, 2001, 2002.

Zhang Xianliang. *Grass Soup*. Martha Avery, tr. Boston: Godine, 1995.

———. *My Bodhi Tree*. Martha Avery, tr. London: Secker & Warburg, 1996.

Zhang Xinxin. *Le courier des bandits* (The Bandit Courier). Emmanuelle Péchenart and Robin Setton, tr. Arles: Actes Sud, 1993. Originally pub. in Chinese, as *Feng • pian • lian* (Envelope, Postcard, Block-of-four). *Shouhuo* 52 (Feb. 25, 1985): 4–92.

———. *Haolaiwu tongjifan* (Hollywood Wanted). Manuscript. 2015, rev. 2021.

Zhou Haohui. *Death Notice*. Zac Haluza, tr. New York: Doubleday, 2018. Originally pub. in Chinese, as *Siwang tongzhidan: Anheizhe*. Beijing: Shidai Huawen shuju, 2014.

Zhu, Aijun. *Feminism and Global Chineseness: The Cultural Production of Controversial Women Authors*. Youngstown, NY: Cambria, 2007.

Zhu, Ping, and Hui Faye Xiao, eds. *Feminisms with Chinese Characteristics*. Syracuse, NY: Syracuse University Press, 2021.

Zhu Xiao Di. *Tales of Judge Dee*. Bloomington, IN: iUniverse, 2006.

Zijin Chen [pseud. of Chen Xu]. *The Untouched Crime*. Michelle Deeter, tr. Seattle: Amazon Crossing, 2016. Originally pub. in Chinese, as *Wuzheng zhi zui*. Changsha: Hunan renmin chubanshe, 2014.

Žižek, Slavoj. "Parallax." *London Review of Books* 25.22 (Nov. 20, 2003). https://www.lrb .co.uk/the-paper/v25/n22/slavoj-zizek/parallax.

INDEX

A Yi, 12, 18, 20, 86, 88, 92, 163n30
abortion, 57, 76, 100
Africa, 8, 23, 73, 80
anime and *manga*, 10, 17
anticorruption literature, 40, 83, 84. *See also*
    corruption
archeology and artifacts, 33, 44, 72, 73, 108,
    109, 110
Army: Chinese (PLA), 36, 37, 45, 79, 81, 88;
    protagonists, 32, 109, 120, 122, 129; US,
    106
Art of War, The, by Sun Tzu (Sunzi), 14, 29
arts, artists, 6, 18, 91, 120–121, 140, 142, 145,
    172n25; musicians, 37, 43, 120
Asian financial crisis, 39, 130
autobiography in fiction, 24, 31, 42, 48–49,
    62, 97, 136–138. *See also* memoirs
awards for crime fiction, 13

Bakhtin, Mikhail, 20
Bao, Judge (Bao Zheng), 77, 167n38
Barckmann, Lee, 5, 54, 72, 91, 106, 137, 140
Baudrillard, Jean, 73
Beijing Consensus, China Model, 6
Beijing Spring(s), golden ages of expression,
    23, 76, 140. *See also* Tiananmen
Bhabha, Homi K., 51, 171n10
biomedical themes, 9, 36–37, 44, 60, 69, 70,
    71, 73, 74–76; COVID-19, 61, 74
blackmail, 12, 62, 63, 66, 71, 108
Bo Xilai, Gu Kailai, Bo Guagua, 40, 53, 81, 82
Bonavia, David, 5, 26–31, 42, 60, 63, 88, 94,
    135; political-social themes, 71, 76, 85, 88
Bourdieu, Pierre, 17
Boxer Rising, 131–132
Boym, Svetlana, 138–140

Brackmann, Lisa, 52, 54–55, 60, 91, 101,103,
    136; culture themes, 141, 142; hero Ellie
    McEnroe, 77, 87, 88, 91, 100, 101,
    106–107, 137; social-political themes, 40,
    56, 57, 69–70, 76–77, 82, 88, 98, 99,
    106–107, 144; style, 52, 91–92
Brookes, Adam, 56, 77, 113, 125, 129, 133
Brooks, Peter, 117
buddy investigators, 110–114
Byron, John. *See* Uren, Roger

Cai Jun, 12, 60
capitalism and critique of it, 8, 23, 25, 50,
    79–80, 144, 146
censorship, PRC, 7, 11, 38, 20, 85, 102,
    119–120, 165n6
Chai Jing, 71
Chan, Charlie, 21, 50, 161n4
Chan Ho-Kei, 7, 11, 136, 163n35; *The*
    Borrowed, 123–124; characters, 88, 92,
    101, 108–109, 112, 115; identity theft
    theme, 78; *Second Sister*, 78, 101, 108, 112
Chandler, Raymond, 3
Chen Cao, Inspector. *See under* Qiu
    Xiaolong
Cheng Xiaoqing, 75, 90
children: as characters, 37, 95, 98, 107; child
    labor, 69–70, 118; childhood, 5, 48, 59,
    95, 99, 108, 121; only children, 43, 121;
    thematized, 12, 39, 77–78, 100, 115. *See*
    also kidnapping; one-child policy
Chinatown mysteries, 2, 71, 161n4
Chinese Communist Part•y (CCP), 2, 7, 8,
    38, 40, 49, 107, 117, 118, 129; characters,
    3, 35, 43, 61, 80, 82, 88, 94, 110, 128;
    discussed, 63, 80, 118, 121; factions, 66,

201

202   Index

80; views, policies, fears, 65, 85, 97, 129, 130, 134, 140

Chinese language crime fiction (pre-1949), 5, 17, 29, 75, 90

Chinese language crime fiction (PRC), 10, 11–12, 13–14, 16, 17, 18, 21–22; qualities, 42, 54, 60, 86, 89, 90, 97, 105–106, 112, 117, 118, 124; restrictions on, 3, 6, 7, 11, 13, 17, 20, 41, 61, 119–120; themes, general, 12, 17, 27, 45, 70; themes, social, 8, 40, 83–85, 102, 124–125, 128–129, 146; works translated, 11–12, 54

Christie, Agatha, 14, 51, 102

Church, James, 8, 47, 55, 56, 60, 135, 13

CIA, 28, 29–30, 37–38, 49, 88, 106, 113, 137

Clancy, Tom, 4, 9

comic, satiric, ironic styles, 18, 51, 90, 98, 113, 128, 141, 175n5; of Flint, 87, 110–111; Qiu Xiaolong, 61, 93, 113; Vittachi, 111; Yung, 87, 111, 112, 130, 137; Zhang Xinxin, 114

construction, substandard, 57, 76, 122–123

consumerism, 51, 84, 144, 147, 162n25

corruption, 7, 36, 44, 51, 60, 62, 64–67, 75, 114, 126; anticorruption, 77, 80, 81, 87, 131–132; bad cops, 64, 88; Chinese concept of, 82, 83; official, 28, 29, 42, 43, 45, 61, 76, 84, 90, 92, 109–111, 123, 134; as sensitive theme, 11, 12. *See also* anticorruption literature

counterfeiting, IP theft, 67, 68, 71–74, 114, 118

crime fiction concept, 15–21, 25, 104, 117, 140, 147

crimes seldom depicted in China mysteries, 51, 76–79, 84

criminology, 75, 76

crossovers, literary, 11, 18, 103

Cultural Revolution, 20, 29, 30, 32, 43, 45, 49, 73, 90, 91, 95, 96; as plot motivator, 88, 123, 125, 126–127; reevaluated, 98, 130, 140, 146

Damrosch, David. *See* world literature

Dashanzi Art District (798 Art Zone), 21, 121

Dee, Judge, 6, 18, 20, 22, 23, 117, 132–135, 137, 164n1, 167n38, 167n39. *See also* Van Gulik

Deng Xiaoping, 27, 93

detectives (as genre definer), 1–6, 10–11, 16, 19–22, 38, 40, 46, 48, 118, 126; women, 3, 101–102, 104–105. *See also* Sherlock Holmes. *See also under* individual author name

diaspora and immigrant communities, 8, 39, 50, 56, 64, 72, 80, 123, 139; exile, 53, 55, 99, 109; self-exile, 7, 12, 20, 36, 64, 128, 139

Draken, L. H., 54, 56, 74, 76, 106, 137, 143

dreams, 78, 100, 122, 133; "the Chinese dream," 116, 144; *Dream of the Red Chamber*, 126

dress, couture, 87, 105, 125, 143, 144

economic crimes, 78

economic growth theme, 7, 53, 55, 57, 60, 79, 144, 145

Eliot, T. S., 48, 54, 90

Erdmann, Eva, 19–20, 21, 51–52

exoticism, 5, 13, 50, 51, 52, 71, 73, 90, 101, 141

Falun Gong, 38, 45, 74, 113, 129–130

family, 12, 33, 43, 47, 52, 58, 67, 79, 97, 113, 115; criminal relatives, 34, 55, 74, 82, 88; discord, 98, 99–100, 105, 108; as metaphor, 37; as neglected topic, 77, 98–99, 105; nonfiction, 39, 41–42, 137; trauma, 108, 132; typical, 99. *See also* children; fathers; mothers

fantasy, 2, 13, 19, 114, 140, 147; as a Sinophone genre, 10, 12, 13–14, 18, 135

fathers, 29, 32, 44, 49, 66, 91, 96, 99, 115, 122; filiality, 32, 48, 92, 93, 99, 108; non-Chinese, 67, 69; unworthy fathers, 43–44, 99, 108, 125

fengshui, 15, 62, 88, 111

fiction, Chinese traditional, 29, 94, 105–106, 110, 119

film. *See* media, moving visual

Flint, Shamini, 8, 47, 51, 54, 60, 74, 83, 101, 129; hero Inspector Singh, 87, 110–111

Index 203

folk literature, 17, 133

food in mystery fiction, 5, 11, 32, 43, 70, 108, 111, 136; in crimes, 70, 72, 161n4

formalist literary theory, 117, 175n1; Viktor Shklovsky, 118

France, 8, 53, 80, 111, 118, 130, 133, 136, 137; China relations, 111, 142; featured characters, 40, 46, 57, 67, 74, 87, 111, 112, 130, 137; French language, 1, 2, 10, 12, 40, 53, 81, 91, 123. *See also* Imbert, Michel; Yung, Alban

Gangxueyin (Gang Xueyin), 12, 175n3

Gapper, John, 60, 68, 77, 81, 83, 88, 101

gay, queer, LGBTQ characters and themes, 3, 101, 102, 104, 105, 122, 133

Gedoie, Rémi. *See* Yung, Alban

Gelder, Ken, 17

gender relations, female heroes, feminism, 29, 35, 40, 43, 101–105

generational divides; in China, 45, 77, 92, 94, 95, 96, 99, 125, 132, 145; among China mystery authors, 119, 135–136

genetic manipulation. *See* biomedical themes

genre concept and popular genres, 5, 14–21. *See also under* individual genre

ghost marriage, 78

ghost towns, 57, 107

ghosts and spectral themes, 10, 12, 111, 121, 147

globalization, 7, 16, 25, 53, 86, 143, 146–147; of literature, 1, 2, 4, 9–12, 16, 19–23, 25, 50, 51. *See also* tourism

Goldblatt, Howard, and Sylvia Li-chun Lin, 23, 41

Golden Age mysteries, 20, 21, 54, 102, 118

Golden Venture shipwreck (1993), 44, 64

gongan ("court case") and Great Judge genres, 22, 85, 165n7, 167n38

Great Leap Forward, 127, 129, 140, 145, 178n10

Guo, Xiaolu, 24, 52, 138

Ha Jin, 23, 24, 52, 138, 168n49, 178n8

Hamilton, Ian, 8, 47, 60, 85, 88, 101, 135–136, 141, 142, 144; global crime, 73; hero Ava Lee, 3, 55, 58, 73, 83, 87, 105, 146

hard-boiled mysteries, 61, 87, 91, 102, 168n52. *See also* noir

Hart, Elsa, 117

He Jiahong, 11, 12, 54, 78

Hiaasen, Carl, 5, 8, 26–27, 60, 71, 73, 85, 100, 135, 136

Higashino Keigo, 10

Hillerman, Tony, 3–4, 6, 23, 56

historical fiction, 4, 5, 10, 18, 42, 45, 103, 104, 105, 123, 147; and mystery genre, 2, 6, 18, 20–21, 117–119, 120, 126, 132–135; source citations in mysteries, 42

honeymoon (in Sino-Western relations), 6, 25, 40, 49, 50, 136, 146, 169n74

Hong Kong, 6, 8–9, 10, 68, 72, 117; 1967 turmoil, 123–124; 1997 handover, 6, 39, 142; Hong Kong characters, 87, 88, 92, 96, 108; literary authors of, 111, 123; mysteries set in, 2, 33, 35–38, 54, 55, 107, 123–124 130, 130–132; reporting from, 27, 30, 35, 38. *See also* Chan Ho–Kei; Küng, Dinah Lee

horror, 2, 12, 19, 74, 76

human rights, 31, 36, 38, 39, 43, 44, 79, 121. *See also* biomedical themes; Tibet; Uyghurs

hutongs, 34, 55, 121, 140, 141

identity, authenticity, 13, 22, 24, 39, 51, 52, 78, 88, 101, 108, 114, 127; multicultural ramifications, 2, 8, 19, 36, 41, 46, 49, 53, 92, 110, 111; and trauma, 132

ideology, 18, 27, 79–85, 110, 132, 145–146; crime fiction as conservative, 102, 140

Imbert, Michel, 24, 39, 44, 60, 135–136; creative path, 3, 146; hero Han Zuo, 120–122; heroes Judge Li and Peng Yetai, 53, 55–57, 72, 129; hero Lt. Ma Gong, 122–123, 145; hero Marc Bernart, 91, 118–119; historical themes, 6, 117–118, 120–123, 125, 127–129; narration, 9, 91; on people's courts, 56, 98; on police behavior, 58, 77–78, 83, 88, 90; social comment, 72, 77–78, 83, 85, 89, 98, 101, 141–142, 145

Information, facts in fiction, 3, 4–5, 29–30, 42–43. *See also* local color

204 Index

Inspector Chen. *See under* Qiu Xiaolong
intellectuals, 25, 49, 90, 91, 92, 94, 98, 113,
142. *See also* scholar novel; Sinologists
Internal Security. *See* State Security
internet, 4, 12, 13, 17, 66, 106, 131–132, 147;
netizen activity, 18
Irony. *See* comic, satiric, ironic styles

Jameson, Fredric, 24–25
Japan, 4, 30, 41, 67, 72, 104, 135; Japanese
American, 103; Japanese fiction, 1, 3,
10–11, 12, 13, 21, 22, 102, 108, 124
Jepson, Duncan, 4, 7, 8, 60, 85, 96, 98, 106,
127; *Emperors Once More*, 130–132; hero
Alex Soong, 54, 87, 131–132
Jia Pingwa, 171n8
Journalism, 54, 60, 62, 83, 106; as
background of novelists, 3, 8, 9, 18,
26–27, 30–31, 35, 41, 51, 137; Chinese, 71,
85; journalist heroes, 36–37, 55, 58, 67,
69, 76, 79, 88, 97–98, 112, 118; press as
court of last resort, 38, 81
June 4, 1989. *See* Tiananmen

kidnapping, 21, 28, 37, 78, 107, 121
kitsch, 140, 141
Kjeldsen, Kirk, 7, 59, 60, 101, 108, 138
Klingborg, Brian, 4, 60, 86, 100, 101, 136;
hero Lu Fei, 4, 55, 92, 94; Myanmar, 52,
54, 55, 71, 146; political and social
themes, 76, 77, 78, 83, 106; style, 4, 52,
55, 60, 90–91, 92, 101
knights-errant, 88, 108, 109
Korea, 6, 60, 76, 129; Church's Korean
Chinese hero, 56, 83, 88, 91; North
Koreans, 56, 88, 137
Küng, Dinah Lee, 26, 35–39, 41, 42, 46, 54,
56, 60, 100, 103, 135, 137; feminism,
101–104; heroes Raymond and Vonalp,
26, 30, 44; political-social themes, 67, 78,
85; publication obstacles, 30–31, 38–39;
religious and human rights themes, 36,
37, 38. *See also* Hong Kong; Tibet
language, 3, 10, 20, 23, 90–92; code-
switching, 51, 91, 171n14; dialogue, 13,
23, 27, 52, 90–91; English language

hegemony, 50; ESL writing, 2, 10, 23, 48,
52; transcriptions of Asian phrases, 52.
See also narrators; translation
laogai, gulags, prison camps: commentary
on, 36, 37, 72, 76, 81, 109, 121, 122, 125; as
plot setting, 6, 56, 98, 109, 120, 128–129;
prison literature from the PRC, 128–129
Laozi and the *Daodejing*, 29, 86
Latin America, 26, 52, 68, 71, 72, 146
law, the legal system, 17, 30, 43–44, 54, 82,
88–89, 97, 112, 114, 119, 134; criticized,
12, 65, 84, 89; law and literature synergy,
126, 134; people's courts, 56, 98. *See also*
lawyers; police
lawyers, 8, 11, 12, 18, 42, 44, 54, 72, 75, 98,
113, 126
Lee, Leo Ou-fan, 7, 10, 11, 60, 88, 101, 112,
135; multiculturalism of, 67, 72, 92, 102
Leitch, Thomas, 20
Leon, Donna, 23, 38, 51–52
Liang, Diane Wei, 2, 3, 7, 24, 42, 48–49, 101,
136, 138, 140; hero Mei, 53, 98, 105,
120–121; and social comment, 3, 56, 73,
77, 78, 88, 144; style, 59, 60, 61
Liu Cixin, 11
Liu Zhenyun, 12, 20, 86
local color, 8, 11, 13, 20, 30, 41, 53–56, 62, 71,
117, 124
Lu Xun, 25, 173n38

Ma Xiaoquan, 12
Mai Jia, 12
Mankell, Henning, and hero Wallander, 8,
60, 77, 79–80, 85, 122, 135, 137
manufacturing, 23, 36, 44–45, 53, 55, 67–71,
81–82, 103–104, 141; illegal, 73, 74, 84,
118; under state ownership, 40; worker
characters, 90, 114, 121, 122; working
class, 40, 61, 62, 68, 73, 89, 101, 104, 113,
128
Mao Zedong, 64, 126–127, 130, 138, 140
Maoism, neo-, 40, 53, 61, 76, 81, 82, 107, 147
Marinina, Alexandra, 22, 179n29
martial arts, 3, 97, 101, 111, 130; chivalric
fiction genre, 10, 13, 105
Marx, Karl, 61; Marxism, 145–146

Mason, Paul, 55, 60, 77, 79, 80, 83, 85, 88
May, Peter, 4, 8, 15, 46–47, 53, 54, 60, 86, 89, 101, 135–136; heroes Li Yan and Dr. Campbell, 47, 74, 87, 91, 100; as historical chronicler, 4, 58–59, 125, 142–143; themes: biomedical, 74–75; themes: social-political, 77–79, 84, 88–89, 90, 97, 106, 113; themes: transnational, 71–72, 73, 97, 98, 137
media, moving visual, 6, 10, 16, 17, 20, 104, 114, 140; and authors, 49, 79, 137; book adaptations, 12, 22, 40, 47, 117; fan activity, 104, 114; film, 23, 41, 50, 81, 91, 103, 114, 127, 140; television, 51, 62, 69, 79, 98, 102, 108, 113–114; video games, 12, 106. See also *anime*
memoirs, 3, 41, 49, 64, 126–127, 136. *See also* autobiography in fiction
metamysteries and quest themes, 47, 61, 75, 106, 120, 126–127
Mexico. *See* Latin America
Mi Lei, 12
migrants, internal, 56, 59, 61, 77, 89, 104, 105, 128
mise en abyme, 114, 134
Mo Yan, 12
modernist tendency, 25, 121; in A Yi, 18, 92; in Qiu Xiaolong, 47, 133
Mones, Nicole, 5, 46, 54, 55, 60, 73, 101, 103, 135, 137, 140; heroes, 46, 55, 108, 137
Mongolia, 55; Inner Mongolia, 55, 80
Montalbano, Bill, 5, 8, 26–27, 30, 60, 71, 73, 85, 100, 135, 136
Moretti, Franco, 53, 147
mothers, 41, 103; as characters, 37, 43, 45, 93, 99, 105, 107, 108, 113, 115–116; motherhood, 37, 39; Oedipus complex, 126
Munro, Robin, 36
murder methods in China mysteries, 60–61
Murong Xuecun, 12
Murphy, Bernice M., 17

narrators: personas, 24, 31, 69, 90–92, 106, 114; styles, 18, 21, 63, 78, 92–97, 112
national allegory, 24–25
nationalism, 7, 25, 45, 97, 130, 132, 146–147

native vs. foreign perspectives, 1, 2, 3–4, 7, 19–20, 22–25, 31, 51, 83
Nieh, Daniel, 7, 52, 54, 58, 87, 136, 138
noir, 3, 7, 61, 79, 84, 102; female, 104; Nordic, 25
nonfiction: "China books," 3, 104; travelogues, travel diaries, 3, 4, 5, 9, 27, 31
normalization of crime, 20–21, 60
nostalgia, 20, 25, 29, 35, 37, 117, 119, 124, 133, 138–142

Olympics, Beijing, 120–122, 141, 142–143
one-child policy, 64, 99, 100, 142, 145
organ extraction and harvesting, 36, 37, 67, 72, 74; bear bile, 44; from pandas, 127
Orientalism, 50, 74, 97; self-Orientalism, 24, 50

pandas, 11, 111, 127–128, 139
paratexts, 15, 47
Pattison, Eliot, 4, 8, 22, 46–47, 53, 60, 135, 136; gulag themes, 56, 99, 109; hero, Shan Tao Yun, 53, 54, 81, 109–110; political and legal comment, 73, 77, 80–81, 84, 109–110, 146; social comment, 54–55, 73, 77, 115, 129; style, 19, 73, 92, 100, 127; women heroes, 102
Pepper, Andrew, and David Schmid, 147
Petty, Cheryl West, 24, 54, 56, 74, 88, 100, 106, 137
Philippines, Filipinas, 37, 38, 42, 56
photography, 24, 61, 62–63, 114, 122, 128, 139, 161n8
poetry: by authors, 3, 47–48, 60, 139, 144; by detectives, 32, 48, 51, 92, 113, 127; poems in mysteries, 48, 60, 61, 66, 67, 70, 92; poets as characters, 125, 126; Van Gulik's *Poets and Murder*, 133–135
police (Public Security of PRC), 32, 143; China mystery authors' contacts with, 4, 24, 28, 42, 48, 89; Chinese disdain for, 35, 63, 88; misconduct and torture by, 37, 64, 72, 74, 83, 88; municipal auxiliaries, 89; People's Armed Police, 37, 77; vehicles, 58–59

206   Index

police procedural (genre): authorship in PRC by police, 8, 18, 61, 86; the global genre, 20–21, 48, 76; PRC authors' strategies, 86; tabooed policing topics in PRC, 11, 61

police procedural (in the China mystery), 1–3, 21, 26, 31, 40, 42–43, 46, 63, 88–89, 127, 128, 129; crimes pursued, 77; foreign police characters, 46, 110–111; heroes, 28, 32, 34–35, 40, 43, 53, 59, 87, 88, 89–90, 91–95, 98, 111, 120; heroes' life-styles, 99, 112; Hong Kong police, 36, 123–124, 131–132; line and jurisdictional conflicts, 63, 76, 106; surveillance, 77, 89

politics (in China mysteries), 4, 26, 29, 30, 32, 66, 76–77, 147; historical, 99, 125–126, 132; lack of, 16, 24, 57, 76, 78–79, 98, 117, 124; policies, 63, 64, 142, 146; PRC mystery comparisons, 40, 86; in Qiu Xiaolong's novels, 91–96, 113, 132–135, 138, 146

pollution, 58, 60, 61, 67, 69–71, 133, 134

pop culture, 12, 29, 111, 141, 142

popular fiction, 1, 3, 10, 15, 16, 17, 18–19, 29, 41, 50, 51, 86, 147; PRC's, 17, 78, 147; Western views of, 16–18, 103

postcolonial crime fiction, 9, 20

postmodernism, 16, 17, 47

princelings, 29, 40, 43, 44, 58, 74, 81, 91, 111; red princesses, 15, 29, 40, 43, 45, 80, 99, 118; HCCs (High Cadre Children), 63, 89, 111

private investigators, 3, 54, 61, 69, 88, 105, 106, 115, 120

progress, theme of, 139, 140, 141, 142, 143–144, 146. *See also* economic growth theme

protests, citizen (local), 76, 146, 174n57. *See also* Tiananmen

pseudotranslation, 24

psychology (themes), 10, 30, 35, 46, 79, 108, 113, 125, 132; authors' training in, 34, 98; profiling, 86; psychopaths, 12, 75, 76, 86, 88, 126, 127, 129

Public Security Ministry and Bureaus. *See* police

publishing industry, Chinese, 7, 11, 20, 23, 83, 102, 123, 124–125. *See also* censorship, PRC

publishing industry, Western, 1, 13, 15, 22, 40, 50, 133; and the China mystery, 6, 10, 11, 24, 26, 30–31, 38–39, 41, 47, 48, 133; on Tiananmen, 78

puzzle, cozy, whodunit, *honkaku* mystery, 10, 20, 21, 38, 54, 61, 122, 124; iconographic puzzles, 109, 127, 131. *See also* Golden Age mysteries

qigong, 32, 35

Qiu Xiaolong, 2, 6, 7, 24, 94, 119, 135, 136, 137, 138; characters, 44, 86, 88, 90; creative life, 3, 7, 20, 24, 46–49, 117, 132–133, 138; hero Inspector Chen, 32, 48, 49, 51, 80, 89–90, 92–96, 99, 138; nostalgia, 138–139; political and legal themes, 28, 40, 53, 76, 78, 81, 82, 84, 106, 119, 134–135, 146; social themes and sources, 54, 56, 61–62, 62–67, 70–71, 80, 82, 85, 99, 111, 125–127, 142, 144–145; style and poetry, 42, 47, 52, 54, 56, 60–62, 66–67, 78, 92–96, 100, 111, 144–145

Qiu Xiaolong's works: novels: *Becoming Inspector Chen*, 99; *A Case of Two Cities*, 64–65, 132; *Death of a Red Heroine*, 47, 62–63, 89–90, 93–96, 144–145; *Don't Cry, Tai Lake*, 70–71, 132; *Enigma of China*, 65–66; *Hold Your Breath, China*, 71, 85, 132; *Inspector Chen and the Private Kitchen Murder*, 133–135, 146; *Love and Murder in the Time of Covid*, 61; *A Loyal Character Dancer*, 64, 71, 90; *The Mao Case*, 126–127; *Red Mandarin Dress*, 92, 125–126; *The Shadow of the Empire*, 133–135; *Shanghai Redemption*, 53, 81; *When Red Is Black*, 64, 145; other prose books, 5, 78, 125, 139. *See also* poetry

racial and ethnic prejudice, 33, 51, 53, 56, 89, 98, 113, 147; anti-Chinese, 50–51, 69, 74, 108, 112, 132, 146. *See also* nationalism; Orientalism; Tibet; Uyghurs

Index 207

realism, 10, 19, 21, 50, 77, 86, 90, 112, 115, 135

Red Corner (1997 film), 41

Red Guards. *See* Cultural Revolution

religion, 19, 34, 43, 76, 109, 111, 129–130, 144; Bon, 109–110; Buddhism, 109–110, 129, 130, 145; Christianity, 34–35, 129–132; Confucianism, 48, 92, 93, 145; Daoism, 35, 75, 92, 97, 108, 130, 145; Islam, 54, 106; Judaism, 107; Manicheanism, 76; reincarnation, 12, 115; sects and cults, 34–35, 45, 129–132, 145; shamanism, magic, 37, 111, 135; Yiguandao, 169n65. *See also* Boxer Rising; Falun Gong; *fengshui*; ghosts; Taiping movement

romans à clef, 64

Rotenberg, David, 4, 46, 54, 60, 77, 113, 129, 135; drama coach Hyland, 87, 91, 136–137; hero Zhong Fong, 55, 75, 80, 87, 88, 98, 100; negative characters, 57, 72, 73, 75, 76, 88, 90

Russia and Eastern Europe, 22, 30, 55, 69, 110, 138–140; Hungary, 138, 179n29; USSR, 4, 9, 71, 138

Said, Edward, 22. *See also* Orientalism

Sampson, Catherine, 47, 58, 60, 78, 83, 91, 101, 115, 136, 144; *The Pool of Unease*, 68–69; hero Robin Ballantyne, 69, 87, 91, 100, 115; hero Song Ren, 54, 69, 88, 100, 115

Satire. *See* comic, satiric, ironic styles

scholar novel, novel for insiders, 67, 133

science fiction (SF), 2, 4, 5, 11, 70, 135m 148

See, Carolyn, 41, 103

See, Lisa, 4, 8, 26, 31, 40–46, 49, 60, 100, 135, 136; Chinese American, 7, 24, 39, 41; feminism, 101, 103–105; graphic puzzles, 127, 131; hero Liu Hulan, 43–44, 49, 53, 138; journalist and historian, 41, 42; themes, 45, 55, 64, 67, 71, 72, 77, 84, 103–104, 106, 130, 132

Segalen, Victor, 51

self-discovery theme, 7, 106, 136–138

Sendker, Jan-Philipp, 8, 40, 56, 57, 58, 77, 100, 115–116, 125, 136; heroes Paul Leibovitz and Christine Wu, 69, 87, 93,

107–108, 115–116, 137–138; social comment, 78, 82, 83, 107–108, 141, 144

serial murders, 12, 60, 61, 71, 75, 76, 86, 117, 128

series mysteries, 2, 15, 31, 38, 42–43, 46–47, 86, 115, 119; series novels, 47

sex, erotic interest, 26, 28, 66, 81, 99, 100–101, 102, 104, 111, 113, 133, 145; Chen Cao love interests, 64, 70, 71, 101, 134; romance, 36, 43, 48, 62, 71, 78, 87, 104, 120–121, 122, 127; sex crimes, 45, 62–63, 65, 78; sexual revolution, 63, 145; sex trade, 63, 133, 141, 145. *See also* gay, queer, LGBTQ

Sha Li. *See* Petty, Cheryl West

Shakespeare, 137

Shan Tao Yun. *See under* Pattison, Eliot

Shangguan Yunzhu, 126, 173n34

Shanghai Gang vs. Beijing Gang, 39, 66, 135

Shen Congwen, 125, 172n27

Shenzhen, 56, 69, 83, 107, 141

Sherlock Holmes and the Great Detective types, 2, 5, 20, 21, 32, 47, 48, 88, 89

Shih, Shu-mei, x, 167n33

Shlian, Deborah and Joel, 5, 54, 60, 76, 82, 100, 106, 137, 179n16

Shteyngart, Gary, 138

shuanggui (double detention), 56, 66, 133, 134–135

Singapore, 6, 8, 35, 110–111, 132

Sinologists, China scholars: as fictional characters, 74, 87, 91, 118, 126, 172n27; Old China Hands, 97, 113, 116; as writers, 8, 18, 28, 60, 136

Sinophone crime fiction. *See* Chinese language crime fiction; fiction, Chinese traditional

Sinophone literature and studies, x, 10, 97

Sjöwall, Maj, and Per Wahlöö, 48

smuggling: of goods, 28, 29, 32–33, 44, 65, 67, 68, 71–73, 109, 110; of humans, 44, 64, 71–72

social crime novel, 3–4, 10, 21, 29, 48, 61–62, 67, 70, 79–85, 103, 111, 140, 146–147

Song Ying, 12, 86

spying and surveillance, 29, 100, 114, 129, 134

spy novels, 2, 4, 9, 22, 26, 28, 105, 116, 147, 172n25; related to China, 10, 12, 46, 72, 113

208   Index

St. André, James, 24
State Security, Ministry of (MSS), 77, 121
stereotypes, 24, 50, 51, 88, 89, 104, 106, 112, 113
Stone, Eric, 9, 47, 60, 68, 72, 113, 129, 135
Strike Hard campaigns, 37, 142, 173n30
subjectivity and individualism, 97–99
subliterature, pulp fiction, 13, 18
Sun Yisheng, 12

Taiping movement, 34, 130
Taiwan, 2, 6, 10, 40, 57, 64, 67, 68, 73; crime
    fiction of, 10, 123
television. *See* media, moving visual
Tey, Josephine, 118, 178n6
thesis novel, 79–85, 103, 123. *See also*
    ideology; politics in China mysteries
Third World fiction, 23, 24–25
Tiananmen (1989), 6, 38, 78–79, 117,
    119–123, 124, 130, 145; 1976 and 1978-79
    protests, 78
Tibet, Tibetans, 4, 52, 56, 62, 73, 102, 113,
    115; as China's internal Other, 54–55,
    142; per Küng, 32, 37–38; per Pattison, 4,
    19, 22, 53, 77, 80–81, 82–83, 98, 99, 100,
    109–110, 146–147
Todorov, Tzvetan, 19
tourism, tourists as readers, 9, 28, 30, 52, 65,
    140, 141
translation, 25, 142; from the Chinese, 1, 11–12,
    13, 22, 23, 24, 41, 48, 54; into Chinese, 5,
    10–11, 17, 20, 22, 32, 48, 124, 142; other, 7,
    10, 25, 52, 81; translator characters in
    fiction, 49, 107, 108, 112, 114, 115
triads, gangs, organized crime, 33, 60, 64,
    72, 73, 74, 76, 121, 122
true crime, 2, 19; as fiction source, 62–67,
    68, 69, 69–70, 70–71, 75
Tsukiyama, Gail, 103

United Nations, 31, 35, 37
universities, 11, 34, 48, 54, 76, 120, 122, 137;
    police, 97, 122, 129
urban life, 3, 4, 7, 21, 29, 32, 53, 55, 91, 146;
    vs. rural, 55, 67, 139, 141, 142, 147. *See
    also* migrants

Uren, Roger, 5, 8, 26–30, 31, 60, 63, 76, 94,
    135, 168n55; themes, 71, 85, 88, 144
Uyghurs, 56, 76, 106, 122, 172n25

Van Gulik, Robert, 6, 18, 20, 21, 22, 23, 26,
    117, 133–135, 137
violence, 28, 60, 101, 125, 126, 129, 132
Vittachi, Nury, 51, 60, 88, 111, 136

Walker, Casey, 84, 138, 141
Walsh, Megan, 17, 102
Wang Shuo, 12, 41
Watson-type characters, 3, 91
weapons of murder, 37, 60–61, 74, 75, 76,
    101, 124
Weng, Albert. *See* Yung, Alban
West, Christopher, 3, 5, 30–35, 46, 60, 61,
    132, 135; on cults and secret societies,
    32–33, 34–35, 130; hero Wang
    Anzhuang, 32–35, 53, 55; political-social
    commentary, 32, 72, 77, 78, 83, 125, 144
Westerns and cowboys, 105, 110
Winks, Robin W., 118
women and crime fiction. *See* gender
world literature concept, 2, 20, 21, 50
Wu Jingzi, 119

Xi Jinping, 6, 40, 132, 133, 136, 139, 146,
    179n19

Yan, Geling, 138, 168n41
Yu, An, 7, 24, 54, 100, 101, 136, 144
Yung, Alban, 7, 8, 40, 46, 58, 60, 91, 101, 132,
    135; on cults, 55, 130; humor, 51, 59, 130;
    and satire of the French, 40–41, 53, 67,
    74, 87, 111–112, 137; Sino-French
    exploits, 57, 72, 88, 130

Zhang Xinxin, 7, 11, 54, 60, 135, 136, 138;
    earlier writing, 12, 101, 102, 103, 114;
    Hollywood Wanted, 74, 91, 114
Zhongnanhai, 57, 88
Zhou Haohui, 11, 12
Zijin Chen, 12, 166n30
Žižek, Slavoj, 22–23

ABOUT THE AUTHOR

JEFFREY C. KINKLEY is professor emeritus of Chinese History at St. John's University, New York, and a John Simon Guggenheim Fellow. He is known for his biography of Shen Congwen (*The Odyssey of Shen Congwen*) and his translations of Shen's fiction (*Imperfect Paradise: Twenty-Four Stories*; and *Border Town*). Kinkley is also the author of *Chinese Justice, the Fiction: Law and Literature in Modern China; Corruption and Realism in Late Socialist China: The Return of the Political Novel*; and *Visions of Dystopia in China's New Historical Novels*.

Printed in the United States
by Baker & Taylor Publisher Services